COMMUNICATION
FOR BUSINESS AND
SECRETARIAL STUDENTS

Communication

for Business and Secretarial Students

Lysbeth A. Woolcott, B.A.

Senior Lecturer in Communication
Windsor and Maidenhead College

Wendy R. Unwin, B.A.

Senior Lecturer in Educational Technology
Windsor and Maidenhead College

SECOND EDITION

MACMILLAN

First published 1974 by
MACMILLAN EDUCATION LTD
Houndmills, Basingstoke, Hampshire RG21 2XS
and London
Companies and representatives
throughout the world

ISBN 0–333–26175–5

A catalogue record for this book is available
from the British Library.

Printed in Hong Kong

First edition reprinted (with corrections) four times
Second edition 1979
20 19 18 17 16 15 14 13 12
00 99 98 97 96 95 94 93 92 91

CONTENTS

PREFACE
to the First Edition

This book is primarily intended for secretaries and would-be secretaries studying for examinations such as those of the London Chamber of Commerce, the Royal Society of Arts and the Scottish Vocational Education Council. The information will also be useful to students on other courses such as the BTEC National Certificate and Diploma in Business Studies.

The exercises in the book are intentionally broadly based and follow the authors' purpose in bringing together aspects of the study of communication which are tested in different examination papers, many of which do not bear the title 'Communication'. The book also offers guidance for use in practical office situations. For these reasons students will need specific knowledge which may be gained from a closer examination of the subject, a degree of common sense and initiative when applying broad principles to particular situations and the ability to apply knowledge of other disciplines.

July 1974   L. A. W.
                                                                                                  W. R. U.

PREFACE

to the Second Edition

This new edition has been made necessary by changes in examinations over recent years, notably the introduction of the Business and Technical Education Council National Awards.

It follows closely the structure of the first, indeed the section headings remain unchanged. However, the authors are happy to have had the opportunity of making extensive changes to the text. More recent information and exercises have been introduced so that the work reflects the latest syllabuses and examinations of the London Chamber of Commerce, the Royal Society of Arts, the Scottish Vocational Education Council. The scope of much of the book has been enlarged and it is hoped that some of the omissions and inelegancies of the first edition have been remedied.

July 1979   L. A. W.
                                                                           W. R. U.

ACKNOWLEDGEMENTS

The authors wish to thank Mrs M. Tucker, Mr E. Evans, Mr D. Sanders and the many colleagues and friends whose advice and help have been so generously given.

Grateful acknowledgement is made to the following for permission to reprint material:

Extract from *The Population Bomb*, revised edition, by Dr Paul R. Ehrlich, © Paul R. Ehrlich 1968, 1971, reprinted by permission of Ballantine Books Inc., Division of Random House Inc.; British Railways Board for an extract from a Sealink brochure; Business Books Ltd for an extract from *Public Relations Advances* by J. H. Crisford, and for an extract from *Recruitment and Selection of Typists and Secretaries* by Eva Roman, Derek Gould (1974); Consumers' Association for extracts from a report 'Shoddy Goods and the Law' from *Which?*, June 1973; The Financial Times Ltd for an extract from an article published in *Financial Times*, 3 October 1977; Hamish Hamilton Ltd for an extract from *Usage and Abusage* by Eric Partridge, Hamish Hamilton Ltd, London, 1947; William Heinemann Ltd for diagrams from *Business Statistics* by W. J. Bell and J. L. Mather; Help the Aged for use of Figure 24, p. 151; The Controller of Her Majesty's Stationery Office for extracts from *Report of the Royal Commission on Local Government*, Cmnd 4040, *Economic Progress Reports*, Local Employment Act 1960, *First Annual Report by the Board of Trade and Trade and Industry*, two figures and an extract from *Energy Trends*, a table from *Economic Progress Report 1974*, and four figures from *Social Trends*; Michael Joseph Ltd for an extract from *The Shocking History of Advertising* by E. S. Turner, and Michael Joseph in association with Rainbird Reference Books for an extract from *The Shell Guide to England*; Link House Magazines (Croydon) Ltd for an extract from the edition of *Video & Audio-Visual Review*, vol. 1, no. 10; The London Chamber of Commerce and Industry for questions from the Private Secretary's Diploma, Private Secretary's Certificate and Secretarial Studies Certificate Examination papers; Management Publications Ltd for extracts from 'Flexible Time-Clock' and 'Managers versus Entrepreneurs' from *Management Today*; John Murray (Publishers) Ltd for an extract from *Parkinson's Law* by Northcote Parkinson; New Science Publications for 'The Language of Clothes' by Keith Gibbons, which first appeared in *New Society*, 4 June 1970, extracts from *New Society*, 28 January 1971, 1 February 1973 and 6 March 1975, and an extract from an article by Dr Claire Whittington published in *New Scientist*, 10 November 1977; The Observer Ltd for extracts from *The Observer*; Penguin Books Ltd for use of extracts from *The*

Economics of Everyday Life, p. 39 © Gertrude Williams 1950, 1964; Progress International for an extract from *Focus on Malaysia*, vol. 3, no. 7 (July 1976); Royal Society of Arts Examinations Board for extracts from *R.S.A. Examination Papers*, and questions and adapted extracts (reproduced by permission of Guardian Newspapers Ltd) from their Diploma for Personal Assistants examination papers; Scottish Business Education Council for questions from the S.H.N.D. in Secretarial Studies examination papers; The Statesman & Nation Publishing Company Ltd for an extract from an article by Peter Paterson published in the *New Statesman*, 22 March 1974; Times Newspapers Ltd for an extract from the *Sunday Times*, 25 March 1973, an article from *The Times*, 9 August 1977, and a table 'Your Personal Guide to Share Buying' from the *Sunday Times Business News*, 11 January 1976; Top Secretary for an extract from *Top Secretary*, November 1973; Derick Unwin for an article by K. Austwick from *Media and Methods*.

Every effort has been made to trace all the copyright-holders, but if any have been inadvertently overlooked the publishers will be pleased to make the necessary arrangement at the first opportunity.

LIST OF ILLUSTRATIONS

1
PRINCIPLES OF GOOD COMMUNICATION

In the past, whenever an organisation had problems with people, the management looked immediately at conditions of work, pay, incentives and other such practical applications. Today more emphasis is placed on the relationships of people with each other and their various attitudes and feelings. Difficulties with such relationships are often ascribed to 'a failure of communication'.

What do we mean by this? That people do not, or cannot, talk to each other? Sometimes it is true that this is the case and then we have to look deeper into the attitudes of the people and find out why there is no communication at all — why, perhaps, they cannot get on with each other sufficiently well even to talk over problems and difficulties.

More often, however, we mean that people do talk to each other, telephone each other, write to each other, but still cannot understand each other. Communication is concerned with understanding. It is the way in which one individual passes a message, an instruction, information, question or idea from his/her mind to the mind of another person. The message must, if communication is to be successful, be received without being altered, confused or misunderstood.

Such a process sounds very simple. In practice it is very difficult, for, however well we plan a communication and however hard we try to consider the recipient, there are many pitfalls that may trap us as we try to 'put our ideas across'.

In this book there is much about the many and varied ways in which we communicate, mainly with words but also by non-verbal means. As you work through it you will learn more of the problems of bad communication and how to overcome them.

COMMUNICATION AND PEOPLE

The starting-point must be to consider what happens between people when they are communicating and to examine the lines of communication that exist in all organisations. This is basic to an understanding of why it is so important to have good communication and why correct grammar, clear speech, good style and the right tone is so important.

Communication is concerned with people. We use mechanical means such as telephones and teleprinters, typewriters and duplicators to help us send our communciations, but they are only machines and do not have voices, vocabularies, memories and feelings. People do. When we communicate we therefore have to think about the human beings with whom we are talking, or to whom we are writing.

WORDS

These people have varying degrees of background knowledge. Thus when talked to they react according to their individual knowledge. For instance, a computer engineer talking to another computer engineer will know that they are both familiar with the concepts and vocabulary and there will be much that he can say without having to add long explanations. If the same man were to talk to an audience unfamiliar with computers he would have to explain concepts such as binary system, computer languages and programming. Words, too, would have to be 'translated': words like Fortran (one of the languages), analogue, digital, terminal, and other much more complex technical terms.

Even simple words can cause confusion. Many words have several meanings and other short and apparently easy words may be difficult for people not familiar with them. The verb *to err,* for instance, causes confusion. Often there is a failure to recognise its connection with the word *error* and, whereas the saying 'to err is human, to forgive divine' used to be commonplace, it is now little known.

LISTENING

If it is assumed that the problems of using the right language in any situation have been overcome, there still remain a number of other problems. The first is that of attracting and keeping the attention of the recipient of a communication. Listening is a skill which is very rarely taught, yet it demands concentration and care if communication is not to fail.

How well we listen often depends on our attitudes to the speaker, the words used, the subject under discussion and a wide variety of other considerations. People often have very strong entrenched attitudes and interests which affect the whole of their lives. Then there are those attitudes which are conditioned by many variables, such as the weather, the time of day (don't ask an employee to do a difficult job at the end of the day!), how well or ill the employee is, any emotional problems she may have, like a quarrel with her boy friend. Relationships between people are very complex and must not be dismissed as unimportant. They introduce problems into the communication process which must be overcome if communication is to be successful.

A BASIC PROCESS

What is certain is that communication is a process basic to establishing links between people, even in primitive cultures. In more sophisticated societies the problems of communication grow and its importance also grows. The technological developments in the transmission, processing, storing and retrieval of information have made it more important than ever that the 'messages' sent shall be as simple, clear and correct as is humanly possible, so that the original meaning is not distorted.

COMMUNICATION FLOW

To help in this process effective systems have to be established. The more complex an organisation is, the more complex are the communication systems which are needed. The simplest analysis of the systems of communication is that which considers a three-way flow — downward, upward and horizontal.

(a) Downward from management levels. Sometimes it will originate at the top and percolate down as far as middle management, sometimes further. At other times it will originate at a lower level and reach the ordinary worker.

Downward communication tends to consist of either instruction or information. The instructions may take the form of orders, or they may be more politely phrased as requests and suggestions. The flow of information is often of a more general nature than are instructions. Much of the information will be appropriate and useful, though some other items will be unnecessary and time-wasting. For instance, an abstract of production forecasts fed through the computer might be useful to a supervisor but he would be unlikely to have the time to plough through the detailed computer print-out, which might comprise twenty or more sheets of figures.

One of the constant grumbles expressed by management from the supervisory level upward is: 'I get none of the information that I need and my desk is swamped with bits of paper that are useless'.

(b) Horizontal communication is the flow of information between people who are at the same level in an organisation, for example between members of the work-force or between members of the Board of Directors.

With the growth of large-scale organisations the desirability of improving horizontal communication has become a necessity. The increased use of specialist departments alone illustrates this. At Board of Directors' level, horizontal communication is partly catered for by Board meetings. Lower down the management structure, meetings are also used for this purpose and personal contact between staff at the same level can be encouraged.

(c) Upward communication is most frequently used in the case of employee/employer consultation, enabling workers to present views to and discuss problems with management. Within individual departments of organisations it exists on a casual day-to-day basis often very successfully. It is, however, sometimes lacking elsewhere in the management structure. Such a lack is often felt by junior management to be a refusal by senior administrators or executives to recognise the contribution that more junior personnel could make.

This is a very much simplified description. There are very many other ways in which communication may flow and, whichever system is used, there will be effects on the patterns of behaviour of the people within that system. For example, in a formal meeting each speaker will address the chairman but what he says will be heard by all the other members of the meeting. They will each react to the speaker's words. However, the behaviour of the people at the meeting will also be very much affected by the way in which the chairman responds to the remarks made. Let us suppose that the speaker proposed a course of action which many of the group supported but which the chairman did not like. The chairman might try to dismiss the suggestion without allowing further discussion. Such action would annoy both the speaker and his supporters and a sense of antagonism towards the chairman would develop. Also, the supporting group would become more sympathetic to each other and would begin to act together.

If the chairman also has some support for his dismissive attitude, then another group will be formed. What commenced as a cohesive single group will have broken into two sub-groups. The flow of communication may then change as the sub-groups begin to talk among themselves and then to argue directly with each other rather than addressing all their remarks through the chair.

The effect of the misuse by the chairman of the existing pattern of communication flow has led first to a change in behaviour and second to the replacement of the formal communication system by a much less formal pattern.

Whatever the systems in an organisation are, and however good they may appear in theory, they will still fail to be effective if the relationships between people are not good. The breakdown of the systems can mean that communication completely or partially ceases, or it can mean that people seek different ways of communicating, outside the prescribed system.

THE GRAPEVINE

In many organisations there is another problem and that is that no effective formal systems of communication have ever been established. Where this is so it is common to find a very strong informal channel, reaching into every level and commonly called 'the grapevine' or 'the bush telegraph'. This spreads rumour and gossip very rapidly. It is very unreliable because, although each rumour might have originally contained a grain of truth, it will have become distorted or magnified through its passage from one person to another until it is almost unrecognisable.

The grapevine can never be completely eradicated. The most that can be done is to reduce its influence by making full and correct information available to the right people at the earliest possible time.

Management sometimes uses the 'grapevine' deliberately, for instance to ascertain staff reactions to possible changes before putting them forward as firm proposals. Such a use must be discreet and careful so that staff do not realise what is being done and so that the meaning of the message is not changed radically. It can be a very dangerous course of action. There are many more reliable and better ways of finding out what the work-force thinks and wants.

UNIONS AND STAFF ASSOCIATIONS

Very many organisations have members who belong to trade unions. Others have staff associations. Systems of communication must exist between management and such bodies and must be so organised that communication with them is effective but does not adversely affect the normal communication flow within the organisation. Management must ensure that communication downward reaches all levels and that it is not possible, for instance, for the production worker to learn of a proposed change from his shop steward before the supervisor knows about it. Also, employees must be encouraged to talk to their superiors about problems and suggestions rather than always going first to their union representatives.

This is not to say that there should be any attempt to deny to the union or staff association full opportunities for consultation and discussion on matters affecting both groups and individuals. Rather, it is a recognition that there are some things which are appropriately channelled through the union, while others should not be. At the very simplest level, if an audio typist has a transcribing machine which goes wrong, one would expect her to report the problem to her supervisor, not to her union. Conversely, however, there should always be a place for union involvement in any grievance procedure.

BARRIERS TO COMMUNICATION

The following summarises the barriers to communication which this section has already mentioned.

1 RELATIONSHIPS BETWEEN PEOPLE

The attitudes, actions and reactions of people to each other can impede or even prevent communication.

2 LANGUAGE

The words that we use may not be understood, may be misunderstood, or may have different meanings. Our background knowledge affects our understanding.

3 LISTENING

An inability or unwillingness to listen effectively will reduce our ability to comprehend and retain information.

4 SYSTEMS

Messages will often not reach the people who need information correctly and speedily if there are no effective formal systems.

THE MEDIA OF COMMUNICATION

There is also the choice of how the communication is to be made. There are three media:

> oral
> written
> visual (non-verbal).

Communication is often an amlagam of two or all of these, but for simplicity they are dealt with separately here.

1 ORAL COMMUNICATION

We talk to people individually, or in groups, direct or via the telephone, more often than we write to them. It is the most important of the media of communication and one that should be given far more attention than is often the case. Thus it is sometimes less effective than it might be.

2 WRITTEN COMMUNICATION

Oral and written communication are closely linked by virtue of their use of language. Written communication is also visual and the presentation of the words, the pattern they make on the page, can help or hinder the reader's understanding. One has only to consider the relative difficulty of reading a page of a serious newspaper compared with a popular one to recognise this. Popular newspapers well understand that it is much easier to follow an article written in short paragraphs with frequent use of sub-headings than a solid mass of print.

There are many written methods used in business. Here are some, though it is by no means an exhaustive list.

written orders	constitutions
messages	handbooks
memoranda	manuals
letters	notices
telexes/telegrams	posters
reports	newsletters
forms	magazines
questionnaires	press releases
surveys	advertisements

3 VISUAL COMMUNICATION

Communication often takes forms such as gestures or facial expressions and these important means of visual communication are frequently linked with speech. Visual communication, however, can also be in the form of pictures. Language itself in its written form evolved from this and many of the older languages contained at least an element of 'picture-writing'.

Modern visual communication, while still including pictures, now also includes complex diagrams, charts and graphs. A visual presentation of, for example, sales figures is often clearer and thus more easy to understand than written communication would be.

Section 14 will consider the choice of media in greater detail, but it should be stressed here that many failures in communication result from an inappropriate use of media, such as using a rather formal letter or memo to convey instructions for unpopular action where these would have been more suitably expressed face to face.

THE ROLE OF THE SECRETARY

Attempts to improve communication are not solely the responsibility of management. They are the responsibility of every member of an organisation and the secretary has a specific role to play. She often represents her 'boss' either directly, in reception duties or answering the telephone, or indirectly in preparing written communication for his consideration and signature.

She should therefore be actively aware of the effect of good communication on the efficiency of, and human relations in, the organisation for which she works. It is to this end that modern examination syllabuses often contain communication theory as well as sections on the effective use of English.

Below you will find a suggested approach to an examination question and some typical questions. Future sections will cover a variety of the problems that arise both in the principle and in the practice of good communication.

SUGGESTED APPROACH TO AN EXAMINATION QUESTION

QUESTION

What do you understand by communication and what is its importance in business?

ANSWER

This is a two-part question.

PART ONE – definition

The problem here is that the standard definition, when 'trotted out' by student after student, begins to sound like an unreal cliché. While it is true that communication is the art of conveying meaning from one mind to another, it is important that the student notes the emphasis on the word 'meaning' and tries to avoid parrot-fashion repetition of a standard definition.

This part of the answer should also contain the following:

(a) the importance of communication as a two-way process
(b) the media employed, with a brief description of some of the major advantages and disadvantages
(c) channels of communication:
    formal – downward, upward, horizontal
    informal – the 'grapevine'.

PART TWO

The importance of communication in business includes the following:

(a)   dissemination of information
(b)   channel for orders and instructions
(c)   provision for discussion
(d)   channel for employee participation.

It should be noted that increased specialisation makes good communication even more desirable. Further, good communication has both internal and external factors, and relations with customers and other outside contacts depends on the existence of a good system of communication.

Additionally, students should be aware that, under the 1971 Industrial Relations Act and the accompanying Code of Practice, some firm requirements were laid down for the establishment and maintenance of systems of communication and consultation with employees. The Code of Practice, in particular, stressed the essential nature of communication and consulation. It proposed areas about which management should ensure employees are kept fully informed, including company plans, organisational changes and management intentions.

Management was urged to provide effective means to establish a two-way flow of information so that employees should have opportunities for discussion and presentation of their views. There is a statutory requirement to provide a contract of employment which gives information about the terms and conditions of employment, rights of trade union membership and grievance procedure. It was recommended that formal grievance procedures should be established and that such procedures should be in writing.

Despite changes in industrial relations law in the years following 1971 the recommendations for the establishment of more effective communication and formal procedures are likely to have considerable long-term influence.

EXERCISES

1. Examine the problems of communication in business. In what ways can communication be improved?
2 Why is it important for the secretary to be aware of the value of good communication?
3. How is communication affected by relationships between people?
4. The management of a national company communicates various types of information to its employees. Discuss the merits of the different methods likely to be used.

(Scottish HND in Secretarial Studies)

5. Define the term 'communication' in industry, and give illustrations of the importance, types and methods of communication in a typical work situation.

(LCC Private Secretary's Diploma)

2

USE OF ENGLISH

This section has been written to help those students who find difficulty with the mechanics of language: grammar, punctuation and spelling. It contains short tests on these topics to help diagnose in which, if any, of these areas students need further help and practice.

Students should work through the three short tests and check their answers with the correct versions in Appendix 1 (p. 274). The number of errors made in these tests will indicate the extent to which the student needs to study the relevant sections.

GRAMMAR

SKIP TEST 1

The following letter contains twelve commonly made grammatical mistakes. Rewrite the passage, correcting any errors you find. Do not alter the letter in any other way. Check your answers against the corrected version in Appendix 1. Score one point for each correct alteration. If you score ten or more correct answers you may choose to skip the following section and move on to Skip Test 2.

Dear Sir,

Owing to the bad weather last week, we were unable to complete the laying of your lawn. I would be very pleased if you could let me know when it will be convenient for us to return to finish the work.

Referring to your query about the price of shrubs. You shall have our estimate for this by the end of the week.

Mr Brown, our consultant, who you met some time ago, will be able to meet you and I next week at a time to suit yourself to consider what herbaceous plants will suit your soil.

We apologise for him not contacting you earlier, but he has unfortunately been ill. He would be glad if you can give him some idea of your preference as to colours in this border. Do you wish them to be different to each other or of similar hues? If you want two colours only, would you like less of one plant or an equal number of each type?

Everyone of the plants we sell have, of course, our usual guarantee.

Yours faithfully

This section covers some of the more common grammatical difficulties including those in the skip test. For students not familiar with the grammatical terms a Glossary is given on page 15.

1   SENTENCES

A sentence is the expression of a complete thought. To be grammatical even the shortest sentence must contain a subject and a finite verb. Errors in sentence structure are most often made in the introduction and conclusion of letters. Neither of these expressions is a sentence:

> *In reply to your letter of 8 May.*
> *Looking forward to your early reply.*

The first contains neither subject nor verb.

CORRECT VERSION: *In reply to your letter of 8 May, I have*
pleasure in enclosing our quotation.

The second has what at a casual glance seems to be a verb, *looking.* However, it is a participle, not a finite verb, and there is no subject.

CORRECT VERSION: *I look forward to your early reply.*

2   AGREEMENT OF SUBJECT AND VERB

Not only must a sentence have a subject and a verb, but these must also agree: that is, a singular subject must have a singular verb, and a plural subject a plural verb.

INCORRECT: *Details of the new contract is to be found overleaf.*

Here the subject *details* is plural so that the verb must also be made plural, *are.*

INCORRECT: *Each of the typists are to have her own type of stationery.*

The subject here is *each*, NOT *typists,* and so the verb must be made singular, *is.*

NOTE: *every, each, either, neither* are all singular.

The following is a very common type of error:

> *This is one of the papers that is to be enclosed.*

The relative pronoun *that* refers to *papers.* Since *papers* is plural the pronoun and verb must also be plural.

CORRECT: *This is one of the papers that are to be enclosed.*

Collective nouns are usually singular, unless the members of the group are behaving as individuals.

> *The committee has decided to increase the membership fee.*

BUT   *The committee were unable to agree.*

3   AGREEMENT OF DEMONSTRATIVE ADJECTIVES

Demonstrative adjectives must agree with the noun they qualify.

INCORRECT: *He could not agree with these sort of proposals.*

CORRECT: *He could not agree with this sort of proposal.*

OR   *He could not agree with these sorts of proposals.*

4   SUBJECT AND OBJECT

Look at the following sentences:

You and I will meet our consultant, Mr Brown, next week.
Mr Brown will meet you and I next week.

The first sentence has *you and I* as the subject and is correct, but the second version has *you and I* as the object and is incorrect. The sentence should read:

Mr Brown will meet you and me next week.

This error is easily avoided. Think of it this way. You would never say:

Mr Brown will meet I next week.

5   GERUNDS

A gerund has the same form as a present participle but serves as a noun. It frequently gives rise to grammatical errors. Consider this sentence, for example:

We apologise for him not contacting you earlier.

This should be:

We apologise for HIS not contacting you earlier.

6   MATCHING PRONOUNS

It is necessary to be completely consistent when using pronouns. Look at this sentence:

One should always read a hire-purchase agreement carefully before he signs it.

Here the writer has changed horses in mid-stream. He began the sentence using the pronoun *one* and then changed to *he*. The CORRECT version is:

One should always read a hire-purchase agreement carefully before one signs it.

7   RELATIVE PRONOUNS

There is some confusion over the use of the relative pronouns *who/whom*, *which* and *that*. The general rule is:

who/whom refers to persons only
which refers to objects and all other creatures
that may refer to persons, objects or other creatures.

These pronouns are used to introduce relative clauses — see also Punctuation 2 (a):

(a)   to define a preceding clause (the antecedent)

> *Uneasy lies the head that wears the crown.*
> *This is the play that Oscar Wilde wrote.*
> *This is the boy who told me the news.*

(b)   to give further information about an already defined antecedent

> *The play, which was directed by Peter Hall, is excellent.*

The examples show that in defining clauses (a) *that* is usually preferable to *which*.

Following a preposition *whom/which* is preferable:

> *He is a man for whom I have the greatest regard.*
> *The box from which she took the chocolate was large.*

8   SHALL — WILL

The use of these two words is governed by specific rules.

(a)   In a statement expressing simply the future tense:
       I, we are followed by *shall*
       you, he, she, it, they are followed by *will*.

> *I shall be glad if you will call on me tomorrow.*

(b)   If determination or intention is to be expressed, the rule is reversed:
       I, we are followed by *will*.
       you, she, he, it, they are followed by *shall*.

> *I will pass the examination however many times I have to retake it.*
> *I will drown and no one shall save me* is definitely suicidal!

It is to be noted that in Scotland this rule does not always apply.

9   SHOULD — WOULD

Like *shall* and *will*, these two words are not interchangeable. Similar rules apply.

(a)   In a statement expressing uncertainty or doubt, or where one action is conditional upon another:
       I and *we* are followed by *should*
       you, he, she, it, they are followed by *would*.

> *I should be grateful if you would visit me.*

Note the difference in tone between this sentence and

> *I shall be grateful if you will visit me.*

This second sentence contains a hint of command, whereas *I should . . . if you would* suggests the asking of a favour.

(b) when the rule is reversed *should* and *would* express regret, a hint that something is unlikely to happen and may also suggest a sense of obligation or duty.

> *I would come but I am unable to leave the children.*
> *He should visit his relatives but he does not wish to see them.*

Do not confuse *would* and *could*.

> *I should be grateful if you would . . .* means 'if you are willing to'
> *I should be grateful if you could . . .* means 'if you are able to'

10 SPLIT INFINITIVE

This is an awkward expression that occurs when an adverb is placed between the word *to* and the other word(s) which together with it form the infinitive.

We must not fail to carefully consider our future development.

The better version is:

We must not fail to consider our future development carefully.

11 FEWER – LESS

Fewer refers to quantities, that is, numbers. *Less* refers to quality or amount.

> *There were fewer seats in the theatre after the reorganisation.*
> *There was less seating accommodation in the theatre after the reorganisation.*

12 USE OF PREPOSITIONS

(a) Avoid the use of compound prepositions when simpler expressions may be used, for example

> *Employees were warned to obey the regulations in respect of (about) safety.*
> *Greater efficiency could result from an improvement in regard to (in) industrial relations.*

(b) A preposition at the end of a sentence is often clumsy and should usually be avoided. In the following sentence, however, Sir Winston Churchill showed that unnatural English can result from following this general guide too closely:

> *This is a practice up with which I will not put!*

(c) Many words may be followed by more than one preposition. However, certain words are linked with certain prepositions. Some of the most common are given on p. 14.

acquiesce in	estranged from
amenable to	exonerate from
coincide with	indicative of
compatible with	initiate in
conducive to	subordinate to
conscious of	negligent of
dependent on	oblivious of
debar from	relevant to

Note the following: *similar to* but *different from.*

Her dress was similar to her friend's but different from her sister's.

Different than is an Americanism

13 AMBIGUITY

It is impossible to give examples of all the possible types of ambiguous expressions. You should be able to spot the ambiguities in the following sentences. They are all taken from letters sent to government offices and were written in good faith by their authors.

(a) I am forwarding my marriage certificate, and two children, one of which is a mistake as you see.

(b) You have changed my little girl into a little boy. Will this make any difference?

(c) Re your enquiry. The teeth in the top are all right, but the ones in my bottom are hurting terribly.

(d) Sir, I am glad to say that my husband, reported missing, is now dead.

(e) The following was a form, issued by the Government, for Maternity Benefits: Every woman by whom a claim for maternity benefit is made shall furnish evidence that she has been or that it is expected that she will be confined by means of a certificate given in accordance with the rules.

Reply: In accordance with your instruction, I have given birth to twins in the enclosed envelope.

EXERCISE

The following sentences contain grammatical errors or ambiguities. Rewrite each sentence correctly.

1. Please express our thanks also to Mr Brown. We are grateful for all the assistance given by you and he.

2. Mr Brown, who you know already, is our chief representative in your area.

3. There were less members at the meeting than had been expected.

4. Due to the bus strike they arrived late at the office.

5. None of the committee members were able to attend the meeting.

6. Referring to your order for the replacement of the Cortina gear box.

7. They were disappointed at him reporting such a poor year's business.
8. She had to carefully compose this tactful letter.
9. Advertisement in a local paper: Wanted; sundial or similar garden ornament for a lady about three feet tall.
10. She did not remember him giving the instruction.
11. He is a man who you cannot but respect.
12. When did he ask you to phone him?
13. This point is not relevant for the discussion.
14. She could not be treated differently to the others.
15. Everyone of those present have copies of the minutes.
16. Further to the report made in your letter of 27 May.
17. Miss Brown told Mrs James that she had won a prize in a competition.
18. The questionnaire was sent to all the parents of children under seven who were asked to complete it and return it to the headmaster.

GLOSSARY OF GRAMMATICAL TERMS

Adjective	a word that qualifies or describes a noun, for example a *beautiful* dress
adverb	a word that modifies or describes a verb, adjective or other adverb, expressing a relationship of place, time, circumstance or manner, for example *greatly, gently, so, now, where, why*
collective noun	a word used in the singular to express many individuals, for example *herd, crowd, committee*
compound preposition	a phrase containing more than one preposition, for example *in respect of, in regard to*
demonstrative adjective	an adjective which points out or stresses a particular noun, for example *that* dog, *those* people
finite verb	what is said of the subject of a sentence, limited by number and person, for example *he walks, I said, they will go, she has spoken, you were saying*
gerund	a form of verb which serves as a noun, ending in -ing, for example *hiking* is an energetic pastime, *eating* is a pleasure
infinitive	a form of verb which is not limited by number or person. It is always composed of at least two words, including *to,* for example *to walk, to discuss, to wash oneself*
noun	a word used as a name of a person, thing or abstract idea, for example *table, chairman, Africa, religion, hope*

object	a noun or noun-equivalent governed by an active verb or by a preposition, for example I kicked *him,* he saw *the man,* I waited in *the car*
parenthesis	a word or passage of comment inserted in a sentence which is grammatically complete without it, for example he said, *and I agreed with him,* that he could never condone such behaviour
participle	(a) a verbal adjective qualifying a noun, for example a *talking doll,* the *spoken* word (b) part of a finite verb, for example *has spoken, were talking*
preposition	a word serving to mark the relationship between the noun or noun-equivalent it governs and another word, for example I found him *at* home, wait *in* the hall, the bed that he slept *on,* won *by* waiting, came *through* the door
pronoun	a word used instead of a noun to designate a person or thing already known, for example the man saw *it, we* were at home, *who* is there? *I* refuse to read *this*
relative pronoun	a form of pronoun which attaches a subordinate clause to an expressed or implied antecedent, for example the man *whom* you saw is my father, the prominent chin *that* characterised the Hapsburgs
sentence	a set of words complete in itself and including, or sometimes implying, a subject and a finite verb and conveying a statement, question or command, for example *I go. Will you go? Go (you).*
subordinate clause	a group of words that contain a subject and verb but which are of secondary importance to the main part of the sentence, for example he asked if, *when you had finished,* you would go home.

PUNCTUATION

SKIP TEST 2

The following passage contains twenty errors in punctuation. Rewrite the passage correcting any errors you find. Check your answer against the correct version of Appendix 1 (p. 274) at the end of the book. Score one point for each correct alteration. If you score ten or more correct answers you may choose to skip the following section and move on to Skip Test 3.

At the Annual General Meeting of Traders Limited held on 16 April 19— the Chairman said it is with pleasure that I am able to announce the results for the past financial year. Profits have risen by 20 per cent after tax and, happily, your Boards concern with the rising cost of raw materials which I expressed last year, has not been entirely justified it is true that costs have risen when do they not do so. Our increased sales particularly on the export side have however enabled us to show increased profits in addition the continued streamlining of the process, rationalisation of staff, together with reorganisation of departments, improved advertising methods and the success of the new name, Tradex, have contributed to progress. I anticipate that in two years time our change-over to the new machines will be complete and that we shall then see even greater returns than are apparent now the dividend of ten per cent that we are able to declare is largely the result of intensive work by the staff and they deserve our thanks. Good staff are hard to come by and we appreciate their many qualities, integrity, intelligence, adaptability, patience and, above all, the will to work hard.

The following section covers, among others, the points raised in the skip test.

1   FULL STOPS

A full stop is used   (a) at the end of a sentence
                       (b) after abbreviations, for example *B.A., Co., Capt.*

Note that if the first and last letters of an abbreviation are the same as those of the word for which it stands, for example *Mr, Mrs, Ltd,* the full stop is usually omitted. It is also becoming increasingly common to omit full stops from the abbreviated names of organisations, for example *BBC, IBM, ICI.*

2   COMMAS

(a)   Commas must be used to separate *commenting* (or non-defining) clauses from the rest of the sentence. For example, in the following sentence the relative clause *comments* on the purpose of the *nut,* which is defined or identified by the word *larger:*

   The larger nut, which secures the high-tension lead, must now be loosened.

However, in this second example

   The nut which secures the high-tension lead must now be loosened.

the relative clause is a defining one which identifies and completes the subject, *the nut,* and no commas are used.

There is a clear difference in meaning between these two sentences:

   The two passengers who were seriously injured were taken to hospital.

> *The two passengers, who were seriously injured, were taken to hospital.*

(b)   A parenthesis must be separated by commas, brackets or dashes from the rest of the sentence, for example

> *The Chairman, Sir Henry Golding, opened the conference.*
> *No one, I am convinced, could have solved so difficult a problem.*

(c)   Finally, commas must be used to separate nouns, adjectives, verbs or adverbs in a list, for example

> *She bought herself a new dress, blouse, skirt and boots.*
> *She typed the letter, read it through, signed it, put it in the envelope and sealed and addressed it.*
> *He summed up the situation concisely, accurately, quickly and without prejudice.*

In addition to these cases where commas are necessary there are many occasions where good style and personal taste call for the use of commas to mark a short pause. Modern practice is to minimise the use of commas where this does not obscure the sense.

3   APOSTROPHES

(a)   Apostrophes are used to indicate omissions and contractions, for example

> *I wouldn't, I've, o'clock.*

(b)   They also indicate plural forms of figures, for example

> *1940's.*

(c)   Finally, they are used to indicate possession or ownership (belonging to). With singular nouns the apostrophe comes before the s, for example

> *the girl's handbag,*

a handbag belonging to one girl. With plural nouns the apostrophe comes after the s, for example

> *the secretaries' typewriters,*

typewriters belonging to more than one secretary. Note that expressions such as

> *in a fortnight's time*
> *two years' guarantee*

require apostrophes. Words whose plural form does not end in s have the apostrophe before the s, for example

the children's toys
women's fashions.

Note that when a proper noun ending in *s* takes the possessive case there is no one rule for the position of the apostrophe. Most proper nouns ending in *s* require *'s*, for example

Charles — Charles's

ITS AND IT'S

Its is a possessive adjective:

Each typewriter has its own cover.

It's with an apostrope indicates an omission, that is, *it is.*

4   SEMI-COLONS

Although they are not greatly used nowadays, semi-colons can still be useful. They represent a pause midway in length between a comma and a full stop. In the following sentence the author found that the two expressions were too closely related to be separated by a full stop. At the same time a comma was hardly sufficiently emphatic a pause.

Do not let us speak of darker days; let us rather speak of sterner days.

                                                    SIR WINSTON CHURCHILL

Note that there are cases where, to avoid ambiguity, a semi-colon must be used to separate items in a list because a comma is also being used in the sentence:

The clothes in the shop window included two dresses, one with a pleated skirt; two skirts; two blouses and matching accessories.

5   COLONS

A colon is used to introduce a list or to amplify a previous statement.

A good secretary needs many qualities: intelligence, common sense, skill, a neat appearance and patience.

It is also used before a quotation to give added emphasis.

What Dr Johnson said is worth remembering: 'Knowledge is of two kinds. We know a subject ourselves, or we know where we can find information upon it.'

6   EXCLAMATION MARKS

They are rarely used in business communication. They may be occasionally used to express surprise, or for emphasis.

7   QUESTION MARKS

A question mark is used after a direct question.

Where have you put the report?

An indirect question does not have a question mark.

He asked where she had put the report.
I wonder where you have put the report.

8   DASHES

Dashes may be used in several ways.
  (a)   They may indicate an interruption.

> *'And in conclusion I might say —'*
> *'And about time too,' interrupted the heckler*

  (b)   They may indicate a break or hesitation in direct speech.

> *'Come,' replied the stranger, 'stopping at Crown — Crown at Mug-*
> *gleton — met a party — flannel jackets — white trousers — anchovy*
> *sandwiches — devilled kidneys — splendid fellows — glorious.'*
>
> Mr Jingle in *Pickwick Papers* (Dickens)

  (c)   They may also be used with a colon to introduce a list. Nowadays, however, the dash is often omitted in this case.

> *Please supply the following:— two white loaves, one can of beans*
> *and a quarter of tea.*

9   INVERTED COMMAS

These are used in four ways.
  (a)   They indicate direct speech.

> *The Chairman said, 'Our company has made great progress this*
> *year'.*

A capital letter is used to open the actual words spoken. A separate paragraph is required for the words of each speaker.

  (b)   They enclose titles of, for example, books, plays, names of ships, trains, houses, trade names, in typed or handwritten material.

> *'The Observer', 'Cellophane', 'Queen Mary', 'Dunromin'.*

Note the use of inverted commas in the following sentence where the title of a film occurs within direct speech.

> *She said, 'I went to see "Gone with the Wind" last night'.*

  (c)   They also enclose direct quotations.
  (d)   Finally, they are used to indicate words used sarcastically or slang expressions, for example,

> *so-called 'experts', 'with it'.*

10 CAPITAL LETTERS

The following list indicates the main uses of capital letters:

(a) The first letter in a sentence and the start of direct speech

This is my book.
She said, 'This is my book'.

(b) The pronoun *I* and the interjection *O*

(c) The forenames and surnames of people

Margaret Smith, Peter Jones

(d) Nicknames and pet-names of people and animals

Dusty Miller, Spud Murphy, Fido, Rover

(e) Registered Kennel and Jockey Club names

Red Rum, Arkle

(f) Titles of people and organisations

Her Majesty,
The London Chamber of Commerce and Industry

Note the less important words such as the articles *a* and *the*, pronouns, prepositions and conjunctions such as *of, by, and* and *for* only have a capital letter if used at the beginning of the title.

(g) Abbreviations of (f)

HM, LCC

(h) Geographical place-names including countries, areas, rivers, mountains, cities and towns

England, The United States of America, The Paris Basin, Nairobi, River Thames, Mount Everest

(i) The names of languages and peoples

Russian, Chinese

(j) The names of political and administrative divisions within a country

Berkshire, Gwynedd

(k) Words used instead of relatives' names as titles when addressing the persons

Father, Grandmother
NOTE: She said, 'My father is an accountant'.
BUT She said, 'May I have some pocket money, Father?'

(l) Deities and pronouns referring to them (also when referring to Jesus Christ)

God, Our Father Who art in heaven

(m)   The days, weeks and months of the year

Monday, February

but not the seasons unless they are being referred to as part of a specific title or date

spring, Autumn crocuses, Spring 19——

(n)   Religious and other festivals

Easter, May Day

(o)   Legal documents

Will, Act of Parliament

(p)   Bills and Acts of Parliament

The Health and Safety at Work Act

(q)   Trade names (whether or not they are the names of companies)

Aspro, Papermate

(r)   Ships and other means of transport

Ark Royal, Concorde, Flying Scotsman

(s)   Stars and planets

Mars, Venus

NOTE the sun and the moon would also be given capital letters when used with names of stars and planets.

(t)   The technical or specific use of common names

the Monarchy (referring to a specific monarchy such as the British Monarchy), *the Standing Committee*

(u)   Books, plays and film titles

Under the Greenwood Tree, Close Encounters of the Third Kind

EXERCISES

Punctuate the following passages.

1. What do we mean when we say that one country is richer than another or that we are better off now than we were fifty years ago how far is it possible to make accurate and precise statements about these things it is much easier to say what we dont mean than what we do we certainly dont mean that a richer country is necessarily happier or better or lives a nobler or more satisfactory life than the poorer one for these are things that we cannot define or measure when we talk about wealth or economic welfare we are referring only to those goods and services which are customarily exchanged for money

(Gertrude Williams, *The Economics of Everyday Life*)

2. if a hottentot desires the wind to drop he takes one of his fattest skins and hangs it on the end of a pole in the belief that by blowing the skin down the wind will lose all its force and must itself fall fuegian wizards throw shells against the wind to make it drop the natives of the island of bilbili off new guinea are reputed to make wind by blowing with their mouths another way of making wind which is practised in new guinea is to strike a wind-stone lightly with a stick to strike it hard would bring on a hurricane so in scotland witches used to raise the wind by dipping a rag in water and beating it thrice on a stone saying i knok this rag upone this stane to raise the wind in the divellis name it sall not lye tilli please againe

(J. G. Frazer, *The Golden Bough*)

3. the archbisop of york dr temple thinks that correct punctuation is more important intellectually than correct spelling he said so yesterday when he presented the school prizes at the royal infant orphanage at wanstead in writing essays said dr temple there are two things one has difficulty with spelling and stops nearly everyone says it is the spelling that matters now spelling is one of the decencies of life like the proper use of knives and forks it looks slovenly and nasty if you spell wrongly like trying to eat your soup with a fork but intellectually spelling english spelling does not matter shakespeare spelt his own name at least four different ways and it may have puzzled his cashiers at the bank intellectually stops matter a great deal if you are getting your commas semicolons and full stops wrong it means that you are not getting your thoughts right and your mind is muddled

(Eric Partridge, *Usage and Abusage*)

4. technical manager within a broad product or activity group he will analyse the design and manufacturing implication of new regulations and standards seek and co ordinate the views of society members and represent their interests both to government and to national/international authorities candidates probably late 30s should have an engineering degree or equivalent qualification mechanical or electrical they will have had senior staff experience in design product development or related fields in the vehicle or vehicle component industries spoken french would be an asset reference S.A. 25144 up to £4500

(Advertisement in *the Sunday Times*)

SPELLING

Skip Test 3

The following passage contains twenty errors in spelling. Rewrite the passage correcting any errors you find. Check your answer against the correct version in the Appendix at the end of the book.

The old-fashioned practise of writing out correctly one's errors in spelling may still definately benifit those students who occassionally find difficultys in this area. An effecient secretary must be able to spell accuratley; even the most capible should keep a dictionery in her desk. Some of the following words are commonly misspelled:

advertisment	*managment*
academic	*phsychological*
conscientious	*recomendations*
explanation	*statistical*
intrepret	*exhibet*
installments	*signiture*
dissappear	*objectionible*

Did you score less than eighteen out of twenty? If so, you must help yourself to improve by concentration, practice and constant use of the dictionary. It is wise to list the mistakes you make in your work and learn them. To learn spelling rules may also be helpful, although unfortunately there are many exceptions.

The list which follows contains some of the most commonly misspelled words. You will certainly need to use them, so learn them.

A
absence
accommodate
acquainted
all right
among
appearance
arrangement

B
beginning
believed
business

C
certain
choice
colleagues
coming
committee
completely
correspondence

D
decision
definite
disappointed

E
especially
essential
excellent
exercise
expenses
extremely

F
faithfully
familiar

G
guard

H
height

I
immediately
independent
instalment

K
knowledge

L
losing
lying

M
maintenance
minutes

N
necessary
noticeable

O
occasionally
occurrence
omitted
opinion

P
planning
possesses
preceding
privilege
procedure
professional

Q
quiet

R
really
received
recommend

S
scarcely
secretary
separately
similar
sincerely
successfully
surprising

T
transferred

U
undoubtedly
unnecessary
until
usually

V
valuable
view

W
Wednesday

3
ESSAYS

Very often, papers on Communication or English today do not require students to write essays but concentrate on more business-orientated, specialised areas such as reports, memoranda and letters. However, for some English examinations and in other disciplines, such as Structure of Business, competence in the technique of essay-writing is required and students also frequently have to write extended essays and projects.

Essays in some papers offer students the opportunity to express their own interests, opinions and attitudes — in fact their own personalities — as well as bringing together acquired knowledge to solve a particular problem. Students also have a chance to show knowledge and understanding of current affairs and topics which can only be acquired by regular reading of newspapers and periodicals. Such a knowledge will be a valuable asset at work and must be developed throughout the business or secretarial course.

Any of the following periodicals, which may well be available in college libraries, will provide useful information:

The *Listener*
New Society
The *Spectator*
New Statesman

Students are also recommended to read one of the quality Sunday newspapers: the *Sunday Times*, the *Observer* or the *Sunday Telegraph*. Their reviews of the week's news and topics provide a survey which will be particularly valuable to students who find it difficult to read a quality daily newspaper regularly. For the student preparing for the more advanced examinations, the *Financial Times, The Economist* and some of the management periodicals will offer useful background information.

EXAMINATION ESSAYS

The writing of a successful essay in an examination demands a series of skills from the student. She must be able to:

1. UNDERSTAND a number of problems, that is the list of topics offered or questions asked

2. SELECT carefully from this list the topic on which she is best qualified to write
3. RECALL the relevant information and knowledge
4. CHOOSE from this body of information and ideas
5. ORGANISE the selected information into a logical order
6. COMMUNICATE this information in an appropriate style and language so that it will be understood by the reader.

All these tasks have to be performed within the limited period of time allowed in the examination.

PREPARATION

The first five items in the list form the preparation stage of essay-writing. Students should plan to spend up to a third of the time available for answering the question on these processes. A satisfactory essay cannot be composed without careful forethought.

UNDERSTANDING the question set is a prerequisite. Dean Inge is said to have once been set the essay topic *Milestones*. Having had a classical education, he failed to recognise a common English word, decided that *Milestones* must be a Greek name and wrote an account of an entirely fictitious Athenian general. Possibly he received a reward for ingenuity, but he could hardly have been said to have understood the question.

Both the scope and limitations of the question must be recognised and defined. The subject *Pollution in the twentieth century* is a general topic and an answer which is restricted to, for example, the pollution of rivers in the United Kingdom has failed to cover the topic adequately. Equally an answer that included more than a brief mention of the pollution inherited at the beginning of the twentieth century as a result of nineteenth-century industrial growth has failed to recognise the limits of the question.

In the essay *The compensations of living in a computerised society* the word *compensations* is the key. Students are being asked to look at the advantages which have arisen from the growth of modern, reliable and versatile computers, not the dangers or problems. The word *computerised* also lends force to the title — students must understand the difference between, for instance, data processing using systems other than computers, between automated and computerised machinery and the possibility that the computer offers for reducing many boring tasks to the mere pressing of keys on a terminal.

Definitive statements, such as *The role of the Bank of England in monetary policy is still increasing,* seem, to a student lacking in confidence, to require an answer supporting the statement. In fact questions phrased as provocative statements may be answered by supporting the opinion offered, by refuting it, or by a discussion presenting both sides of the argument. Such a question is seeking to test the student's ability to present views supported by logic and reasoning, and the logic and reasoning are as important as the point of view.

The wording of the question *Describe the role of the Building Societies in the United Kingdom during the 1970s. To what extent did they contribute to investment by individuals, pension funds, or other big investors and what contribution did they make to easing the housing problem?* is lengthy but helpful. The wide-ranging subject *investment . . . and . . . contribution to . . . housing* is further defined and some helpful hints follow. The expression *other big investors* must be noted. The student is being requested, not merely invited, to consider the role of other relevant groups.

SELECTION of the question or topic most suited to the individual candidate is the next step. It may be helpful first to *reject* the topics which are unsuitable. This will leave a short list for consideration. The student would ask herself such questions as:

> *Do I have the specialised knowledge required by this topic?*
> *Am I more skilful at descriptive writing, narrative writing, or in the logical presentation of argument?*
> *Which type of writing is required for this particular subject?*
> *Have I some personal experience which will enable me to write in an original manner and not produce a stereotyped essay on a rather well-worn topic?*

Examiners mark many essay answers to the same question. Higher marks will be awarded to students who can produce refreshing new ideas or approaches to rather commonplace subjects. As in all communication, consideration of the reader is vital and any essay must have as its first aim that of interesting the reader.

RECALL. At this third stage the student is ready to put pen to paper and jot down, *in note form*, as it occurs to her, all the information she can remember and all the ideas she can formulate on the topic. A new line should be used for each new idea, even if it consists of a single word, to allow for later elaboration. This first list of ideas and information should be as wide-ranging as possible.

CHOOSE from this preliminary list those ideas which best fit the emerging theme. Two criteria to use are, first, relevance to the subject and the approach chosen and, second, the length of the essay required. A short essay, in an examination where six questions have to be completed in two and a half hours, will require the students to be more selective in the choice of words and more concise in the development and expression of ideas than where more time and greater length are available. Ideas that are rejected at this stage should be crossed out.

ORGANISE the selected matter into an appropriate order. In practice this may be most conveniently done by numbering those points which have been selected as a framework, without rewriting. A considerable rearrangement of one's orginal flow of thought is usually necessary. An essay must have the quality of unity. The development of the subject must be smooth and logical. Too abrupt a change of direction or subject will be difficult for the reader to follow.

Chronological order is often the most simple approach, and the most suitable, for the narrative types of essay and for such questions as *What preparations must be made before a committee meeting is held?* A topic such as *The future of the trade-union movement* may also be planned on the basis of time by reviewing the past origins and development of the movement and the present trends before developing the main theme which is the future of the movement. In this case the student must be careful to keep her subject constantly in mind and not devote too much time or space to the consideration of the past and present. The inclusion of these must be justified by demonstrating the logic of the development from past and present towards the future.

Where a number of facts or points such as advantages and disadvantages have to be presented, the most sensible approach is to present them in descending order of importance. Such a plan would suit a topic like *What are the advantages of recording statistical data in graphic form?*

Questions requiring discussion of arguments for and against a viewpoint or a discussion of problems and their remedies present problems of planning. Two such questions are: *Marshal the arguments for and against comprehensive schools* and *Down and outs and drop-outs. Say what you consider to be some of the causes of various types of apparent failure in life or in career, and suggest remedies.*

There are two possible approaches to such questions. The student can either

(a) present all the advantages (or all the problems) and follow these by all the disadvantages (or the suggested solutions), or

(b) present each advantage in turn, followed by an associated disadvantage (or each problem followed immediately by the suggested solution).

WRITING

Once the subject has been thoroughly thought out and the organised notes have been prepared, the essay can be written. Here are some guidelines.

1. Although new ideas, illustrations and examples will come to mind as the essay progresses, stick as closely as possible to the original plan. Otherwise there is danger that the essay may lose its logical flow, may stray too far from the subject, or that the conclusion will not follow logically from the reasoning.

2. Pay particular attention to the introduction and conclusion. The first aim is to interest the reader, and this interest must be attracted in the first sentence of the first paragraph. First impressions are important. So are last impressions. Does the conclusion complete the essay satisfactorily or does it leave the reader in mid-air?

3. Take care with paragraph construction. Each paragraph should contain one main idea expressed or implied in the key sentence. The other sentences will introduce, support, elaborate or draw conclusions from this main point.

4. Link each paragraph carefully with the previous and following ones to demonstrate the smooth flow of ideas.
5. Use a style and language appropriate to the subject. A 'business' topic such as *British business methods* will require formal language and an objective tone. An objective tone is also necessary in an essay which presents the pros and cons of a case. Even if the writer's own opinion is made clear, an objective tone, recognising that other views are tenable, will help persuade the reader to appreciate the writer's point of view.

Descriptive and narrative writing is much less frequently required in Business and Secretarial examinations than used to be the case. Should the need arise, students should remember that a more vivid and even dramatic style of writing is required to convey subjective impressions or enhance the interest of the subject-matter.

Some newspaper articles (see below) can suitably be written in an informal style. Such informality should never be allowed to degenerate into colloquialisms or slang except, possibly, in direct speech in inverted commas.

EXAMINATION REQUIREMENTS

1 ESSAYS

In many examinations the length of the written answers is largely determined by the number of questions that must be answered in a given time, for instance six questions in two and a half hours. If it is assumed, as should be the case, that each student will read through the whole paper and then select the questions to be answered and, at the end, read through the answers, then the time allocated for each answer will be, perhaps, only 20 minutes or half an hour.

Not all of this time can be used for writing. The process of recall, choice and organisation will take up to ten or fifteen minutes. Therefore, the essay itself will often be quite short, from 250-350 words, perhaps, but must be very clear and contain much factual information or solve a problem. So the essay is an exercise in the student's ability to write concisely yet avoid appearing limited in knowledge or outlook.

2 NEWSPAPER ARTICLES

At work secretaries may be asked to prepare information to be included in a variety of publications, including:

> magazines
> technical journals
> house journals or newsletters
> newspapers.

The format that should be used for articles is similar to that for press releases and is detailed in Section 8.

Examination papers also require students to write articles such as those given in the exercises at the end of this section and in the examination papers in Appendix 6. Some of the types of articles which may be required are discussed in the following pages.

(a) *Reviews*

A review of a book, film or play does not require an account of the plot or content of the work. Only an outline of either of these should be given, sufficient to provide a basis for an assessment of the work that is the purpose of the review. An assessment of the work includes comment on such topics as characterisation, style and organisation. What was interesting, admirable, unusual about the work? How does it compare with previous works by the same author, or comparable works by other authors? What shortcomings does it have? A review of a play or film will also involve some criticism of the production, the interpretation, setting, costumes, and so on.

Reviews may be presented as criticisms but students should remember that the function of a critic is to consider the merits as well as the demerits of a book, performance or production. Criticism should be, as far as possible, objective and constructive.

As opposed to a question on a literature paper which requires a review of a closely studied set book; play, book and film reviews in newspapers and journals are often presented in a more informal style. They are also frequently quite short. An example of a book review follows:

BAD LANGUAGE!

Shop Stewards at Work

by Eric Frink

MacNelmans 305 pages £9.00

This is a good book, spoilt to some extent, unfortunately, by the writing. Regrettably the findings are presented in language calculated to deter any but the most determined of readers or those who are familiar with the jargon which is nowadays used in sociology. It is not the hallmark of scholarship to use this kind of language when the same ideas can be presented in everyday English.

The book studies trade-union work-place representatives in a particular factory, and is informative about a relatively little described subject. It considers the shop stewards' functions, their view of their trade-union role, their motivation, actions and reactions.

The author finds, first, that shop-floor stewards regard their relationship with employers more as a conflict of interest than do the clerical staff representatives. Second, their conception of trade-union principles is more radical and related to ideas of social justice and prevention of exploitation. Third, there is strong emphasis among stewards of the need for leadership.

The books suggests that shop-floor workers with grievances take them first to the stewards whereas clerical staff often take complaints direct to management. Staff workers are less committed to trade unions and often critical of union activity. There was marked contrast between staff and shop-floor support for union goals.

Workers benefited from strong shop-steward leadership with fewer stoppages of work. Stewards often play conciliatory roles and are aware of wider social objectives.

The response to leadership depends on expressed ideas evoking a sympathetic reponse, which itself depends on the conditions under which people are employed. Strikes are not caused by active trade unionists but by grievances. Active trade unionists with the consciousness of the need for collective bargaining help to resolve grievances constructively. This book will underline this truth.

M. J. Ermitor

(Based on a review in *Personnel Management*, vol. 9, no. 11)

(b)   *Magazine articles*

The examination question is likely to include the subject on which the article is to be written and an indication of the type of magazine for which the article is intended.

Students must plan their writing with their readership very much in mind. The whole approach, together with the language, tone and style chosen, will vary with the nature of the magazine. An article written on UFOs for a teen-age magazine would be very different from one written for a serious scientific journal.

(c)   *Newspaper reports*

These may be for any of the following:

(i)   daily national papers
(ii)   weekly national papers
(iii)   daily local papers
(iv)   weekly local papers
(v)   newsheets published by a firm for its employees.

The content, as well as the style, must be adjusted according to the style of the paper for which the article is designed. We all know that there is a considerable difference between reports in *The Times* or the *Sun*, to say nothing of the different kinds of articles (and pictures) which appear in these two papers.

Reports should be written with short sentences and fairly short paragraphs. Remember that most will, if printed, appear in two-inch-wide columns. They often have to be exercises in summarising, since many relatively unimportant items will only merit space for 100-200 words or less. It might be as well to try and estimate how much might be printed and write to an appropriate length. In an examination a suggested length should be given in the question by the examiner.

ESSAY, REVIEW AND ARTICLE TOPICS

ESSAY TOPICS

1. A friend is joining a class at your college or taking a job in your office and asks you to explain the daily routine. What would you tell her?

2. Our life is restricted by many government regulations, for example opening hours, cinema hours on Sundays, shopping hours, and so on. Choose any regulation which you find irksome and say why you think it should be changed and how you would change it.

3. We are always being told that we should save for the future. How would you encourage people to save?

4. The future of the trade unions.

5. In what English skills do you think this examination should test an adult like yourself? Why should it test these skills?

6. 'Council housing is now an anachronism.' Do you think this is true?

7. Take a business or an industry known to you and show how it is organised locally, and where appropriate, nationally.

8. Describe a well-run office and indicate the underlying reasons for its success.

9. Discuss the point of view that the setting-up of branches of US firms is dangerous for the future of the United Kingdom and Europe.

10. Consider a situation, known to you or imagined, in which an area of national beauty or recreational value is threatened by a proposal for a development that has some other kind of value, for example an oil plant on the coastline, a nuclear station, an army range in wild country, a large housing estate in a green belt, a reservoir drowning farms and fields. Put forward the arguments for and against, in report form or otherwise.

11 'Temps'. Discuss the advantages and disadvantages of the life of a temporary secretary as compared with that of a permanent one.

12. The provision of a good network of transport facilities for goods and people seems essential for the prosperity of a region. Describe the situation in your own area and make some suggestions for improvement.

13. Towns and counties are administered partly by elected members of the public, partly by permanent paid officials. Briefly outline the system and indicate its strength and its weakness.

14. Mention some new developments in office layout and machinery and justify their introduction.

15. How to deal with hijacking and kidnapping when used as political weapons.

16. The affluent society has changed into the violent society. Do you agree?

17. Is it right that the main industries and services of a country should be controlled by the State?

18. Does the Welfare State reduce personal responsibility?

19. Racial discrimination in Great Britain.

20. The mass of men lead lives of quiet desperation. Discuss.

21. Love, friendship, respect do not unite people as much as a common hatred for something. Discuss.
22. The promotion of tourism in any **one** area of the United Kingdom.
23. The industrial and commercial applications of closed-circuit television.
24. Your evaluation of the improvements in reprography in the last decade.
25. The problems of agriculture and the EEC over the last fifteen years.
26. The implications of a declining population.
27. The effects of office-sited vending machines.
28. The secretary and word-processing systems.
29. Industrial stagnation.
30. Assess the benefits and disadvantages to men of the Sex Discrimination Act.

REVIEWS

1. Prepare a review of this book in about 300 words for inclusion in a monthly magazine entitled *Business Training*.

2. Your employer has seen an advertisement for a book entitled *Office Efficiency*. You happen to mention that you have read it and he asks you to prepare a concise review for him so that he may judge whether to purchase it or not.

   The main contents of the book and some comments on it are given below. You must decide whether or not your review will favour purchase. Invent realistic details.

   > *Office Efficiency.* Contents cover: training of clerical and secretarial staff; supervision; work planning and procedure; office layout; furniture and lighting; equipment; stock control.
   >
   > In the main a direct style of writing, a little verbose at times. Some good detailed information and sources, e.g. equipment suppliers, but sample costs are two years old although the book has only recently been published. Training and supervision covered in rather general terms. Nothing included on job descriptions and staff appraisal.
   >
   > Other books of similar type exist but are older. There are also specialist books on, for example, Organisation and Method. Journals give more up-to-date information of some items. Very good introduction to the need for greater office efficiency. Would start people thinking.

3. Take any film on business organisation, office procedure and practice or other related subjects that you have seen during your course of study. Prepare a review in not more than 350 words for inclusion as an appendix in a report proposing a training course for junior management.

4. You have recently read a book which advocates that all office managers should receive training not only in management skills but in relevant basic clerical and secretarial skills such as book-keeping and mechanised accounting or typewriting. Prepare a critical analysis of the suggestions,

relating them to the management development programme of a commercial organisation

5.   Write a review for your local paper in about 500 words on a recent local operatic or dramatic production.

6.   Review, for your company magazine, any recent very successful film which will shortly be shown in the vicinity.

7.   A publisher has recently reissued the collected works of one author to celebrate an anniversary (centenary, birthday, etc.). Review the works, commenting on the author's use of language, style, the relevance of the writings to the present day and the philosophic, moral or entertainment appeal.

MAGAZINE AND NEWSPAPER ARTICLES

1.   Write an article of about 500 words for **one** of the following:

    (i)   a careers magazine for school-leavers, on the pros and cons of the view that a woman wishing to make a career in business should seek to start off as a secretary;

    (ii)   a staff newspaper issued fortnightly to 180 office and factory employees, on the findings of a survey of attitudes to the firm's proposal that the standard lunch break should be reduced from one hour to ¾ hour, with compensation at leaving time.

(RSA Diploma for Personal Assistants)

2.   Write an article of about 500 words for **one** of the following:

    (i)   a women's weekly magazine read by many working secretaries, on *The Male Secretary: A Threat or a Benefit?* (Consider why women secretaries predominate at present: the pros and cons of males entering secretarial work: the possible preferences and reactions of working secretaries and employers.)

    (ii)   a local newspaper, about a firm's forthcoming centenary. (Provide some brief historical background: up-to-date information on the firm and details of activities designed to commemorate the centenary.)

(RSA Diploma for Personal Assistants)

4

LETTER WRITING

Business organisations spend considerable sums of money on building, maintaining and projecting their firm's image. Handsome buildings, decor and furniture, beautiful receptionists and glossy literature all help to impress clients with a picture of a flourishing, progressive concern. More mundane perhaps, but just as vital in projecting an image of efficiency and helpfulness, are the letters sent out by an organisation.

The fact that business letters involve a considerable investment of time, and therefore money, is often overlooked. As long ago as 1976 a major London secretarial agency assessed the cost of one dictated and typed letter as lying in the range £4-7.

The humblest copy typist is responsible for the attractive and clear presentation and correct punctuation of letters. Further up the ladder, a secretary responsible for the composition of letters must also contribute clarity of content and suitability of language, tone and style. In letter writing, therefore, a secretary is able to make perhaps her greatest contribution to her organisation.

The writer of a business letter has two objectives to attain. The explicit objective is to provide a record of communication. (If no record for the file is required, then a telephone call may well be both speedier and less costly.) The implicit message of any letter is the impression it makes upon the reader. This message is carried in both the appearance and content of the letter. A well-typed letter (on good-quality paper with a well-designed letterhead) whose content is both clear and courteous conveys a favourable impression of the writer and the organisation. It is, in fact, an excellent 'image-builder' and a valuable exercise in public relations.

In this section three aspects of letter writing are considered: the presentation of the letter; the logical planning of the contents; and the use of suitable lanaguage, style and tone. These divisions are convenient but to some extent artificial, for they are all interrelated. The presentation of the letter may include the use of headings, sub-headings, hanging paragraphs and possibly a numbering system. All these devices are closely related to the content of the letter, indeed their sole purpose is to help the reader understand the writer's 'message'. Similarly, the language, style and tone must match the message. A letter of complaint will be written in very different terms from those of a sales-promotion letter.

LAYOUT

The layout of letters is largely determined by custom and convention and at work you will also be guided by the house-style of your organisation. Basically there are two main forms of layout in use: the older semi-blocked form and the fully blocked form, which is now widely used. The fully blocked form of layout is often unpunctuated. Typed examples of the two styles are given in Figures 1 and 2, but similar rules apply to hand written letters.

Figure 1 shows a letter sent from a private address on unheaded notepaper. The sender's address if typed, indented, at the top right-hand corner. Note that the sender's name is **not** included. The date appears beneath the address, and is neatly aligned with it. The recipient's address on the left-hand side is not indented but kept in line with the margin.

Although the letter is very short it has none the less been divided into two paragraphs, the first containing the **topic** of the letter, the second giving amplifying information. The start of each paragraph will normally be five spaces in from the left-hand margin for a typed letter, or the equivalent for a handwritten one.

The complimentary close, *Yours faithfully,* begins from the centre of the page. The signature is aligned under the complimentary close. Since many people's signatures are illegible, it is courteous to print the name under the signature so that a reply can be correctly addressed.

Note that in the fully blocked layout shown in Figure 2:

(a)   the letter is typed on headed notepaper

```
                                              5 Green Lane,
                                                 BURBERRY,
                                                 Wilts.
                                                  BB3 6XZ

                                              10th March, 19--


Contemporary Furnishings Ltd,
11 James Square,
MANCHESTER.
MC1 6BG

Dear Sirs,

        I should be grateful if you would send me further
information about the chairs you advertised in
'The Mercury' last week.

        I am particularly interested in your plywood
rocking chairs.

                        Yours faithfully,



             W. Penrose (Mrs)
```

Figure 1   Semi-blocked letter

THE TIN CAN PRESERVING CO
HUNSTON LINCOLNSHIRE
HU5 5TF   TEL HUNSTON 194


```
Our ref   ABC/DE
Your ref  GH/IJK


12 December 19--


A J Eyre Esq
Ideal Estates Limited
9 Timmins Lane
YARBOROUGH
Norfolk
YB1 6SZ


Dear Mr Eyre

Thank you for your letter of 1 December 19--, enclosing
detailed plans of Site No. 12.

A preliminary sketch of our proposed new factory is
enclosed so that you may have time to consider it
before we meet.

I am pleased to confirm the tentative arrangements we
made on the telephone yesterday and shall look forward
to meeting you on Friday, 10 December, at 2.30 p.m.

Yours sincerely



J Gotts
General Manager

Enclosure
```

Figure 2   Fully blocked letter

(b)   the typing begins at the left-hand margin (with the exception of the
      printed heading)
(c)   the layout has open punctuation — the content of the letter is, of
      course, conventionally punctuated.

A useful variation to this fully blocked layout puts the date on the right-
hand side of the sheet, which may assist filing.

These two sample letters demonstrate most of the features of the layout of
letters listed below.

1   LETTERHEAD

Limited liability companies use printed notepaper which by law must include
the following information in the letterhead: full name of the company, the

names of the directors, the place of registration, the registered number and the address of the registered office. The telephone number and telegraphic address are usually included.

Some firms prefer to print only the name of their organisation (or even a monogram) at the head of the page and to put all the other necessary information at the foot. This style gives an attractively uncluttered and 'modern' appearance to the notepaper.

When you write a letter from your own address on unheaded notepaper you must write your address in the top right-hand corner. Add your telephone number (if this is likely to be useful to the recipient) at the left-hand margin, opposite your address. Write words like *Street, Road, Square* in full, but the recognised abbreviations for names of counties may be used.

Postal codes should always be used. The Post Office recommends that:

(a)   the post code should be the last item in the address
(b)   it should appear for preference on its own
(c)   if this is not possible, six spaces should be left between the post code and the preceding item
(d)   the code should be written in block capitals, without punctuation and with a space between the two halves of the code.

2   REFERENCES

In a reply to a letter you should quote the correspondent's reference, if he has used one. References are either numerical, usually referring to a filing system, or may consist of the writer's initials followed by those of his typist.

In a fully blocked layout references usually appear immediately above the date. Where the semi-blocked form is used, they appear at the left-hand margin, opposite the date.

3   DATE

The most logical order is day, month, year, for example *1 May, 19 − −*. Unless open punctuation is used, there should always be a comma after the month. It is not necessary to put a full stop at the end. The shorter form, *1 December 19 − −*, is now increasingly used with open puncutation.

Never abbreviate the month, or, worse still, write the date numerically as 12. 4. − −.

4   RECIPIENT'S ADDRESS

Except in purely personal letters, this must always be included. It may appear either immediately above the salutation or at the foot of the letter, but always at the left-hand margin.

Often letters are addressed to a company:

> *The Ideal Motor Co. Ltd,*
> *LONGHAM,*
> *Beds.*   *3LO4 8JB*

and the customary abbreviations *Co.* and *Ltd* may be used. (If you do not know why a full stop has been used after Co. and omitted after Ltd, refer back to p. 17)

Messrs is falling into disuse. In any case it may be used only when addressing a company whose title includes personal names, and which is not limited, for example

> *Messrs J. Brown and Sons*

When a letter is addressed to a department within a company, the name of the company sometimes appears first, for example

> *The Ideal Motor Co. Ltd,*
> *Accounts Department,*
> *LONGHAM,*
> *Beds.   3LO4 8JB*

or the address may be written

> *Accounts Department,*
> *The Ideal Motor Co. Ltd,*
> *LONGHAM,*
> *Beds.   3LO4 8JB*

At the higher managerial levels, letters are very often addressed to an individual within a company. The name of such an individual appears as the first line of the recipient's address. The form *R. Brown, Esq.,* is slightly more formal than plain *Mr R. Brown* and is not often used nowadays.

It is always courteous to use the correct form of address and title of an individual. These forms are not listed here but can be found in many reference books. It is also tactful to remember that most people like their qualifications, for example MA, or decorations, for example CBE, to be mentioned.

Finally, a letter may be addressed to an individual by his title:

> *The Sales Manager,*
> *The Ideal Motor Co. Ltd,*
> *LONGHAM,*
> *Beds.   3LO4 8JB*

The use of the phrase *For the attention of . . .* is not generally recommended. However, it may be useful when a letter is being sent to a firm following, for example, a telephone conversation with a member of staff who will be dealing with the ensuing correspondence. The phrase is inserted between the recipient's address and the salutation, for example

> *Accounts Department,*
> *The Ideal Motor Co. Ltd,*
> *LONGHAM,*
> *Beds.   3LO4 8JB*
>
> *For the attention of Mr Smith*
>
> *Dear Sirs,*

5 SALUTATION

Dear Sirs is used when addressing a company, *Dear Sir* when formally addressing an individual. Letters to women, married or unmarried, begin *Dear Madam*. If in doubt as to the sex of your correspondent use *Dear Sir* but **never** *Dear Sir or Madam*.

6 SUBJECT HEADINGS

If a subject heading is used, it appears immediately beneath the salutation. In a semi-blocked layout it should be centred and in the fully blocked form it will be aligned with the left-hand margin. Always use a subject heading when it will be helpful to the reader, either by quoting, for example an order or account number, or when it will immediately identify the subject under discussion and thus shorten the letter.

7 COMPLIMENTARY CLOSE

Chinese mandarins are reputed to have ended their letters to their underlings with the not very complimentary close, *Tremble intensely*.

More recently, it was the custom for civil servants to conclude:

I am, Sir, your most obedient servant,

Less dramatically, or less hypocritically, the following forms are now most generally used:

Dear Sir/s ... Yours faithfully,

for a formal letter, or less formally

Dear Mr Brown ... Yours sincerely,

Yours truly may be used to conclude both formal and informal letters, but it is now rather old-fashioned.

8 SIGNATURE

The written signature appears below the complimentary close and the name is typed or printed beneath. Very often the writer's position in his firm also appears:

Yours faithfully,

J. Dimwiddie
Company Secretary

The firm's name is frequently, but surely unnecessarily, included with the signature, for example

Yours faithfully,
J. Brown & Co. Ltd,

J. Dimwiddie
Company Secretary

If a letter is signed on behalf of a superior, this should be indicated:

Yours faithfully,

Penelope Digby

for J Golightly
Sales Manager

Sometimes the expression *Dictated by Mr Golightly and signed in his absence* is added at the foot of the letter.

p.p. (which stands for *per procurationem* meaning *for and on behalf of*) has a special legal meaning and should not be used for general purposes.

When a woman signs a letter she should indicate her status as follows:

(a)   if she uses her forename in the signature and does not put *Mrs*, it will be assumed that she is single, for example *Jane Smith*

(b)   if she uses an initial, she should define her sex and status, for example *J. Smith (Miss)*

(c)   if she uses her forename and wishes to indicate her married status, then she signs herself *Jane Smith (Mrs)*.

The expression *Ms*, which is the equivalent of *Mr* and does not distinguish marital status, is now widely used and generally acceptable.

9   ENCLOSURES

When any documents are included in the envelope with the letter this must be indicated by *Enc(s)* or *Enclosure(s)* written at the foot of the letter at the left-hand margin.

10   PS

Don't use it. If a letter is so ill-planned that the writer has afterthoughts, then the letter **must** be rewritten.

CONTENT

In both planning and writing a letter the interests of the reader, **not** the writer, must be the prime concern.

All but the simplest letters need to be planned carefully and this is most conveniently done by making a list of the points to be covered and then arranging them in the most logical sequence. Some of the possibilities are given below.

(a)   In a reply, use the order of the original.

(b)   Ascending order of importance. This implies that minor items will be presented first before one reaches the main topic of the letter.

(c)   Descending order of importance. Here the major topic is presented first, followed by the minor details.

(d)   Chronological order is often a logical choice. Thus a series of events will be presented in the order in which they happened.

As a very general guide, the use of the following plan is suggested:

(a)   subject
(b)   information
(c)   purpose
(d)   conclusion.

1   SUBJECT

It will obviously help the reader's understanding if he is told, first of all, what the letter is about. If the letter has just one topic, a heading may be ideal. Otherwise the opening paragraph must immediately state the subject of the letter. It should be short, as indeed should all the paragraphs of a letter.

Frequently the letter will be a reply, when the simple opening sentence, *Thank you for your letter of 15 June, 19 − −, about . . .,* is perhaps the most satisfactory form. (The date quoted is, of course, that appearing on the previous letter, **not** the date on which it was received.)

Avoid beginning letters with the phrase *With reference to . . ..* It all too often beguiles the writer into long, rambling or incomplete sentences, such as *With reference to your letter of 1 March.*

2   INFORMATION

A second paragraph, or series of paragraphs, may often be required to amplify the subject of the letter mentioned briefly in the opening paragraph.

3   PURPOSE

Having introduced and explained the subject of the letter, the purpose is now reached. This may, for example, be a request for action, the statement of a decision, or the information required.

4   CONCLUSION

It is not always necessary to add a concluding paragraph. Remember that letters should be as brief as courtesy and clarity will allow and do not conclude with some meaningless (and often ungrammatical) padding such as *Assuring you of our best attention at all times.* If your letter is a prompt reply and to the point, your best attention will already have been demonstrated.

However, the last message the recipient receives should, wherever possible, guide him towards the next stage. Here are some useful concluding sentences:

> *We look forward to receiving your instructions/reply.*
> *Please tell us if we can give you any further help.*
> *I hope this information will be of use to you.*

LANGUAGE

Once the content of the letter, **what** you wish to say, has been planned, you must give thought to **how** you will express it. Just as manners have become much more informal over the past decades, so has the language of letters.

Stilted 'commercialese', using expressions derived from Latin, like *re, ult., inst., prox.* and old-fashioned phrases like *We are in receipt of your esteemed favour* have almost disppeared. The sooner they do so, the better.

Simple, direct and concise language will be the most easily understood by your reader, and therefore is most appropriate. Nelson's famous message at Trafalgar was not:

> *With reference to previous instructions appertaining to naval discipline, it is felt that all personnel in the immediate vicinity of Cape Trafalgar will carry out the navigational and/or combative duties allocated to them, whichever is applicable, to the satisfaction of all concerned.*

BUT

> *England expects that every man will do his duty.*

This is not to say that all the words and expressions we use should be simple or monosyllabic. A limited vocabulary always makes dull reading. But current clichés, such as *at this moment in time,* and pompous expressions, or any words which are unlikely to be understood by the reader, should always be avoided.

```
Dear Sirs

We shall be pleased to receive at your earliest con-
venience details of your organisation for distribution
within our own organisation in order to confirm these
facts to members of our own staff.

If you could publish details of this organisation in
detail it will simplify our task to achieve the
objective of having the information available at an
early date.

We would suggest that a meeting be held at these offices
during January with your UK agents if preferred on a
date to be agreed to give you the opportunity of out-
lining your proposals and ensuring our interpretation is
correct and in accordance with our own interpretation
of the main requirements.

Yours faithfully
```

Figure 3   Faulty letter (a)

Figure 3, a genuine letter, demonstrates how the writer's message can be lost in a jungle of pompous verbiage and repetition.

Three helpful guides are:

(a)　use short simple words wherever possible
(b)　use short sentences wherever appropriate
(c)　use short paragraphs almost always.

JARGON

Jargon is defined by H. W. Fowler in *Modern English Usage* as: 'talk that is considered both ugly-sounding and hard to understand: applied especially to the sectional vocabulary of a science, art, class, sect, trade, or profession, full of technical terms'.

Figure 4 well illustrates the pitfalls of the use of jargon. The two expressions

> *currently met an out of stock situation*

and

> *resume a stock position*

conjure up delightfully comic pictures, but how pretentious they are. It would have been so much more straightforward to say

> *unfortunately this material is out of stock at the moment and we regret that we shall not be able to deliver your order until the end of February.*

```
Dear Sirs

CUSTOMER ORDER NO. F.58294

In response to your card regarding the above
and the non-delivery of one box of 352 Typing
Paper, we are writing to inform you that this
has currently met an out of stock situation
and that delivery cannot be met until the end
of February.

We trust that you will be receiving the above
immediately we resume a stock position.

Yours faithfully
```

Figure 4   Faulty letter (b)

The phrase, *the above*, repeated twice, is not helpful to the reader. It would have been more sensible to say *this order*, instead of directing the reader's eye back to the heading each time. *We are writing* is far too commonly found in letters.

Finally, the writer of this letter appears to have been so carried away by his flow of jargon that he forgot to make perhaps the most necessary point in a letter of this kind, namely an apology for the inconvenience caused to the customer.

The following suggestions should help you to avoid the use of jargon.

1. Use active, not passive forms of verbs, for example

> *we feel,* **not** *it is felt that . . .*

2. Avoid circumlocution, in other words always prefer the shorter, simpler expression. Use for example

> *for* **not** *for the purpose of*
> *about* **not** *with regard to*

3. Don't use padding. It has been said that 30 per cent of the content of business letters is 'dead wood'. Sir Winston Churchill quoted the following example of padding, of which he strongly disapproved.

> *consideration would be given to the possibility of carrying into effect . .*

4. Choose the more common, shorter words, for example

> *send* **not** *forward*
> *end* **not** *terminate*
> *go* **not** *proceed*

No doubt you can substitute suitable alternatives for the following:

commence	peruse
materialise	utilise
assist	deem

After having emphasised the value of brevity, we shall conclude with the warning that even virtues can be taken too far. George Bernard Shaw was a master of brevity, and also when he chose, of devastating rudeness. He once received an invitation which read 'The Countess of Blank will be at home on . . .', to which he simply replied, 'So will George Bernard Shaw'.

STYLE AND TONE

The style we choose will be a compromise between several different elements. First, it will to some extent reflect our own personalities. This is not to say that we should use too idiosyncratic a style, for we are seeking to project an image not only of ourselves but also of the organisation on whose behalf we may be writing. But an element of originality is desirable.

Originality in this context implies that the letter will both avoid the use of stereotyped phrases or jargon and will also impress the reader as having been written with him in mind and to meet his particular needs.

Second, our style, in the choice of vocabulary, sentence structure, and so on, will seek primarily to be comprehensible to the reader. A letter to rate-payers, explaining the need to increase rates, will be phrased in very different terms from a report on the same subject circulated within the Treasurer's Department.

Third, the style must be suitable to the subject. Formal circumstances, such as debt collection or complaint letters, require a formal, though not threatening, tone. When one is asking a favour the style will be much more in-formal, though it should never be allowed to slip into colloquialisms. Figure 5 shows a letter written in a pleasantly informal style. It is, in fact, a standard

letter which reflects the house style of the organisation from which it origin-
ated — friendly, informal, but never casual and always efficient.

```
Dear Sirs,


                 Our letter:
             Subject-matter:


     We cannot trace having received a reply to our
letter.  It would help us if you could make enquiries
and let us have your comments.  If you have already
replied, we apologise for having troubled you - but
will you please let us have a copy of your answer?
     We shall be grateful for your co-operation.



                 Yours faithfully,
```

Figure 5   A good letter

So our style in writing letters will reflect ourselves, our reader's needs and
the demands of the subject matter. But the final aim will be to write well.
This does not imply the use of literary flourishes but of accuracy, brevity and,
let us hope, a touch of elegance.

The examples of letters shown in Figures 6, 7, 8 and 9 were written in
reply to a circular letter sent to publishers requesting materials for display at
an educational conference. They all contain examples of common errors.

The letter in Figure 6 was, no doubt, satisfactory to its recipients in that it
contained an offer of the help which had been requested, but it has many
flaws. There are also grammatical errors. Letters must be promptly answered.
It should not be necessary to apologise for delay. If for some reason it is not
possible to give a detailed reply immediately, an acknowledgement will re-
assure one's correspondent.

```
Dear Mr X,

    Thank you for your letter of 20th June,
and I apologise for the delay in answering
it.  I have recently returned from holiday
and have had a great many things to attend
to.  If you will be kind enough to give me
the address to which you would like the
material sent, I will despatch a quantity
of our latest catalogues and bulletins to
you.

         Yours sincerely,
```

Figure 6   Faulty letter (c)

Dear Sir

We thank you for your letter giving information
on your conference on 9th September at Blank
Technical College.

We would be interested in exhibiting our equipment and wonder if it would be possible to have
a representative in attendance.

We enclose leaflets giving details of the equipment we would exhibit and, as you are so close,
we would welcome the opportunity to meet you at
our works in Blankford. Please let us know if
this can be arranged.

Yours faithfully

Figure 7   Faulty letter (d)

Dear Mr X,

    Thank you for your letter dated 1 June 19--,
but I am sorry the only way I can help is to let
you have some catalogues, which I am pleased to
do with this letter, though they are limited in
number, for we have a continuing expanding demand
throughout the country, but I do hope that these
will be helpful to you.

                Yours sincerely,

Figure 8   Faulty letter (e)

Dear Mr X,

    I am writing to you in connexion with the one day
conference being held at Blank Technical College. Since
the date of the conference is the 9th September I should
like to make arrangements to send a selection of our
books in compliance with your wishes.

    I would therefore be most grateful if you could let
me know who will be dealing with the publishers' exhibits.
I have made a provisional list of books which I feel
would be suitable, however I am enclosing our 'Education'
subject list for you to look through; you will find that
certain of the titles have been marked for your attention.

    Any further information which you can supply me with
would be most appreciated.

    I shall be away for the next two weeks, but when I
return I shall be in contact again. Should any of the
books be of interest to you for your teaching commitments
please do not hesitate to send for 'Inspection copies'.

    If I can be of any further assistance, please do not
hesitate to contact me.

                Yours sincerely,

Figure 9   Faulty letter (f)

Now look at the second sentence. The writer is somewhat discourteously concentrating on his own problems, not on those of his correspondent. It also wastes the reader's time, as it tells him nothing he needs, or wishes to know. Finally, it detracts from the small courtesy of the apology in its implication that the writer had much more important things to do than to write this reply. One paragraph is clearly not sufficient, even in so brief a letter, for the variety of topics mentioned by the writer.

Figure 7 shows a helpful and friendly letter, but note the number of times that the word *we* occurs. Note also the very commonly made grammatical error, *we would*. The correct form is, of course, *we should.*

The specimen shown in Figure 8 seems to be the result of a boss dictating his amiable but muddled thoughts to a secretary whose contribution to the general disorder is a scattering of commas. It is a combination of the man who cannot dictate and the secretary who cannot edit. Whom would you blame most for this particular horror?

Figure 9 provides an even better example of muddled thinking, and a whole rogue's gallery of errors of grammar and punctuation. Rewrite it, correcting the errors and reorganising the content.

```
Dear Mr X

CONFERENCE AT BLANK TECHNICAL COLLEGE

We are indeed interested in your Conference to
be held on 9th September and should be pre-
pared to man a display.  Further details of
how you intend to run the Exhibition would be
welcome.

Yours sincerely
```

Figure 10   A helpful letter

The letter shown in Figure 10 is a refreshing change from the four earlier ones. Note how the writer combines brevity with clarity and infuses into two short sentences a tone of warmth and helpful interest.

Figure 11 shows a letter which is friendly and helpful in tone. The reader may well find it officiously helpful. The first paragraph seems to assume that she does not know what to do with an application form, while the second paragraph implies a lack of confidence in the form. A well- designed form will elicit all the information required. You may think that this letter was completely unnecessary and that a compliments slip would have been a more suitable and economical substitute. Perhaps the worst fault, though, it that the letter is so writer-orientated: notice how every paragraph begins with the word 'I'.

It is always difficult to view one's own work objectively and critically. None the less, if you can view your own compositions from the reader's point of view, asking yourself how you would feel if you received this letter, you are unlikely to go far wrong.

```
Dear Sir

I enclose a form for application for employment with
this organisation for you to complete and return to me.

I understand that you are interested in working for
the Company in an engineering capacity and it will be
helpful if you can provide as much information as
possible.

I shall contact you again when I have received your
completed form with a probable view to arranging a
formal interview.

Yours faithfully
```

Figure 11   Faulty letter (g)

SOME TYPES OF BUSINESS LETTERS

1   CIRCULAR LETTER

These are most frequently sales-promotion letters, but you may also be asked to compose, for example, begging letters on behalf of charitable organisations, letters to ratepayers, members of societies, or employees of a firm. An example is shown in Figure 12.

Circular letters are unsolicited: the readers often have no particular interest in your message. You must therefore catch the reader's attention in the first sentence and hold it to the end. This can best be done by showing that your 'message' will somehow benefit your reader.

Frequently, circular letters are sent to a large number of people. A conversational style and friendly tone will help to make them less impersonal.

Finally, the presentation is important. A badly duplicated letter on cheap paper is much less likely to be read than one which has an attractive appearance.

2   LETTERS OF COMPLAINT (see Figure 13)

A dissatisfied customer who feels that she has been unfairly treated is likely to be angry, but she must resist any temptation to show this by rudeness or sarcasm in a letter seeking redress. A moment's reflection shows that such a tone can hardly fail to antagonise the reader and it is unlikely to persuade him to consider the complaint with sympathy.

The tone of a successful letter should therefore be reasonable but firm. All the relevant information should be presented clearly, and copies, not originals, of any documents involved should be included if possible.

If the complaint is about faulty goods, they should not be returned with the letter, but be retained as evidence, or possibly returned personally to the shop.

Renderdri Ltd,
9 Oak Lane,
Billington,
Surrey.
B14 6XZ

2nd May, 19--

Dear Sir,

    A local advertising campaign is to take place shortly
to introduce 'Renderdri' into your area. A limited
number of home owners will be given the opportunity of
having 'Renderdri' applied to the exterior walls of their
homes at a substantial discount.

    'Renderdri' is an exterior coating up to 20 times
thicker than ordinary paint. It can be applied in any
weather. The long lasting properties of Fibreglass,
Asbestos and Titanium are combined in a product which
gives a decorative surface with a high degree of insulation and is impervious to all climatic extremes.

    Eliminate constant and costly repainting. 'Renderdri'
is guaranteed for 20 years against chipping, flaking or
peeling.

    If the exterior walls of your home could do with a
facelift, take advantage of our special introductory
offer by completing and returning the enclosed reply
paid card.

        Yours faithfully,

        Marketing Manager
        RENDERDRI

Enclosure

Figure 12   A sales letter

The plan of a letter of complaint will follow the general rules already set
out:

(a)   the subject of the complaint
(b)   supplementary information
(c)   purpose (what action you seek), for example replacement of goods,
a refund, a further repair or service call free of charge
(d)   a complimentary conclusion, possibly expressing confidence and the
expectation of a favourable and helpful reply to reinforce one's
purpose — an indication of urgency which expresses the hope of a
reply 'within seven days' may be helpful.

3   LETTERS OF ADJUSTMENT (see Figure 14)

Replies to complaints will be as varied as the complaints themselves. Obviously
many unreasonable complaints are received by firms and replies cannot always
satisfy the complainant.

```
                                        5 The Larches,
                                          BLANKTON,
                                          Exshire.
                                             BL5 4JS

                                        16th October, 19--

The Manager,
Blank Electricity Board,
BLANKTON,
Exshire.
BL1 6BD


Dear Sir,

              Electricity Account No. NB.456/H

       I was concerned to receive your final demand of
    13th October, 19-- for payment of my quarterly elec-
    tricity account of £35.78.

       I wrote to you on 25th September querying this
    account and my letter was acknowledged by a card from
    you stating that my letter was receiving attention.  I
    have not yet received a full reply.

       In my earlier letter, of which I enclose a copy, I
    questioned the amount of the account, which I believe
    is far too high an estimate for a summer quarter during
    which electricity was used only for cooking and lighting.

       The meter now reads 52405 units.  Will you please
    send me a revised account based on this actual reading
    or, if this reading is unacceptable, send your meter
    reader to check.

       In view of your threat to cut off my electricity, I
    hope that you will reply promptly.

                      Yours faithfully,



                      B. Bloggs

    Enclosure
```

Figure 13   Letter of complaint

A letter of adjustment, however, should always contain an apology which will demonstrate the firm's concern at, and recognition of, the inconvenience caused to the customer, without committing the firm. The tone should be conciliatory and if the firm is unable to meet the complainant's demands, the reasons should be explained carefully. No reputable firm will wilfully lose business or antagonise customers and a sympathetic tone will go far to create good will.

4 A LETTER REQUIRING TACT

As a local dignitary you have been invited to become President of a society in the town. You feel that its activities are time-wasting and pointless, though

```
19 October 19--

B Bloggs Esq
5 The Larches
BLANKTON
Exshire
BL5 4JS


Dear Mr Bloggs

Electricity Account No NB 456/H

Thank you for your letter of 16 October 19-- about
the final demand for payment of this account.

We apologise both for the delay in replying to your
letter of 25 September 19--, which appears to have been
mis-filed, and for the final demand which you were
mistakenly sent.

Your meter reading of 52405 is indeed acceptable and a
revised account, which will replace the previous
estimated account, is being sent to you.

Yours sincerely


J Kincaid
Area Manager
```

Figure 14   Letter of adjustment

worthy, and you wish to refuse, but without giving offence. An appropriate letter is shown in Figure 15.

5   LETTERS OF APPLICATION FOR JOBS

There is a growing tendency for job advertisements to invite applicants to reply by telephone. However, it is still far more common to apply for a job in writing. Some firms will, in their advertisement, ask you to apply for further details and, perhaps, an application form. The application form, when completed, should be returned with a covering letter.

If the advertisement simply invites you to apply, you have the choice of writing:

(a)   a letter containing all the relevant information, or
(b)   a short covering letter together with a *curriculum vitae* containing the relevant information set out on a separate sheet.

You will also have to consider whether your application will be hand written or typed. Typing will give a neat appearance and is obviously particularly appropriate for applications for secretarial posts. However, many employers still wish to see a specimen of your handwriting. Indeed, some employers, especially in the United States, employ experts to examine applicants' handwriting.

If your application consists of a covering letter together with a *curriculum vitae*, the letter should be handwritten and the *curriculum vitae* typed. If you

```
                                        The Beeches,
                                          Castle Road,
                                            RAVENFIELD,
                                              Exshire.
                                                RA5 6JS

                                        18th April, 19--

     Miss I. Dogood,
     Honorary Secretary,
     Ravenfield Festival Society,
     5 Green Lane,
     RAVENFIELD.
     RA8 5TT

     Dear Miss Dogood,

          I should like to thank you most sincerely for your
     letter of 16th April inviting me to become President of
     the Ravenfield Festival Society.

          I have followed with interest the growth of the
     Society over the past two years.  The effort being made
     to promote the Arts in Ravenfield with the ultimate
     aim of holding a Festival is one which I applaud.

          Although I am very fond of music, my knowledge is
     limited to the popular classical range, rather than to
     the more serious music to be featured at the Festival.
     I understand that, apart from the actual performances,
     there will be discussions between artists and members
     of the Society.  With my lack of technical knowledge of
     music, I do not feel able to take a sufficiently intel-
     ligent part in such activities nor to represent the
     Society in the capacity which would seem to be required.
     I feel therefore that to accept your invitation would be
     to do the Society a disservice.

          I trust that you will appreciate my reasons for
     declining to be President of your Society and that you
     will convey to the members my very best wishes for the
     future success of the Ravenfield Festival.

                         Yours sincerely,


                         Charles Martingale-Smythe
```

Figure 15 Tact

apply by letter only, the choice of handwriting or typing is a matter for your own discretion. You will probably choose on the basis of the legibility and elegance, or otherwise, of your handwriting.

A covering letter should follow this plan:

(a) reference to the advertisement and statement of application
(b) reference to enclosed *curriculum vitae*
(c) amplification of details of *curriculum vitae*, if relevant
(d) complimentary close.

PLAN OF CURRICULUM VITAE

> Name
> Address
> Telephone number
> Date of birth
> Schools/colleges attended (with dates)
> Examination results
> Examination results awaited
> Other qualifications
> Experience (with dates)
> Referees (1)
>   (2)

Usually two referees are sufficient, though sometimes three are asked for. If you are still a student, the first referee should be from your school or college. If you are already at work, you should name your present employer. This is a professional reference from someone who is qualified to give information about your qualification and experience. The second reference may be called a character reference. Preferably the person should be of some standing and have known you for some time.

Courtesy demands that your referees should have been asked to act for you **before** you give their names. If you are able to give them some information about the post for which you are applying, they will be able to make their reference more relevant and helpful.

Testimonials are of very little value and are rarely asked for nowadays.

The sample letter of application shown in Figure 16 was written in reply to the following advertisement:

THE AVA GOE COMPANY
requires

a Senior Secretary to the Sales Manager. The Company is a long-established one, specialising in the manufacture of plastic containers, and has a wide home and overseas market.

We are seeking to recruit an experienced secretary to join a vigorous and expanding sales team.

Candidates should preferably be in the age range of 25-40 with shorthand and typewriting speeds of 120/50 w.p.m. respectively.

Salary by negotiation. Good working conditions. Luncheon vouchers. Three weeks annual holiday. Pension scheme.

Apply in writing, giving details of background, qualifications, experience and salary required to:

> Personnel Officer
> Xford Trading Estate
> Xford XY3 2ZA

This advertisement is also used in Section 12 'Interviews'.

```
                                           12 Rough Lane
                                           CUTSTONE
                                           CT4 6BL

                                           16 May 19--

        The Personnel Officer
        The A V A Goe Company
        Xford Trading Estate
        XFORD
        XY3 2ZA

        Dear Sir

        SECRETARY TO SALES MANAGER

        Your advertisement for the above post in this week's
        Xford Gazette aroused my interest as I am at present
        working in a similar capacity in a smaller firm.  I
        should welcome the opportunity to move to a more res-
        ponsible post in this field and hope that my appli-
        cation will merit serious consideration.

        I obtained eight 'O' levels and 'A' levels in English
        and French at my grammar school and then attended a
        secretarial course at the Northshire College.  I passed
        130 Pitman's Shorthand, The London Chamber of Commerce
        Advanced Typewriting (speed 55 wpm) and The Institute
        of Linguists Intermediate French.

        My first post in 19-- was as secretary to the Deputy
        Sales Director of Marchandise et Cie, 16 Rue Clébert,
        Paris 6ième.  I worked in Paris for two years, gaining
        useful experience of the European market.

        In 19--, I took up my present post with Sales Limited,
        272 Field Avenue, Cutstone.  The firm produces a range
        of packaging products.  The relatively small size of
        the organisation has given me experience of a wide
        variety of work.

        At present my salary is £       p.a.  I should hope that
        a move would improve on this, with prospects of further
        increases should my work warrant them.

        Both my present and previous employers have expressed
        their willingness to act as referees on my behalf.  I
        can be available for interview on any weekday, but
        should appreciate being able to give my employer some
        prior notice of my impending absence from work.

        Yours faithfully



        Mary Banks (Miss)
```

Figure 16   Letter of application

EXERCISES

1. Write a letter to an estate agent saying you wish to rent a furnished
    house or bungalow near the sea for yourself and three friends for three

weeks during late August or early September. Give your requirements, for example number of bedrooms, garage, etc., and the weekly rent you are prepared to pay.

(LCC Private Secretary's Certificate)

2. Prepare a letter for your employer's signature accepting the invitation for him to be President for the next year of the professional body to which he belongs. He will also be delighted to give his inaugural address at the headquarters in London in two months' time. He will, however, inform the Secretary later of the actual subject of his talk. Since your employer is about to travel abroad, and is unsure of the date of his return, he asks the Secretary to get in touch with you, his secretary, with any queries and to give you full information about the address and overnight hotel accommodation on the occasion.

(LCC Private Secretary's Certificate)

3. As Secretary of your local literary and arts society, write a letter to a well-known figure (of your own selection) inviting him or her to address your society at the first of the next season's meetings. In your letter give some brief introductory details of your society as well as the arrangements for the lecture and for the reception of your speaker, who will be travelling some distance and will have to stay overnight.

(LCC Private Secretary's Certificate)

4. As Chairman of your local residents' association, write a circular news-letter to all your members, giving an account of the activities, successes and failures of the past year, together with some indication of your proposed future actions. You may use the following notes if you wish: fund raising and social — new bus service to estate — road repairs (now complete) — residential development on Sandford Farm — play spaces — gravel pit nuisance.

5. You have been employed for five years by your present firm as a private secretary in a post which you have enjoyed and where you have been able to progress, but now you wish to resign. Write your formal letter of resignation to your employer, at the same time requesting a reference you may use for any future job. (In your letter invent your own reasons for your resignation.)

(LCC Private Secretary's Certificate)

6. You are the manager of a firm of wholesale fruit importers. Lorries belonging to a firm whose warehouses are adjacent to yours often block your right of way. As manager, write a letter of complaint in a firm but tactful tone, giving a recent instance of obstruction and requesting an end to the inconvenience.

(SCCAPE Advanced Secretarial Certificate)

7.   Jones, the Managing Director of Farm Foods Inc., has indicated to Brown, an Area Manager, that higher-grade appointments in his area should not be made without consultation with Head Office. Jones learns indirectly that Brown has made such an appointment without that consultation. He wishes to convey to Brown that he is aware of this and feels that it calls for an explanation. In the character of Jones, write a letter to Brown, friendly in tone, but which indicates the writer's displeasure at the breach of instructions.

(SCCAPE Advanced Secretarial Certificate)

8.   Reply to the following advertisement:

Personal Secretary

A personal secretary is required for the Head of the Purchasing Department of a large international company with offices opposite Holborn tube station.

This is a varied and responsible position and applicants should have shorthand and typewriting speeds of 100/40 w.p.m. Previous secretarial experience is preferred but an intelligent college-leaver would be considered.

Commencing salary £2600 per annum, plus proficiency allowances up to £550 per annum according to speeds. Salary rises by increments to £3800 plus.

Hours 8.45 a.m. - 4.45 p.m. (4.30 on Fridays). Four weeks holiday per annum. Subsidised staff restaurant and sandwich bar.

Letters of application should be addressed to the Personnel Office (Recruitment), Danum House, French Street, W.1.

9.   Write a letter of application, enclosing a *curriculum vitae,* in reply to the following advertisement:

GIRL FRIDAY

Long hours. Endless demands, Brutal slave-driving boss thinly disguised as director of new dynamic multi-million-pound property company in Mayfair.

Speaking just English won't be enough for the executive secretary who chains herself to this job.

She must speak French too. Possibly an additional European language. And be capable of slaving away at both shorthand and audio. Why should any girl suffer like this? For the pay (£3400) per annum), that's why. It's definitely way up.

Also, write a letter to your headmaster, asking him to act as a referee.

10. Qualbest Pharmaceuticals Limited is a British company which manu-
factures drugs and medicines. These have saved many lives in British
and European hospitals. Some of the drugs have been invaluable in
curing diseases in the developing countries. Of course, it is not possible
to cure every sick patient, whatever drug is used. The high cost of research makes the drugs very expensive. An (imaginary) British newspaper has recently published an article attacking the company for over-
charging and for marketing drugs which do not cure people. This attack
in unjustified when all the facts are known. For example, the company
donated a large consignment of drugs after an earthquake disaster in
one of the developing countries.

EITHER

(a) A Director of the company decides to write a letter to the newspaper, which he hopes the editor will publish, in which he will
defend his company against the attack. He asks you as his secretary
to draft a suitable letter which he will use as a guide when he writes
his final draft. Prepare a letter as requested, basing it on the facts
given above. You may invent minor details to lend realism. No
expert knowledge of drugs is required, and you should **not** discuss
diseases except in general terms.

OR

(b) An official working for an international relief organisation asks you
as his secretary to draft a letter from him to Qualbest Pharmaceuticals Limited. He wants to express his gratitude for the firm's
generous help during a recent disaster, and to comment on the newspaper attack which he has just read. Prepare the draft as requested,
basing it on the facts given above. You may invent minor details to
lend realism. No expert knowledge of drugs or relief work is required.

(LCC Private Secretary's Certificate)

11 In your answer to this question you may invent minor details where
necessary, but keep your letter reasonably brief. Remember that you
are **not** using headed paper, and set out your letter ready for signature.
A new London symphony orchestra plans to go on tour in a foreign
country in 19 – – for about three weeks, giving a number of concerts
in various towns. Assume that English is well understood in the country.

EITHER

(a) As secretary to the orchestra's General Manager, prepare the draft of
a letter which he will send to the Chamber of Commerce of one of
the towns in which he hopes to hold a concert. He will need to find
out if there is a suitable concert hall available for booking, and what
the hiring charge would be. He will also want to know such things as
the hotel accommodation available for members of the orchestra,

what airport facilities exist in the area, and whether there are any special local tastes in music.

OR

(b)   Imagine that the above letter has been received by the Chamber of Commerce. As secretary to the official who will reply, draft a helpful and informative letter from him to the General Manager of the orchestra. Include suggestions about advance publicity, mentioning any ways in which your Chamber of Commerce might be able to assist.

(LCC Private Secretary's Certificate)

12   The Personnel Director of Dunslop Ltd has just received a letter from a university group inviting his company to be sponsor for their proposed August 19—— expedition to North-west Greenland. As Personal Assistant to the Personnel Director, write a letter of refusal which does not cause offence.

(Scottish HND in Secretarial Studies)

13   Hobson and Harkins Ltd, who have been good customers of Smalltown Electronics Instruments for a number of years, now owe £762. This sum has not been paid within the usual trade terms and a standard reminder has brought no results. As Accounts Manager of Smalltown Electronics Instruments, write a tactful letter dealing with the situation.

(Scottish HND in Secretarial Studies)

14   A well-known British motor-car manufacturing company has been suffering from recurrent production losses for a variety of reasons in the summer months of 19——. As Personal Assistant to the Director of Home Sales, draft a letter which seeks to explain the need to adjust again the delivery dates of quotas of particular cars to main dealers and which attempts to reduce the anticipated exasperation.

(Scottish HND in Secretarial Studies)

15.   The following letter to the Editor of the *National Gazette* appeared in last Monday's edition, 30 May:

Sir,

  Can nothing stop bureaucracy from despoiling the English countryside in the name of profit?

  I refer to the British Coal Authority's threat to exploit the newly discovered reserves in the Vale of Floristone, a matter calling for immediate national debate.

  The Vale contains farms and village communities set amid some of the finest scenery in the country. The Authority's plan to mine coal here is shocking to all those who care for the preservation of Britain's rural landscape.

In any case the Authority's bland argument that the coal can be sold abroad to improve our balance of payments goes completely against the nation's long-term economic interests and therefore nullifies any possible case for mining. As a once great power we still exist by using native and imported raw materials to create and export manufactured products. In this present period of world energy surplus we must do all we can to conserve our raw materials for the future.

It is patently obvious that coal in the ground is a much more worthwhile asset than coal out of the ground, which reflects merely a depreciating national bank balance. With all those who love this as yet unspoiled corner of England I shall do all I can to thwart the Authority's intention.

Yours faithfully,

J. H. Masham

The Chairman of the British Coal Authority (BCA) means to answer this letter and asks you, as his PA, to collect some relevant facts and comments from senior staff. Their responses are set out below. Edit these items and compose a draft reply letter for the Chairman's approval. Only the body of the letter is required.

BCA has already had contacts with round about 40 local authorities, etc. about the seams we've located in the Vale. We've had news conferences and endless chats and letter exchanges with pressure groups and what not. There's a mountain of files on this already. Truth is, we're keen to keep everyone as happy as we can. Anyway, there's a lot of the locals are backing the BCA; not surprising when you think there's not much work going outside of farming and horticulture. If we can get cracking with our arrangements there'll be more cash in people's pockets and less dole money to fork out. How *can* Masham talk such tripe about an 'immediate national debate' when we've leant over backwards listening to people? And that's only for starters. BCA hasn't even begun to get down to brass tacks yet in sorting out a plan for *mining* the stuff. Our backroom boys reckon there are 450 million tons under the Vale; that's £7000 million in the national kitty.

Masham's wrong about shipping the coal abroad anyway. The Midland power-stations will be first in the queue. Besides, if we get the green light on the scheme we'll all be less likely to end up buying expensive foreign coal in 15-20 years' time. Be warned; a lot of people who know what they're on about are saying that round about then world energy supplies will be getting short. That will jack the price up. Everyone else will be scrambling for what's going while we're all sitting pretty here at home.

Britain's dead lucky; we've got food and fuel as our biggest natural resources. We'd better start all pulling together to boost output in both departments. Heaven knows, it's time we did something to give a facelift to our balance-of-payments situation. BCA wouldn't be earning its keep if it didn't do its bit to help get the country out of its economic mess. Apart from all that, no one gives a higher rating than BCA to looking after the environment and dodging the grottier social effects of sinking new pits. Our track record's second to none on this sort of thing.

(RSA Diploma for Personal Assistants)

16   Your employers, Traveltours of Bridge Street, Eastbury, who arrange package holidays, have just been informed that some of the new hotels on Ibiza which were to be used during the forthcoming holiday season will not be completed in time; there have been difficulties with the supply of building materials and a protracted spell of wet weather has created further problems. There will be sufficient vacancies for your clients in other established hotels, but not all of these can offer the same amenities and standard of comfort as the new ones; they are situated in pleasant surroundings but are not on the coast. Clients who are asked to accept a stay at one of these as an alternative will be offered a choice of a cancellation (with full refund of all money paid so far) or a discount of 15 per cent on the cost of the holiday. The company will provide free transport from the alternative hotel to the coast for the duration of the holiday and your permanent representative on Ibiza will be on hand to assist in minimising upsets and inconvenience.

Write a letter to be circulated to all clients whose holidays will be affected, expressing your regrets, explaining the situation to them and assuring them that the company will do its utmost to ensure that they will have an enjoyable holiday. You would like to hear from them as soon as possible.

(LCC Secretarial Studies Certificate)

5

MEMORANDA AND REPORTS

It is possible (and it has been done) to write a complete book about report-writing. This section seeks to distinguish between different types of report and also to help students plan, organise and write them. First, you need to know about a document frequently used in business for many purposes, including short reports. That document is a *memorandum*.

MEMORANDA

Memoranda ('memos' for short) are the equivalent within a business of the letters sent to people outside it — internal correspondence, in fact.

The paper on which they are written or typed is usually pre-printed and, so that staff may be encouraged to keep memos short, it is often of A5 size. Figure 17 shows some examples of memo headings, but there are many variations. For instance, one organisation uses a pre-printed set of three A4 size sheets, coloured white, blue and pink respectively, with no carbon required. The top half of the set is used for the original message, the white and blue sheets are sent to the recipient and the pink sheet is filed. The recipient writes his answer on the bottom half, returns the white sheet and files the blue one. This has the advantage that question and answer appear on the same sheet of paper.

The important items that must appear on a memorandum heading are:

1. The word 'MEMORANDUM' (sometimes shortened to 'MEMO').
2. The words 'TO' and 'FROM', indicating the space where the names and/or titles of the recipient(s) and sender of the memo are written.
3. 'DATE' followed by a space in which the date is written.

Also included sometimes are:

1. Name or cipher (monogram) of the company above the word 'MEMOR-ANDUM'.
2. 'REF', as for a letter.
3. 'SUBJECT' — this word means that a heading or title for the memo must be given. This is a desirable practice in correspondence, for a heading immediately identifies the subject-matter.

```
                          MEMORANDUM


                                      DATE:
        TO:                  FROM:


```
1.

```
                    Name of Firm
                    Memorandum
        From:.................. To:..................
        Date:.................. Ref:..................
        Subject:....................................
```
2.

FIRM	MEMORANDUM	FORM NO 632
TO	SUBJECT	FROM
		DATE

3.

Figure 17   Memoranda forms

The salutation and complimentary close found in letters are omitted from memoranda and, as they are used for internal correspondence, there is no need to include addresses.

Memoranda, like letters, may be formal or informal. An example of a short formal memo, with copies sent to several people, is shown in Figure 18. In this case four copies plus a file copy would be typed and the name of each recipient underlined on the copy sent to him. On other occasions a single copy of a memo may be sent out with a circulation list attached. Each reader will tick his/her name on the list to indicate that the memo has been read.

MEMORANDUM

DATE: 6th June 19--

TO: FROM:

    Mr Black Production Manager   J. Jones
    Mr Gray   Chief Accountant   Managing
    Mr Green Export Manager   Director
    Mr White Sales Manager

MONTHLY REPORTS

Please note that there will be a meeting of the
Board of Directors next month to discuss expansion of exports to Europe and I shall therefore
require the monthly reports by 26th June, a
week earlier than usual.

J. Jones

Figure 18   A formal memorandum

Memoranda are no longer merely reminders. The format is used very widely, even, as will be seen later, for informal reports. In examinations students are required to write quite long memos, such as in Exercise 6 at the end of this section.

The layout for long memos should follow closely the layout suggested for reports later in this section. As they are business documents it is inappropriate to write them without using whatever headings, sub-headings and numbering systems will assist the reader to understand and use the documents.

REPORTS

Before looking at some of the ways in which reports may be presented, let us consider what a report is. Briefly it is a written document, or oral presentation, in which a problem is discussed and examined. Information will be conveyed, findings and conclusions reported, hypotheses and theories stated and analysed and, sometimes, recommendations for future action, or suggestions for further consideration, made.

This section is concerned with written rather than oral reports and, for the most part, with short reports of 500-600 words at maximum. Managers are busy people. They do not want long-winded discursive documents which take a long time to read and understand. They want reports which are very much to the point. It is essential to establish at the beginning what the report is to contain and how it is to be used.

TERMS OF REFERENCE

The first task is to define your terms of reference; that is, the subject, limits and purpose of the report and who is to read and use it. A true report is one which you have been asked to write by a superior. He will therefore provide you with terms of reference. Make sure that you understand exactly what you have to do and what he wants and *write it down.* (It is always safer not to trust your memory.)

If you are preparing a report on your own initiative, then you will devise your own terms of reference. Again it is desirable to write your purpose so that it is very clear in your mind.

For instance, suppose you know that the annual budget is about to be decided and you would like your manager to submit plans for some new equipment for your office. You may decide, rather than just going to talk to him, to prepare a report on the state of existing equipment, the reasons for buying new items, the choices of machinery available and costs. You will have to decide whether to:

1. give him the main facts only and let him ask you for any supplementary information
2. give him all the facts
3. give him one of the two above and make suggestions about what you would like
4. give him one of the two above and make firm recommendations on essential equipment (and perhaps some suggestions for other items).

PREPARATION

Before commencing your report, think carefully about:

1. the subject and purpose of the report
2. the information your reader/readers already possess
3. what the reader/readers need to know
4. the use to be made of the report.

COLLECTING INFORMATION

Gather together all the information you will require. It can be obtained by:

1. reading, for example, technical journals, newspapers, sales literature
2. looking — observe what is the present work method, what problems there are, etc.
3. talking to people about the problem you have to solve, which may also affect them
4. carrying out a survey, devising a questionnaire or having work recorded
5. experimenting, either by a formal controlled experiment or by 'trying something out'.

Write your information in note form, on separate sheets of paper, so that it will be simple to organise into the correct order.

ORGANISATION

When you have collected all the information:

1. check it carefully for accuracy
2. decide on your main sections and their order — devise appropriate headings and then work out the most logical sequence for the information in each section
3. arrange your facts under the appropriate headings
4. analyse the facts and decide whether your analysis and findings are to appear with the facts in each section or to be contained under a separate heading
5. note down any recommendations you wish to make
6. consider summarising complicated or long pieces of information and putting the information itself in appendices
7. prepare any diagrams or illustrations which will help the reader to understand the report or speed the reading.

DRAFTING THE REPORT

The preparation, collection of information and organisation completed, the process of writing the report is relatively easy.

1 STYLE

The author must first choose a style and language for the presentation of the material. The style must be suitable to the subject and the reader. It should:

(a) be objective and accurate, based on facts not personal views (any of these must be clearly shown to be views)
(b) distinguish clearly between facts and conclusions which can be inferred from the facts
(c) be impersonal, unless the reader has required the author to state personal arguments
(d) only very occasionally be controversial or provocative
(e) always be as concise and as simply worded as possible, keeping technical language to the level that the reader will understand and avoiding jargon
(f) consider the reader or readers all the time and maintain a suitable formality according to the relationship between writer and reader(s).

2 PRESENTATION

The writer must decide whether the report should be presented:
(a) within a letter
(b) within a memo
(c) as a separate document with a covering letter or memo
(d) as a document to be presented on its own or, for example, as a paper to be sent out with an agenda for a meeting.

3   LAYOUT

(a)   *Titles*

Reports must have apt and definitive titles or headings. Some examples are shown below:

(i)   A report from the National Council for Educational Technology:
Towards more effective learning

(ii)   A report of a working party:
Working Paper No. 1
Computers for Education
Report of a Working Party under the
Chairmanship of Professor J. Black
NATIONAL COUNCIL FOR EDUCATIONAL TECHNOLOGY

(iii)   A progress report:
NATIONAL GIRO RENT PAYMENT
The first three months of the new scheme
(Report prepared for the meeting of the
Westshire District Council, 3 September 19——)

(iv)   An informal report to a superior:
SUGGESTIONS FOR REALLOCATION OF SECRETARIAL
WORK IN THE SECRETARIAL BUREAU

As has been shown, report headings often need additional information presented as supplements to the main heading.

(b)   *Sub-headings and numbers*

Each section of a report, after the introduction, should have its own clear, brief heading. It is often helpful to number the sections as well. Certainly numbers should often be used within each section to identify the separate elements.

Several numbering systems are in common use. Government reports may use the simple one of having main section in roman numerals and each paragraph numbered in sequence in arabic numerals (see the sample Contents page, p. 74).

In this book, for example, the sections have a system of letters, numbers and indented sub-sections as follows:

MAIN HEADINGS

1   SUB-HEADING

(a) *Sub-sub-heading*

(i)

(ii)

A third possibility is the decimal system. Examples are found in the publications of the Business Education Council:

14   PUBLIC ADMINISTRATION AND PUBLIC SECTOR STUDIES
BOARD

4 INTRODUCTION

The introductory sentences of a report should state the terms of reference, refer the reader to existing situations without restating them, state the manner in which information was gathered and, if necessary, refer to and explain specialist words frequently used.

5 THE MAIN SECTIONS

Each main section should ideally be written in its entirety at one time. It is not, however, always necessary to draft the main sections in the order in which they will appear in the final report. Sometimes it is an advantage to draft a section for which all information is available even when some of the facts for other sections are not yet to hand.

All main sections should follow the same pattern, for example all or some of the following:

(a) statement of the facts
(b) analysis of the facts
(c) inferences
(d) detailed conclusions.

6 FINDINGS, CONCLUSIONS AND RECOMMENDATIONS

These may be:

(a) stated at the beginning of the report, immediately after the introduction
(b) stated within each section
(c) stated as the last section or sections of the report
(d) summarised after the introduction, but stated in full within each section or at the end of the report
(e) stated in full in each section and summarised at the end of the report.

The shorter the report, the more likely it is that (c) will be the format chosen. At work the custom and practice of the organisation or the wishes of your superior will generally determine your choice.

Findings and conclusions must be clearly related to the introductory section of a report and must be based on the facts. Recommendations must be made in an appropriate manner. You must not, for instance, *tell* your 'boss' what to do. Far better to suggest possible courses of action, giving facts such as costs, and leave it to him to make the decision — which is his job. It is possible to propose, say, that one of three decisions might be preferable because it will be the most efficient, but usually it is better to let facts and figures speak for themselves. They will be more effective than any special pleading.

Reports should be signed and dated at the end.

7 ILLUSTRATIONS

All diagrams, plans, charts and other illustrative material should have been prepared when the report was organised. Now a decision should be taken on whether they will be incorporated in the text or presented as appendices (see 8 below). If they are to be put in the text:

(a) number each illustration and refer to that number at the appropriate point in your writing

(b) place each illustration as near as possible to the point at which it is first mentioned in the report.

8 APPENDICES

Wherever possible material which is supplementary to the main thread or argument in the report, but to which some readers will wish to refer, should be removed from the body of the report and presented in appendices at the back. The following guidelines should be remembered:

(a) in the body of the report, summarise or refer to material included in an appendix

(b) number appendices and give the reference number at the appropriate point in the report

(c) consider including the following types of material as appendices (this is not by any means an exhaustive list)
> plans, layouts, complex diagrams and charts
> statistical data including financial information and costings
> brochures and price lists
> detailed results of surveys and questionnaires
> method study results
> systems analyses
> experimental data
> manpower planning
> training plans
> glossaries of technical terms
> sources of information/bibliographies.

REVISION

When a report has been drafted and, preferably, typed in double spacing, it must be examined critically before it is re written or typed for final submission. It is difficult to detect one's own mistakes immediately after making them and so revision should if possible take place after the manuscript has been put aside for a few days.

A helpful revision procedure is now provided:

(a)   re-read your draft, concentrating on the content, meaning and system of headings

(b)   check the title, introduction and conclusion to make sure that they relate satisfactorily to one another

(c)   examine the text in detail, looking in particular for mistakes of grammar, spelling, style

(d)   check the illustrations and appendices

(e)   ask a knowledgeable colleague to read the draft and criticise it for you.

EXAMINATION REPORT QUESTIONS

Examination reports can be prepared by following most of the suggestions previously made. They will frequently have to be written within memos or letters or with a covering memo or letter. Appendices that are felt to be necessary should be mentioned in the report but, because of the time element in an examination, will not have to be written.

The question will usually indicate the formality of style required. For instance, a report in memorandum form to a Manager from his Secretary would be more informal in tone than one from a salaried official to a local government committee, which would probably be a report sent out with a covering letter or as an agenda paper.

WORKED EXAMPLE

The following example of a report presented in memo form is based on the following question:

> You are secretary to a Sales Manager whose staff is soon to be increased. To accommodate the additional sales representatives and typists the office will require additional equipment and reorganisation. It is not in a good state of decoration. Write a memorandum to your Manager proposing the changes you think will be necessary.

Points to consider

1. *Content.* The question immediately suggests three topics:
   (a)   new equipment
   (b)   layout of office
   (c)   redecoration.
2. In addition you must write an introduction defining the purpose and the terms of reference, summarising the recommendations and announcing the arrangement of the main sections.
3. The conclusion and recommendations should give an estimate of the cost

of the changes recommended. The recommendations can best be justified by demonstrating the relatively low cost of the improvements suggested.

4. This will be too long a report to be typed on a printed memo form so it would be preferable to present it with a short covering memo.

(Appendices are mentioned but not included in the example.)

Suggested answer

MEMORANDUM

TO: Mr S Wilson   DATE: 11 December 19——
FROM: A B Jardine

I have pleasure in submitting for your consideration the attached report on the redecoration and reorganisation of the Sales Office.

ABJ

THE
REDECORATION AND REORGANISATION
OF THE SALES OFFICE

As the Sales Office will soon need redecoration and reorganisation to accommodate an increased number of staff, I suggest the additions and alterations detailed below. A plan is attached to the report as a guide to layout (Appendix 1), together with a colour scheme (Appendix 2), and a detailed estimate of costs (Appendix 3).

1   NEW OFFICE EQUIPMENT

   (a)   Desks. The existing desks are in good condition and can be retained. New desks will be needed for the shorthand typist who will join us shortly and for the two new sales representatives. As the desks in present use are of teak, it would maintain uniformity if similar desks were ordered.

   (b)   Cabinets and cupboards. The office filing cabinets and cupboards are in very poor condition. It would therefore be preferable to order six new cupboards in a bright colour. One of the new circular filing systems would prove indispensible to the secretarial staff and would not take up as much space as the old filing cabinets.

   (c)   Carpeting. The existing floor covering seems to be quite adequate; this grey corded carpeting is hard-wearing and will fit in with any colour scheme.

   (d)   Chairs, telephones and typewriters. The appearance of the office would be improved if new chairs were ordered in some bright colour, the same colour perhaps as the filing cabinets. These chairs should be comfortable. The three existing telephones are adequate for the needs of the office, but a new typewriter will have to be ordered before the new shorthand typist begins work.

2 OFFICE LAYOUT

I have included a diagram of the proposed layout (Appendix 1), which is self-explanatory. I should, however, like to make the following comments on the reasons for my choice of layout:

(a) <u>Windows.</u> I have made every effort to ensure that desks are placed as near to windows as possible so that all employees are aided by a certain amount of daylight. The present lighting is adequate.

(b) <u>Doors.</u> I have placed the desks in such a way that anyone entering the office may immediately see all members of staff at work.

(c) <u>Heating.</u> By next month under-floor electric central heating will have been installed in the entire office block. I have not proposed any air-conditioning system as this would prove very expensive. However, electric fans could be most useful in the summer months.

3 REDECORATION

In deciding upon a colour scheme (see Appendix 2) I had to consider several factors. Too much bright colour would be overwhelming and so I confined this to chairs and cabinets. Walls should be painted with a hard gloss so that they can be cleaned easily, and walls and ceilings should be of a colour that is light but easy on the eye.

4 ESTIMATE OF COSTS

The total estimated cost of these alterations is £1750. A detailed breakdown is given in Appendix 3.

I hope that the plans for the reorganisation meet with your approval and that this total estimated cost does not appear to be excessive.

A B Jardine
11 December 19——

LONGER REPORTS

In business, reports with their accompanying appendices may well run into many pages. Government reports can run to several volumes, each containing several hundred pages.

Such reports may be planned and written in the way already described but will be more elaborate in order to present a larger volume of material effectively. The main differences are found in:

    the title page
    contents pages
    summary or synopsis.

1 THE TITLE PAGE

There will be a separate page at the beginning of the document bearing:
    the title of the report

    any explanatory sub-titles
    the name(s) of the author(s)
    the body responsible for publication
    date and /or reference number.

2   CONTENTS PAGE(S)

Figure 19 is taken from the Redcliffe-Maud *Report on Local Government*.
This table refers to the section headings, the sub-sections and, in this case, the
sub-sub-sections, with their relative importance indicated by typeface and in-
dentation. The sections have, in addition to their title, a reference to their
paragraph (see numbering system explained earlier in this section) and the
page number. A list of appendices is also included at the end of the contents
page. Obviously the compilation of the contents pages is done after the writing
of the report.

	Para.	Page
CHAPTER IV		
THE CHANGES NEEDED: EVIDENCE OF WITNESSES		
THE CASE FOR LARGE AUTHORITIES	110	33
PLANNING, TRANSPORTATION AND HOUSING	113	34
EDUCATION	126	37
PERSONAL SERVICES	139	39
LINKS BETWEEN SERVICES	145	40
DELEGATION	150	41
NEW STRUCTURE - MAIN PROPOSALS	156	42
City regions	158	43
Two tiers of authority	163	44
Authorities for most purposes: provinces above	171	46

Figure 19   Sample contents page

3   SUMMARY OR SYNOPSIS

It is common with long reports to give at the beginning a summary of the
conclusions and/or recommendations, and sometimes of the whole report. It
is often a marathon to read right through a very long report and many of the
readers have no need or wish to do so. Others may wish to find out the
general purport of the report but leave detailed consideration to a later time.

EXERCISES

1.   You have worked as secretary to one man in your organisation for the
     past five years. Each year you have received a small increment to your

salary. Recently your boss has been promoted from Sales Manager to Sales Director. Invent any additional details you think necessary and write a memo to your superior in which you ask for, and attempt to justify, an increase in your salary.

2. Your firm's social club has a strong membership of older employees but has failed to attract much support from younger members of the firm. As a member of the social club committee write a memo for discussion at the next meeting outlining the ways by which you think membership might be increased.

3. Write a circular memorandum for the office staff of your organisation, explaining the new canteen facilities and revised lunch periods.

4. Your company is acting as host for a one-day conference to take place in six weeks' time on industrial handling techniques, which representatives from firms throughout the country will attend. The Public Relations Officer is responsible for the organisation of this conference and requires you, his secretary, to assist him and initially to present in a written memo a time-table, in a logical order, of the arrangements to be made up to and on the day of the conference.

(LCC Private Secretary's Certificate)

5. Your firm has decided to remove its commercial offices to a country market town. Premises are available, but before a final decision is made the Personnel Director, your employer, with one or two other executives, is visiting the area to investigate the availability of labour, housing, transport facilities, etc. His visit will cover three days.

As his secretary, prepare a memorandum detailing the arrangements with which you have been concerned for hotel bookings, appointments with Town Clerk, Youth Employment Officers, transport officials, etc. (Add as much detail as you can to your memorandum to make it as informative as possible to your employer for his visit.)

(LCC Private Secretary's Certificate)

6. Each month the Leisure Record Club offers a new, low-priced LP record to its members, who agree when they join that they will buy at least five records each year. To attract new members a 'free' record is sent on approval to enquirers, who may keep it if they decide to enrol.

Mrs Adamson, a housewife, sent for the 'free' record which she thought would make a useful birthday present for her husband. She did not buy any records during the next twelve months and you have recently written on behalf of the Membership Controller to remind her of the strict rules. This has caused some distress, as she is unable to afford to buy records. You wrote back to suggest that she should return the original 'free' record, but this would obviously cause domestic embarrassment. Using your discretionary authority you have finally written to waive the Club's requirements — and to admit that there was a very long interval between her original application and your first reminder.

Submit a memorandum to the Controller in which you set out full details of the problem and the ensuing correspondence. Indicate what action you took, your reasons, and how the matter has been settled. Include an appropriate comment and/or suggestion regarding the Club's policy of 'free' offers and its follow-up procedure. The Controller is not likely to be sympathetic. (See also Section 6, pp 93–4.)

(LCC Private Secretary's Certificate)

7. The firm you work for has a total office staff of twenty. As it is now experiencing some financial difficulties, you have decided to suggest ways in which economies could be effected in the office. Submit your recommendations in the form of a memo to the Office Manager, inventing as necessary any details concerning the current organisation of the office.

(LCC Private Secretary's Diploma)

8. In this question all the major details are provided for you, but you may need to supply minor details such as names or dates. You may also need to be selective when examining the data.

As Secretary to the Manager, prepare a memorandum from him from the information given below for distribution to all 100 members of staff, They have not heard of the scheme. You must set out the proposals clearly and reasonably briefly, present them as favourably as possible and made suitable arrangements for obtaining the views of every employee without delay.

The Manchester Branch of Bon Voyage Limited, a very large travel agency, opens from 9.00 a.m. to 5.30 p.m. This means a loss of valuable business in the early morning and the evening. The Manager, who only recently joined this branch and is very enthusiastic, wishes to extend office hours to run from 7.30 a.m. to 7.30 p.m., provided that his staff will co-operate in a staggered-hours system.

Under this system the length of the working day for each employee will remain as at present, but the time of arrival (and hence of departure) will vary. In this way staffing can be spread out over the longer opening hours.

Of course, if the scheme proves successful the total quantity of work handled by the branch will increase, but the new scheme might well lead to higher profits for the company and thus to higher staff bonuses.

Some members of staff might wish to have the same time of arrival for each working day; others might like different times for different days. However, once a duty rota had been fixed it would be necessary to give one or two weeks' notice of changes.

If the staff are willing to try this new scheme for a trial period, particularly to see whether their rush-hour travel problems are eased by it, the Manager hopes to introduce it in six weeks' time. He first needs to know quickly and fully what staff reactions to the proposal will be.

(LCC Private Secretary's Certificate)

9. The Sales Manager, whose assistant you are, has been asked at short notice to visit Vinland to discuss with a Government representative the possibility of a large contract with your firm. He has never visited Vinland and knows little about it.

   You have made a hasty visit to the library and collected the following information. Incorporate what is relevant into a report for your Sales Manager, inventing and adding any information you think necessary, for example your firm's business, what clothing he will need and topics on which further information should be sought during his visit.

Vinland is situated in the N. Atlantic Ocean. It is 250m. from the S.E. coast of Greenland. Length 298m. and breadth 194m. Pop. (1967) 156,033. Vinland is an ice-covered plateau built up of volcanic rocks and pierced on all sides by fjords and valleys. The lowlands cover about one-fourteenth of the whole area and are almost the only part of the island which is inhabited, the central tableland being absolutely uninhabitable on account of its extreme barrenness. Glacier fields cover over 5,000 sq. miles. There are several active volcanoes. A large portion of Vinland is covered with lava and hot springs or geysers are scattered throughout the island. The chief products are salted and frozen fish, meat and fish oil and much of this goes to the U.K. Olafsfjord is the capital with a pop. of 62,035.

(The Universal Encyclopaedia)

HOLIDAY WITH THE HEROES

– IN VINLAND. This summer Olaf Olafsson leads two special Saga tours. Sites made famous by the Sagas and talks illuminating Vinland's epic past. These tours bring history thrillingly to life for the academic and the enthusiastic layman alike. See also Vinland's natural wonders, active volcanoes, geysers and lava flows. A really adventurous holiday in this unspoiled Norse haven.

For the sportsman trout and salmon fishing or pony trekking over lonely moorland. For the birdwatcher many exotic species like the ptarmigan or golden eagle. The marvellous scenery alone is sufficient reason for a visit.

Travel is easy – 3 hours from London by air or sail twice weekly from Leith.

(From a travel brochure)

In the last few years Vinland has been gradually emerging from the northern twilight. The changes began with the Second World War and the Anglo-American occupation. Capital was pumped into the country and the forces brought powerful machinery for road making and similar purposes. Farm machinery was bought and land reclamation undertaken on a large scale. Electrification and housing schemes were embarked upon. There was a considerable influx of people from neighbouring countries and Germany.

There are now acres of greenhouses heated by water from thermal springs and a great many farmhouses, as well as several whole villages, are heated in the same manner.

But the economic situation has remained precarious and the standard of living low. There are few manufacturing industries and not many manufactured goods and little farm produce for export. For exports Vinland still depends mainly upon the fishing industry and the fishing grounds are showing unmistakable signs of depletion.

These hard economic facts, together with a growing awareness of its strategic situation have combined with a growing urge to 'progress' and prosperity to lead the Vinland government to take an increasingly aggressive attitude towards its Western neighbours.

The unilateral extension of territorial limits from 12 to 50 miles offshore has led to ugly incidents between Vinland fishery protection vessels and foreign fishing fleets.

The recent demand for payment of £3m. a year from NATO for use of the Vinland bases has led to further acrimonious exchanges but seems likely to be met.

In future, however, Vinland's economic prosperity is likely to rely most on the recent discovery of large deposits of the radio-active ore, thorium, in the interior of the country.

Vinland has already shown herself ready to take on her powerful neighbours. The strategic importance of these deposits will enable her to strike some very advantageous bargains and the country is undoubtedly on the brink of a period of great growth and development.

(Article in *Watchword*)

10. Over the past eighteen months there has been a larger-than-average turnover of staff in the Typing Pool of the firm for which you work. The Personnel Officer, whose assistant you are, has asked you to investigate and write a short report on the causes and possible solutions to this problem. Use the following notes as the basis for your report:

Supervisor conscientious — rather strict, overworked — working conditions poor — typewriters and duplicator need replacement — large volume of work — some of the girls' skills inadequate — only one girl promoted from pool in last two years.

11. The Personnel Manager, whose secretary you are, is responsible for training in your company. He has received suggestions that a refresher course might be organised for secretaries who have been with the company for some time, not only to keep them up to date and informed

of the latest practices, but also to prepare them for higher secretarial posts.

Since you are a senior secretary he has asked you to write a brief report giving your opinions on such a course, how and when it might be held to cause the minimum inconvenience to the employers of those attending, and suggesting the topics you think should be covered by the course with your reasons for their inclusion. (Invent any details you think necessary to give reality to your report.)

(LCC Private Secretary's Certificate)

12. The Personnel Director of Electronic Products Ltd had invited the Head Office Manager to give his comments on the present recruitment methods for clerical and secretarial staff.

As the Personal Assistant to the Personnel Director of Electronic Products Ltd, write a report with any recommendations on the present recruitment methods for the clerical and secretarial staff.

(Scottish HND in Secretarial Studies)

13. Read the following passage about the problems of the Printing Department. Use the information it contains to write the 'Recommendations' section of the O & M Officer's report.

THE PRINTING DEPARTMENT

TERMS OF REFERENCE

The Office Manager expressed concern over the delay in printing material called for by departments. The Print Room Supervisor didn't seem able to cope. Extra staff had not solved the problem. Office Manager asked O & M to 'have a look at it'.

FACT-FINDING

Interviewed the Print Room Supervisor. He said that difficulties could only be solved by giving him another machine and operator. Asked what work load he had on hand he showed us three wire trays full of masters. He had no records of the number of print runs completed or the number of impressions printed (I've got my work cut out printing them, without having to count them too!).

MACHINES

Three offset machines, photographic equipment, plate-making equipment, guillotine, heavy-duty stapler, spine-taping machine.

GENERAL OBSERVATIONS

It was noted that a great deal of the Supervisor's time was taken up in dealing with queries, 'urges' and dissatisfied customers generally.

It was observed that, whilst everybody appeared to be busy, it was seldom that more than one machine was actually printing at any given moment.

Machine operators selected their next job for themselves, except when actually told to give priority to a particular one,

A great deal of work of dubious value (for example, personalised note pads for junior members of staff) was being done.

No formal stock-control methods governed the frequency or the quantity of print runs to replenish stocks of standard forms and letter-heads.

STAFF AND DUTIES

Print Room Supervisor. Buys paper and other supplies. Costs and charges out all printing jobs to departments. Spends about 40 per cent of time on artwork (for example, form design) and chasing work when customers phone.

Assistant Supervisor. Does some artwork. Helps with accounts and stands in for Supervisor when absent. About 60 per cent of time occupied with camera and plate-making work.

Three Machine Operators. Occupied in printing, cleaning up masters, cutting paper from the flat sheet, collating, stapling, binding and moving work.

(From O & M Case-Study Notebook, *Management in Action*)

14. You are secretary to the Managing Director of a garden centre. This consists of several acres of shrubs, rose-beds, glass houses, and so on where plants of all kinds are grown for sale to the public. A busy main road passes the site and the public can drive straight in and park on a forecourt. A large shop section sells all kinds of gardener's requirements such as tools and fertilisers. There are also work-shops and offices, but there is no cafe. The garden centre does not deliver to customers, who must pay cash and collect their own purchases. The public are allowed to wander about freely, inspecting and handling plants.

The Managing Director is thinking of making some changes in the organisation of the garden centre and has asked you to carry out a general survey of the way it is run, particularly where you think there are shortcomings. Where possible he would be glad of helpful suggestions. You are to present him with a formal report that he can circulate to members of the Board of Directors. He is quite aware that you are not an expert and that your inquiries have been mainly confined to walking round the site and talking to staff and the customers.

Prepare a suitable report. You are free to use or ignore the following points which you have noted down during your investigations.

Point	Good features	Bad features
Self-service	Customers prefer it, and buy more	Plants get dropped; pilferage occurs
No delivery	Keeps prices low	No sales to people without cars
No credit	Keeps costs down	Lower sales
Much rain	Good for plants	Customers get wet
Small forecourt	More space for plants	Cars queue to get into centre
No playgound space	More space for plants	Children run about and cause damage

(LCC Private Secretary's Certificate)

15. You are secretary to the Product Development Manager of Comlon International Cash Registers Limited. He has recently held a special sales convention at which some new types of cash registers were demonstrated and business customers (e.g. shopkeepers) could discuss their requirements, and he wishes to prepare a brief report about what took place, with suggestions (a) for any improvements in the organisation of the next convention to be held in six months' time, (b) for any improvements in cash registers that might be considered. Draft a report for him, using the following data as your guide.

The convention lasted all day, with demonstrations, talks and a question-and-answer session. Refreshments and meals were provided by the company, but were not free of charge. Lunch cost £2.50 and there were some complaints about this. The convention was publicised by circular letters to trade customers and advertisements in trade magazines. It was estimated that about one in ten potential visitors actually came or sent a representative. Some visitors had difficulty in finding their way to the convention building once they arrived at the large factory site. Great interest was generated, and considerable sales were made at the end of the day, especially of electric cash registers suitable for small shops. The more elaborate (and very expensive) machines did not sell so well, and not a single manual cash register was sold. Few visitors came from the north of England or Scotland (the factory site was in Middlesex).

(LCC Private Secretary's Certificate)

16. You work in a large textile factory as secretary to the Safety Officer (male or female, as you choose). He is responsible among other things for ensuring that adequate precautions are taken against dust, exposed machinery, fire, and hazards such as falling objects.

There is a Safety Committee, composed of workers' representatives. members of the Board of Directors and the Safety Officer. The Committee meets regularly and issues advice and directives when necessary. However, the employees tend to ignore directives, largely because work would be slowed down if they were obeyed, and hence wages would be lost. As a result there have been several serious accidents recently.

The Safety Committee has now asked the Safety Officer to report on the general standard of safety in the factory. He must briefly investigate the causes of the recent accidents, and find out how the employees regard the directives of the Safety Committee. (He is free to consult other members of the Committee.) If necessary there could be sanctions against employees who break safety rules, such as suspension (which might cause a strike). There could also be an education programme to inform people about the vital need for safety (though this might be very expensive to arrange).

You have assisted the Safety Officer to carry out his investigations and have been asked to compose a suitable report, which he will sign, for submission to the Safety Committee. Inventing minor details to add realism, write your draft report. (*Note:* No expert knowledge of factories or industrial safety is expected.)

(LCC Private Secretary's Certificate)

17.   You are employed as Secretary to the Office Manager of a road-haulage company. The office staff includes two accountants, seven male and four female clerks, one secretary and four typists. Staff turnover has been high, although salaries and working conditions are good. At a staff meeting it was found that employees did not feel sufficiently involved in the business. In particular they felt that work could be reorganised so as to give everyone a more meaningful job.

Following this meeting your employer has asked you to write a short report summarising the causes of the high staff turnover and suggesting specific ways for improving staff participation in the management of the business.

(LCC Private Secretary's Diploma)

6

SUMMARISING

At school summarising may have seemed an academic exercise. In business it is a practical skill which has a very wide range of applications. Composition of, for example,

> telex messages
> telegrams
> abstracts of information
> minutes
> synopses of reports
> telephone messages
> summaries of correspondence

all demand of the writer the ability to select, often from a mass of information, the relevant matter and to express that information as concisely as possible. Practice in summary-writing for examination purposes will assist the potential secretary to develop a necessary and most useful skill.

Summaries for secretarial examinations follow very closely the pattern of abstracts and synopses prepared in commerce and industry. They are unrealistic only in some details, such as having to devise memoranda headings, names and other minor additions. Also, examiners usually set a limit on the number of words which may be used.

However, the presentation should very often be in a format similar to those mentioned in Section 5 'Memoranda and Reports'.

THE EXAMINATION

Most English and Communication examinations test the candidate's ability to write a summary.

Students should be careful not to take a disproportionate time over the summary and should note carefully and follow the instructions given in the examination paper.

Examination questions may take one of a variety of forms:

(a) You may be asked to write a summary of the whole or part of a given message. This is the most straightforward form the question can take.

(b) You may be asked to summarise some of the ideas contained in the passage, for example: *Summarise the arguments contained in the passage for and against . . . .*

(c)   You may be asked to extract and rearrange some or all of the information contained in the passage so that it falls under given headings.

(d)   You may be asked to present information in a specific form, for instance for use in a court of law (see Worked Example 2).

(e)   The content of the summary, or the purpose for which the examiner suggests that it shall be used will often determine the format, for instance a fact sheet (see Appendix 6, p. 285).

(f)   Some examining bodies now ask students to abstract information and present it in note form, a practice quite common in business.

GENERAL CONSIDERATIONS IN SUMMARY WRITING

1 VOCABULARY

Unfamiliar words in the passage for summary may present some difficulty for those candidates who are not allowed to use a dictionary in the examination. However, you should be able to establish the general meaning of a word or phrase from the context in which it is used. Even where the vocabulary is familiar, students must remember that words often have more than one meaning so that it may be necessary to study the context to choose the most appropriate one.

2 INTRUSION OF A STUDENT'S OWN IDEAS

The summary should be only of the information that has been presented in the original passage. No other ideas, digressions, illustrations or opinions of your own should be added. You are concerned solely with the writer's ideas. Therefore, be careful to follow the following rules:

(a)   do not let your own opinions colour your interpretation
(b)   do not add examples of your own
(c)   do not discuss the opinions given
(d)   do not give additional information
(e)   do not alter the balance of any arguments presented.

3 CONTINUITY

If it is appropriate to write a summary in the form of continuous prose, a logical connection of ideas in the summary should be made clear. Words such as *but, however, nevertheless, because, therefore* and *although* are useful to establish continuity and a smooth flow of ideas, but they must be used with care and accuracy if the original meaning is not to be distorted.

TECHNICAL PROBLEMS

1 LAYOUT

The layout for a summary must be appropriate to the purpose for which it would be used. In secretarial examinations, if an examiner indicates that the context is a business one, the format should usually be of a type suitable for use in business.

This will mean that the student, in addition to giving the summary a heading, will need to consider writing a memorandum, using sub-headings and numbering items within the summary.

2 PARAGRAPHS

The problem of how to paragraph a summary can be eased by the application of common sense. Where the summary is a short one it can often most suitably be contained in one or two paragraphs, according to the subject-matter. On other occasions the paragraphs of the original passages, always providing that they were sensible in the first place, can serve as a useful guide.

You may be asked to summarise the arguments for and/or against a policy, attitude, etc. In this case the summary will fall quite naturally into two paragraphs, one containing the arguments for and the other against.

In other cases information will need to be listed and numbers used. Sub-headings can often add to clarity (see Worked Example 1).

Paragraphing a summary of correspondence is a separate case and has been dealt with under that heading (p. 93).

3 LENGTH

Examiners will usually indicate the length of summary they require. Often they will instruct the candidate to write a summary in about 120 words, that is, between 110–130 words. A shorter answer than this may well have omitted important points and should be revised. More than 130 words may well result in the student being penalised for excessive length. When the candidate is instructed to write a summary in not more than 120 words, the instruction should of course be strictly obeyed.

If no particular length of summary is specified, the student should reduce the passage to about a third of its original length.

In an examination the main heading need not be included in the number of words used. Neither does the student need to include memoranda headings, covering memoranda, or, providing that it is suitably placed, the source of information. Suitable placing for the source of information could include:

(a)   as, or within, the subject heading of the summary or covering memorandum
(b)   within the content of the covering memorandum
(c)   in brackets after the completed summary.

However, sub-headings and numbers used within the main body of the summary must be counted and included in the total number of words, which must be stated at the end.

4 TENSES AND REPORTED SPEECH

Whereas it was once obligatory to write a formal summary in reported speech, that is, using an impersonal tone and past tense, this is now considered rather pedantic. The rules to follow are:

(a)   the tense of the original may be retained in most cases

(b)   personal pronouns must be avoided

(c)   where the passage is written entirely in the first person, it is sometimes preferable to change it to reported speech

(d)   where a quotation in direct speech is included in a passage for summary, this should be changed to reported speech.

If reported speech is being used, care is needed with pronouns, tenses and adverbial expressions. Consider the following example:

> *In his Annual Report the Chairman said 'Our company has had a successful year but your Board of Directors hopes to have even better progress to report next year.'*

In reported speech, the passage is as follows:

> *In his Annual Report the Chairman said that their Company had had a successful year but that their Board of Directors hoped to have even better progress to report the following year.*

The present tense is retained if the stated facts are still true, for example:

> *He said, 'Everyone dies sooner or later.'*
> *The author said that everyone dies sooner or later.*

Note that the word *that* should be used to introduce reported speech, as in the above example.

Questions need particular care:

> Direct speech   *Can we meet next week?*
> Reported speech *He asked whether they could meet the following week.*

But rhetorical questions need more rephrasing:

> *Shall we suffer such a trading loss again?*
> *The Chairman said that they could not suffer such a trading loss again.*

5   FORMS OF REPORTED SPEECH

	Direct speech	*Reported speech*
Verbs	reports	reported
	is reporting	was reporting
	has reported	had reported
	shall (will) report	should (would) report
	may	might
	can	could
	must	had to
Pronouns	I, you (sing)	he, she
	we, you	they
	me, you (sing.)	him, her

Pronouns	us, you	them
(continued)	mine, yours (sing.)	his, hers
	ours, yours	theirs
	myself, yourself	himself, herself
	ourselves, yourselves	themselves
	this, these	that, those
Adverbial	now	then, at that time
expressions	today	that day
	yesterday	the day before
	last week (year)	the week (year) before
	tomorrow	the next day
	next week	the following week
	here	there

6   EXAMPLES AND ILLUSTRATIONS

These may often be omitted, or, if they are retained, be generalised. Consider the following passage:

> *I think people ought to be allowed a second crack at their names, re-registering at, say, eighteen. Indian tribes do this. No squaw leans into the birchbark cradle and names its contents 'Great Swift Buffalo Hunter': they probably wait until he's met a few buffalo first. Plenty of people do it already, of course: Justin de Villeneuve, Englebert Humperdinck II; John Wayne was christened Marion.*

(Katherine Whitehorn, the Observer)

The illustrations in this passage should be treated by omission:

> *She thought that people ought to be allowed to change their names, re-registering at, say, eighteen.*

Statistics may often be generalised, as the following example shows (the *original* precedes the *generalisation*):

> *Some of the population-doubling times in the UDCs (underdeveloped countries) are as follows: Kenya, 24 years; Nigeria, 28; Turkey, 24; Indonesia, 31; Philippines, 20; Brazil, 22; Costa Rica, 20; and El Salvador, 19.*

> *Population-doubling times in many underdeveloped coutnries are less than twenty-five years.*

In some summaries prepared for businessmen it will be appropriate to retain some detail. For example, if a manager had asked for background information prior to visiting Brazil, it might be relevant to include for him the actual population-doubling time in that country.

7   QUOTATIONS

Since these are frequently used as illustrations of a point they may often be omitted. If they are retained, however, and turned into reported speech, care must be taken to attribute them to the correct author, **not** to the author of the passage in general.

8   ORDER

You must not gratuitously change the order of ideas in a summary of a passage. Indeed, you should never do so except then you are summarising parts of the passage, for example the arguments for or against the policy, or if there is repetition in the original. The safe rule is to stick to the original order whenever possible.

9   BALANCE

An author will generally write at greatest length on his most important ideas. In summarising a writer's ideas you should aim at giving them the same weight in terms of comparative length as he has done, unless you are instructed to include only some of the information — otherwise you may distort his meaning. It is a common fault among the inexperienced to find that too many words have been used on the first part of a passage, leaving the temptation to compress the second half into a quarter of the words allowed.

METHOD

A suggested method of writing a summary of a passage is given in Figure 20 in the form of a flow chart or algorithm.

WORKED EXAMPLES

EXAMPLE 1

Your employer is an official in a local government transport department. He is interested in trends affecting cars and driving habits. Summarise the following passage in not more than 160 words ready for placing in his 'in' tray. You will need to draft a brief explanatory memo because he has not heard of the article from which the passage is taken. The memo does not count as part of the 160 words. There are 494 words in the passage.

The most drastic response to higher petrol prices is simply not to buy a car. Economist Intelligence Unit figures show that there has been a drop of nearly 10 per cent in new car registration over the past twelve months. But, again, this is complicated by factors like the imposition of credit controls — which make it less easy to buy through hire purchase. And the figures disguise the bustle of activity in the second-hand market. Here there is more conclusive evidence of petrol-related changes in behaviour. In this market, buyers are choosing cars with a smaller engine capacity. Yet in the same week that a pop star traded in his Rolls Corniche for a Mini, an American bought five Rolls-Royces, a dealer's entire stock, in one sale. So that dealers' returns, on which evidence of this shift is based, should be treated with caution.

HOW TO WRITE A SUMMARY

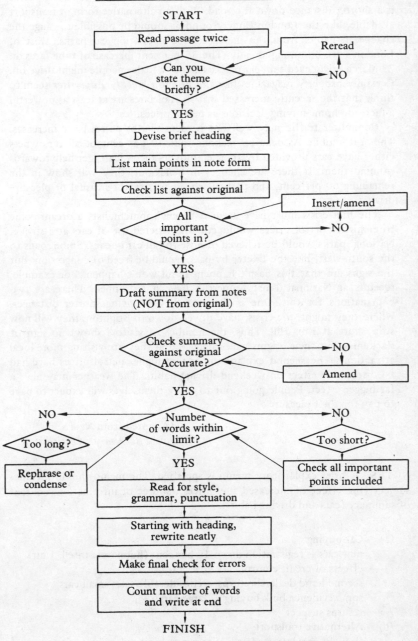

Figure 20 How to write a summary

Less drastic is the decision either to take the car off the road or to drive it a shorter distance down the road. With an alternative form of transport available, like the London Underground, it should be possible to gauge the change in habits from the increased use of station car parks. Most of London's are brimming already. The 35 per cent increase of tube fares on 23 March might even thin car park users out a little: people might drive on. Certainly property magazines like the *London Weekly Advertiser* seem to think that the recently increased British Rail fares are at least as powerful a factor in home-buying decisions as petrol prices.

Commuter traffic may well not be sensitive to petrol price increases. The Automobile Association reckons that 40 per cent of all car-owners either have cars provided by their employers or, at least, get help towards running them. If there are changes in behaviour, they will show in the remaining 60 per cent, and particularly in that sector's casual or pleasure driving.

The fuel crisis must have seemed to environmentalists a dream come true: higher petrol prices would cut unrestricted use of cars at a stroke. National parks would be relieved of nose-to-tail car queues. Spine roads to the south-west, like the Exeter by-pass, would be freed of congestion. But the signs are that this hasn't happened and won't happen. For example, receipts at National Trust properties have not dropped. There are two explanations for this. One is that people are driving shorter distances. Where they might, pre-crisis, have driven down to Brighton, they will now stop short at Box Hill. Thus, the number of visitors shows no sign of slackening but their origins have changed and they are visiting more local attractions. The second explanation is that higher petrol prices have had no discernible effect on weekend driving habits. The weather may have a far bigger effect. People going out to enjoy themselves will expect to have to pay for their pleasure.

(Adapted from *New Society*)
(*LCC Private Secretary's Certificate*)

NOTES: A brief explanatory memo is specified. The memo should include: subject (the effect of increased fuel prices), source of information, content of summary (cars and driving habits).

(a) Car buying
new cars — registration down 10 per cent (Economic Intell. Unit)
effects of credit control
second-hand dealers' returns — considerable sales small cars
some evidence bulk-buying of large cars
returns suspect

(b) Alternative transport
thought cars less used or just to get to local rail
probably negated by fares' rises, particularly London Transport

(c) Company cars
   40 per cent company-owned/subsidised
   Only 60 per cent to judge changes

(d) Leisure motoring
   environmentalists vain hope less road and parking congestion
   people restricting length of journey
   visiting local attractions
   leisure motoring affected by other than fuel prices

SUMMARY

MEMORANDUM

To ... Transport Manager ....   From .. M Robinson ....
Date . 18 June 19––..............   Subject . The effect of increased ....
                                  fuel prices ....

I recently read an article in the March 19–– edition of *New Society* and, as it concerns cars and driving habits, I thought you might be interested in the attached summary of its contents.

                                                                MR

THE EFFECT OF INCREASED FUEL PRICES

The article makes the following points:
CAR BUYING
New Cars
Registration has fallen by 10 per cent (Economic Intelligence Unit) but this may have been affected by stricter credit control.
Second-hand Cars
Dealers' returns show considerable activity in sales of smaller-capacity cars but, with some evidence of bulk-buying of large cars, the returns are suspect.
USE OF ALTERNATIVE TRANSPORT
It was thought that cars might not be used, or merely used to drive to local stations. However, this trend is probably negated by rises in other transport fares, particularly the London Underground.
COMPANY CARS
Forty per cent of cars are company-owned or subsidised. Thus changing trends will only show in the remaining 60 per cent.
LEISURE MOTORING
Environmentalists hoped vainly for less road and parking congestion. It seems likely either that people are restricting journey length and visiting more local attractions, or that weekend motoring is governed by factors other than higher fuel prices.

                                                     (158 words)

EXAMPLE 2

The following passage is taken from an article by Tony Gould in *New Society*. Imagine that John Adams has subsequently been charged with a shoplifting offence. Your employer, a solicitor, is preparing Mr Adams's defence, and he has asked you to summarise all the points in the passage which might be helpful evidence (for example, personal hardship, mental strain, evidence of good character). Prepare a summary of not more than 120 words which could be read out in court.

Vivian Adams and her husband John, who hasn't worked for the last four years, are in their early fifties. They live in a bungalow near Southport.

JOHN: 'The business was packing cases, wooden packing cases. I was one of the family — not a partner. They suddenly decided to close and they sold the land and buildings and everything else of the business, gave the goodwill to another firm and the men went to this other firm — all bar myself. I was told that because I had gone to law to query the trustee's action in closing the works they wouldn't find me a job at this other firm. It was a family business: my father was a partner. He died and then mother had a life interest and it was willed to my sister and myself afterwards: but it was during my mother's's life interest that the business was sold, so I had no real control to stop it being sold.

'Well, I was in the office, more or less general dogsbody. I was getting £1,300 a year, gross — just under, actually. With taxes and everything, I only got about £14 a week. When I went on the dole, the first six months were nearly a par, but after that it was less than half; and after twelve months it was cut dead. I just go down each week now and get the card stamped. We had a small amount of cash savings which we've had to use up, so we're not entitled to draw from social security. I haven't had any offer of a job from the employment exchange, so we're just fighting this law case and that's the only hope at the moment.

'It was a shattering experience, absolutely shattering. You see, insecurity has always been a sort of bogey with me; I've always felt that security was an absolute must. Desperate when that went; been desperate ever since, really. I'm not used to it yet, going down to the dole, although I can't say a word against the people there: they have been perfectly friendly.

'It makes you feel very bitter and it's very morale-reducing, because normally if you had so long off you would decorate the house and do repairs; but you don't feel you can do it. You haven't the morale to do it somehow and anyway where could I find the money to get the paint and stuff?

'We used to like to go to places, to friend's houses, but we've cut all that out. Our friends have been more than willing to cut us out, you know. That's one thing — in fact, we've said that if we ever come off right at the end of this, such friends really aren't worth bothering about afterwards who haven't bothered about our plight.'

VIVIAN: 'We never lived a high life. We never wanted to do more than keep up the appearances that we'd always been able to keep up.

'We haven't any children. I just hate to think what our kids would have turned round and said to us now. In fact, we are put down as guardians for two children because their father lost his wife through cancer, and I've often thought, "Well, heaven help us if anything happened to *him*."

'It's been a psychological shock. Our whole world collapsed. John has been terribly good to me. The screws and scrapes to make sure I get the things I really need. But you can't have any ambition because you haven't any brass to go with it.

'The only brass John's got now is his war medal. Not that bravery gets you anywhere; perhaps we'll sell it when we're starving.'

(LCC Private Secretary's Certificate)

COMMENT

The passage consists of statements made by Mr and Mrs Adams. The summary must distinguish carefully between fact and opinion, and hence the use of the expressions 'he claims', 'Adams emphasised', 'Mrs Adams stated'.

SUMMARY

Statement in defence of John Adams

John and Vivian Adams, both in their early fifties, live near Southport. Adams has been unemployed for four years.

Adams alone was made redundant on the closure of the family business. He claims that this resulted from his legal action querying the closure.

Unemployment pay ceased three years ago. His small cash savings, now spent, prevented entitlement to social security benefits.

Adams emphasised the desperation and bitterness he feels because of his present insecurity.

Mrs Adams stated that they were childless. They had never lived extravagantly. John Adams is a good husband. He had a decoration for bravery and was nominated joint guardian to two motherless children. They had suffered great shock and were now penniless.

(117 words)

SUMMARISING CORRESPONDENCE

A summary of correspondence may be required, for example by management for a decision, or to be presented at a meeting, or to be circulated to several departments whose managers can then ask for the original of any correspondence that is their concern.

The general rules of summary writing will apply and the following special points should also be observed.

1 THE HEADING

A simple standard heading should be used.

> *Summary of correspondence between . . . and . . . on the subject of . . .*

2 DATES

If the dates of the letters in a series have no particular significance, the first and last letter dates may be incorporated in the heading after the second address and before the subject, for example

> *from 12 October to 17 December 19——*

However, the dates of the letters may be important and, if so, must appear at the beginning of each letter summary.

3 PARAGRAPHS

Each letter in the series should be contained in a separate paragraph.

4 IMPORTANT DETAILS

Such facts as delivery dates, specifications, quotations, numbers and sizes cannot be generalised but must be quoted in full.

5 ACKNOWLEDGEMENTS

Acknowledgements and complimentary phrases and conclusions can be omitted. Mention of a complete letter which is simply an acknowledgement may usually also be left out of the summary.

6 THE EXAMINATION

If you are asked to summarise correspondence in the examination, you should state at the end the number of words used. However, the words used in the heading are not included. The best format to use is the one suggested above. However, if the examiner sets a long series of letters to be summarised in relatively few words, such as those in Exercise 12, an alternative format may be easier. In this case the examiner accepted the letter by letter format, a summary into a single whole or one stating the arguments for and against and ending with possible alternatives.

WORKED EXAMPLE

The following six letters are summarised in Appendix 1 in 120 words.

LETTER 1

5 Maple Grove,
BINGLEY,
·Wilts.
WB4 6LM
14th March 19——

The Reliable Insurance Co.,
Broadgate,
BRADFORD.
BD1 5CX

Dear Sirs,

Thank you for your letter dated 10th March, giving a quotation for insurance cover on my car. I note that your premium is £65 per annum.

My present insurance company allows me the maximum no-claim bonus on my premium and I wish to know whether you are willing to do the same. I see from your quotation that this allowance would reduce my premium by £18.50.

They also made a further deduction from my premium since I agreed to pay the first £25 costs on any damage incurred. What is your policy in this respect?

I look forward to your reply.

Yours faithfully,
John Maggs

LETTER 2

The Reliable Insurance Co
Broadgate
BRADFORD
BD1 5CX

Ref EH/JW
16 March 19——

J Maggs Esq
5 Maple Grove
BINGLEY
Wilts
WB4 6LM

Dear Sir

We acknowledge receipt of your letter dated 14 March.

You will receive a full reply to the points you raised during the next few days.

Yours faithfully

E Higginbottom
Motor Insurance Department

LETTER 3

The Reliable Insurance Co
Broadgate
BRADFORD
BD1 5CX

Ref EH/JW
18 March 19——

J Maggs Esq
5 Maple Grove
BINGLEY
Wilts
WB4 6LM

Dear Sir

Further to our letter of 16 March, I note that you have received our quotation for a comprehensive motor insurance premium of £65. You ask whether we can allow you a no-claim bonus and a reduction for your agreement to pay the first £25 of any damage incurred.

If you can let us have evidence of your no-claim bonus by sending us a copy of the insurance schedule from your previous insurers, we shall be able to offer you a similar reduction in premium of £18.50.

We are pleased to be able to offer you a further reduction of £10 for your agreement to pay the first £25 of any damage. Your revised quotation with these two reductions will be £36.50.

I hope this answers your queries. If you require any further information I shall be pleased to help.

Yours faithfully

E Higginbottom
Motor Insurance Department

LETTER 4

5 Maple Grove,
BINGLEY,
Wilts.
WB4 6LM
22nd March 19——

The Reliance Insurance Co.,
Broadgate,
BRADFORD.
BD1 5CX

Dear Sirs,

Thank you for your letter dated 18th March.

I enclose my insurance schedule for the Apex Insurance Company which shows that they allow me the maximum no-claim bonus of £18.50. I hope you will find this satisfactory.

If so, I shall be pleased to accept your revised quotation for £36.50 for comprehensive motor insurance.

Yours faithfully

John Maggs

Enclosure

LETTER 5

The Reliable Insurance Co
Broadgate
BRADFORD
BD1 5CX

Ref EH/JW
25 March 19——

J Maggs Esq
5 Maple Grove
BINGLEY
Wilts
WB4 6LM

Dear Sir

Thank you for your letter dated 22 March.

We are pleased to enclose our revised quotation of £36.50 for comprehensive motor insurance.

We also enclose the proposal form for your signature and look forward to receiving your instructions.

Yours faithfully

E Higginbottom
Motor Insurance Department

Enclosures

LETTER 6

>5 Maple Grove,
>Bingley,
>WILTS.
>WB4 6LM
>28th March 19——

The Reliable Insurance Co.,
Broadgate,
BRADFORD.
BD1 5CX

Dear Sirs,

Thank you for your letter dated 25th March.

I am pleased to accept the revised quotation and return the signed proposal form.

I also enclose my cheque for £36.50 and wish you to arrange the commencement of cover as soon as possible.

>Yours faithfully,

>John Maggs

Enclosures

EXERCISES

1. Using the information contained in the following passage, describe the help given by the Department of Trade and Industry to British business-men promoting their products abroad. Write about 100 words.

   Apart from tourists, Eastern Europe is playing host every year to an ever-increasing number of British businessmen, many of whom are attending the trade fairs which are very much a part of the commercial life of the Communist bloc countries.

   The whole question of exhibiting at trade fairs is one which many companies tend to side-step, simply because they have little or no idea of how to go about it. Yet a great deal of help is available, both from trade delegations maintained by overseas markets in London and from British government agencies such as the Department of Trade and Industry.

Probably the easiest way to find out which trade fairs are particularly relevant to your own company's products is to contact the Department of Trade and Industry's Fair and Promotions Branch, based at Hillgate House, 26 Old Bailey, London EC4 7HU.

The DTI supported some 5,000 firms exhibiting at 270 trade fairs in 38 countries last year, as well as staging various British weeks, store promotions and outward missions, which were supported by another 1,700 companies.

The DTI has an extremely comprehensive list of fairs being held throughout the world. But as well as supplying information, the Department can also supply practical help, and even finance, for companies planning to undertake export drives at overseas fairs. For example, under the joint venture scheme, the DTI provides space and a shell stand for firms taking part in a group display sponsored by a trade association or a non-profit-making body at an overseas trade fair.

In addition, for joint venture schemes outside Western Europe, the DTI will pay half the return tourist air fare for two representatives of each firm taking part, and half the freight charges for returning unsold goods exhibited at the event.

In the case of major fairs, where participation is normally organised on a national basis, the DTI organises a British pavilion in which space and shell stands are provided to exhibitors.

Once again, in the case of events held outside Western Europe, the Department gives help and assistance towards the cost of representatives' travel and in returning unsold exhibits.

The Department is also instrumental in organising British weeks, British shopping festivals and store promotions in overseas centres. Often it will give financial support to companies taking part in approved Outward Missions sponsored by a trade association, chambers of commerce or similar non-profit-making bodies with the objective of assessing the prospects for British exports to a selected market or to sell or promote the sale of British products (422 words).

(From *Top Secretary*)

2. As a member of the Child Poverty Action Group compose under the heading *Advice to Claimants* a list of 'do's' and 'don'ts' for people in situations similar to those of the Baths and Longs. Base your answer on the information contained in the following extracts from an article entitled 'The Clothes Line' by David Bull and Christopher Iveson.

Although the weekly supplementary benefit is expected to cover its normal replacement, clothing is by far the most common item for which the Supplementary Benefits Commission makes lump-sum, exceptional needs payments (ENPs). Bedding, which is not provided for in the weekly payment, follows some way behind, in second place.

The average ENP is worth £8.20 and only two per cent exceed £20. Our sights were raised, however, when the Child Poverty Action Group acquired a copy of the SBC's internal document B/O 40 which officers use to determine a household's clothing and bedding requirements (see Table 1).

TABLE 1   The B/O 40 standard: items allowed per household

Clothing, each member
  2 pairs shoes; 1 coat; 2 nightclothes; 2 vests; 2 pairs pants; 3 pairs hosiery
Females
  2 petticoats; 1 corset; 1 cardigan or jacket; 2 dresses (housewife only); 2 bras
Males
  1 jacket or (boys only) anorak; 2 pairs trousers; sweater or (householder only) waistcoat; 2 shirts
Bedding
  1 pillow and 2 pillowcases per person; 3 blankets; 3 sheets per bed

---

Bristol University social work and administration students, on field-work projects with local CPAG branch, recently checked the needs, on the B/O 40 standard, of some 40 families. The outcome will be published later; this article describes only the first two attempts. These left us asking why the two families received so much more than the claimants we had helped before, and why, in spite of similar circumstances, they fared differently from each other.

Both families have four dependent children, are long-term claimants, and pay identical rents for houses on the same council estate. A casual visitor to their two homes would expect the 'Bath' family to need more than the 'Longs'. Their home is ill-kept and sparsely furnished, and Mrs Bath is invariably badly dressed; while the Longs' home looks so warm and comfortable as to disguise, at first, the threadbare carpet and the family's worn furniture.

The Baths lacked, by the B/O 40 standard, 68 items of clothing and 33 of bedding; the Longs needed 57 and 21 respectively. These needs were spelled out in letters to the SBC, whose officers duly made a call. The Longs' visitor stayed half an hour, examined the bedding and asked to see all clothing — even tights! But the Baths' visitor examined neither clothing nor bedding.

The Longs received £44.90 and the Baths £50.15 (including £3.60 that the officer added, unsolicited, for lino in one room). The payments, however, were allocated for very different requirements. The Longs' award covered all of their bedding needs except for pillowcases; the parents received none of the garments they required; and the 20 items of clothing for the children were mostly inexpensive ones. The Baths, on the other hand, obtained only two sheets and no blankets, but nearly all the pillows and pillowcases that they requested and the clothing award, which was spread across the household, concentrated on the dearer items.

The discrepancy on bedding can be attributed to the different approaches of the visitors; but the clothing variations make nonsense of the commission's argument, at subsequent tribunal hearings, that the two families were expected to make 'normal replacement' of clothing.

We advised each family to appeal on two counts: the amounts awarded for some items; and the missing items. In his letter, Mr Long made clear his appeal on the first count, then added: 'Also, the grant did not cover all the items I required.' The tribunal chairman ruled that this was an aside and would only hear the first part of the appeal. The Longs were duly awarded £2.30 to make good the underpayment. The tribunal later agreed to hear the rest of the appeal; but meanwhile Mr Long had submitted a new, much reduced, claim. The chairman would not go through the outstanding items, one by one, and the tribunal arbitrarily awarded £16.20 for only eight of them.

The chairman at the Baths' hearing, on the other hand, methodically noted each outstanding requirement. He reprimanded the commission for failing to examine bedding and adjourned the hearing for a thorough revisit. Moreover the family had not received a properly completed form B/O 40A, telling them which items the grant covered and how much was allowed for each. It was therefore agreed that the revisit should take account of all the items that were needed now. We asked that it include also an examination of all floor coverings, as there were no grounds for singling out one room: all were as bad.

The officer who revisited agreed: he awarded £18.48 for four remaining rooms. Bedding to the value of £34.55 was awarded, leaving only two blankets and three sheets outstanding. Most of the £29.97 worth of clothing was underwear. Mr Bath's needs were mostly met, but his wife received nothing, possibly because she stormed out of the house when the officer, with all due thoroughness, asked 'whether I had any knickers'. When the hearing was reconvened, the tribunal decided that £131.15 was enough.

It certainly exceeded the Baths' wildest dreams — and ours. But why had the Longs received only half as much? It is, at best, difficult and, at worst, futile to attempt to monitor something so deliberately unscientific as the administration of discretion by the SBC and tribunals. Notwithstanding, we hope that our analysis of subsequent cases will offer a lesson or two. Indeed, a few tips for advocates emerge from the two initial cases.

(*New Society*)

3.   In about 160 words summarise the benefactions conferred by advertising, and the reasons for the 'periodic qualms of the advertising man' described in the following passage. Give your summary a suitable heading.

No one doubts that advertising has done much to raise the standards of physical wellbeing. The catalogue of its benefactions, real and claimed, is a long one. It has speeded the introduction of useful inventions to a wide as distinct from a select circle. It has brought prosperity to communities which did not know how to sell their rotting crops. By widening markets, it has enabled costs of raw materials to be cut, accelerated turnover, lowered selling prices. It has spread seasonal trade and kept people in employment. It has given a guarantee of dependability — for who (as that advertisement used to ask) would buy a nameless motor-car put together in a back-street workshop? Its defenders claim that advertising has abolished heavy underwear, made people clean their teeth (which was more than the dentists could persuade them to do), and made them Nice to be Near. These gratifying results have been achieved, not only by informative, but by persuasive and indeed by intimidating advertisements. The prime object of the exercise was not, of course, to benefit humanity but to sell more fabrics, more toothpaste, more disinfectant.

Not least important, advertising is also the buttress of a free and cheap press, which otherwise would exist only by the conditional subventions of governments, parties and pressure groups. It is also the provider of free radio and television entertainment for millions daily. Here, the prime object may not be to entertain, but to sell goods; yet millions are reasonably satisfied with and grateful for the fare they provide.

Perhaps the periodic qualms of the advertising men spring from the knowledge — as Professor J. K. Galbraith has hinted — that the keenest brains are employed to sell fringe commodities which fulfil no urgent need, but which do something to lighten the rat race for which advertising is in some measure responsible — goods like tobacco, liquor, drugs, sweets and gum. In a prosperous society there comes a point, as the professor indicates, when advertising no longer rewards the community with lower prices and greater efficiency. The manufacturer in a competitive market cannot conquer by price-cutting, for that way lies suicide; all he can do is to battle expensively, ingeniously, and perhaps unscrupulously for a bigger share of the existing market. This is unlikely to be achieved by a calm presentation of the facts about his product, or by a plea for loyalty, but it can be done by a variety of tricks, among which is to invest the product with subjective qualities — offering romance with chocolates, poise with perfume, popularity with dance lessons, social prestige with motor-cars. In Shepherd Meade's 'The Admen' (1958) a character says that toothpaste presents the real challenge to the advertiser, since there is not enough difference between one brand and another 'to put in your eye'. The same could be said of many cigarettes, most whiskies, nearly all petrols. Somehow the advertising man must _persuade the public that his brand is different, or more desirable; and if he does not do so, factories are going to close down and agencies disappear. He must find what arguments he can to solace his conscience. If, for example, it is ethical for doctors to prescribe useless medicines, with a purely psychological value (placebos) why is it unethical to sell a sound product by investing it with a fanciful appeal?

(E. S. Turner, *The Shocking History of Advertising*)

4. Prepare a summary of the principles underlying containerisation and its advantages, using only the material in the following passage. Your summary will be used by a group of businessmen who are examining their firm's freight transportation methods. Give the summary a suitable title and do not use more than 150 words.

There have been many important developments in international transport during the last twenty years, such as the jumbo jets, the supersonic airliner, the hovercraft, giant oil tankers and so on. But one of the most far-reaching developments tends to be overlooked by the general public, who are more interested in spectacular events. This crucial development is that of containerisation.

What exactly does 'containerisation' mean? The concept is simple enough − containers are used in which goods are packed. There is surely nothing very original about that. The containers are, moreover, contructed to standard international specifications. For example, they all measure eight feet in width, eight feet in height, and ten, twenty, thirty or forty feet in length. But again, there is nothing unusual in having a lot of similar-sized boxes. What is so special about containers?

The really significant impact of containers is their transmodality. This is a new term which is best illustrated by the following example. One of the chief worries facing any manufacturer is that of ensuring swift, cheap and safe transport for his goods. Consider the problems facing a British factory exporting machinery to Malaysia. The goods must first be taken from the factory, by road, to a railway depot. The railway carries the goods to the docks, where they are stored in a transit shed. Then they are loaded on to a ship. When the ship reaches Malaysia, the goods are unloaded. Then they are carried by rail and, later, perhaps by road or even river.

Every one of these steps entails delay, handling expenses, paperwork, and the danger of damage to the goods or pilferage. But consider how a container overcomes these problems. The manufacturer packs his cargo into a tough standard container which fits neatly on to a special lorry trailer. The lorry drives to a railway depot, where a special, crane lifts the container off the trailer and directly on to a flat railway wagon within minutes. The freight train, consisting of perhaps a hundred such waggons, speeds to the docks. Within a couple of hours a massive crane has swiftly lifted each container off its waggon and on to a specially built container ship waiting in an adjacent dock. And so on, whenever the mode of transport changes from road to rail, sea, river or (with limitations) air. The saving in labour is tremendous, and the speed is amazing. Within a single day a container ship can arrive fully laden at a port, unload, reload and leave on her next voyage. Within an hour or two a container train or 'freightliner' can unload and reload.

Containerised cargo is very secure against breakages and theft. The old danger of cargo breaking loose during a storm no longer applies when the ship's holds are completely filled with a neat stack of containers like so many bricks. And the containers need not be sent back to the factory, they can be re-used for different cargo just as a taxi carries passengers from place to place. Imagine a taxi which could use road, rail or sea as it wished, and you have a rough approximation of transmodality, which is the concept of using all methods of transport for a single vehicle. Containers can, in fact be looked upon as vehicles.

There are some drawbacks to containerisation, of course. Ports need to be equipped with very elaborate and expensive handling equipment, and a container ship cannot use ordinary ports. A small consignment of goods may not be enough to warrant a container.

But the advantages are tremendous for most kinds of freight. The high speed means that the exporter's goods arrive quickly, so that he receives payment sooner, and even the insurance charges are much lower.

(LCC Private Secretary's Certificate)

5.   Write a summary of the following passage in about 180 words. Give your summary a suitable heading and state the number of words used.

Educational technology is providing us with a wide variety of new aids to learning and teaching, helping to combat the increase in demand for all levels and the shortage in the supply of skilled teachers. The use of such aids has considerable implications for the design of spaces in colleges and universities. The simplest and most obvious way to match large numbers of learners with a small number of teachers is to increase the group size for teaching and learning, in other words, to have larger audiences for each teacher. This may be superficially efficient in dispersing rare talent over a wider audience; it is not necessarily effective as a learning situation. For instance there may be little opportunity for student participation, little opportunity for students to discuss and clear up difficulties and misconceptions with the lecturer, and hence little immediate feedback to advise the teacher on the success or otherwise of his teaching. Wherever group sizes increase, there is a corresponding need for supplementary small-group follow-up or for the incorporation of methods whereby students may seek clarification or help as the instruction proceeds. The first solution brings us back to the shortages of the teachers concerned, unless a highly skilled or specialised lecturer can be supplemented by assistants of an intermediate level; for instance, the use of post-graduate research students as 'demonstrators' in some university departments. The second solution, namely the opportunity to interrupt the lecturer, must inevitably be limited to few students and few occasions if the lecture is to make progress. A third and more profitable solution is to provide greater opportunities for students to teach themselves.

Paradoxically, and perhaps fortunately, while the new mass media such as film and television can be employed to assist in the teaching of large groups, other new developments in the field of aids and media in education are helping to cater for increased individualisation of instruction and, in fact, much may ultimately depend on the degree of sophistication which can be achieved with such aids. These two opposite trends, towards the teaching of large audiences and towards individualised instruction, have obvious implications for the shapes as well as the sizes of rooms and theatres; in addition, the servicing required for electronics or other equipment may exert some contraint on the actual dispersal of different types of teaching space — for instance, in some senses the teaching of language can be regarded as a laboratory subject (541 words).

(K. Austwick, *Media and Methods,* ed. D. Unwin)

6. The following extract is taken from *Public Relations Advances* by J. H. Crisford. It discusses what a businessman should do if his company wants to put up a stand at an exhibition. Prepare a summary of not more than 170 words, clearly setting out the steps (and their alternatives) to be taken by an executive who seeks a well-designed stand. NOTE: A 'brief' means a set of detailed requirements given to a designer.

A problem facing executives when planning exhibitions is, who shall they get to design the stand? Usually the executive will have the task of selecting a designer, and as the design of the stand can be critical to the success of the exhibition this is obviously an important decision.

There are two main alternatives: you can either first approach the designer and then, usually with his participation, choose the contractor who will build the stand that the designer has designed; or you can go first to the contractor and get his own designer to design the stand.

If your first choice is the designer you are then faced with the further alternatives of employing your designer's choice of contractor — which may not be your *own* choice — or of finding a contractor who satisfies both you and your designer. One of the worst situations to find yourself in, prior to a big exhibition, is a squabble between your designer and your contractor.

Whatever you decide, you are about to entrust a large budget to designing and building the stand which has got to be superbly efficient at its job for the vital days of the exhibition. I believe — and this works very well — you should commission three designers to prepare plans and make a model.

You must be honest and tell each of the three that you are asking for competitive designs. You must give them all identical briefs. Ask each to come to your office (separately) to discuss your requirements, and give each the same number of working days to complete the plans and the model. Explain that you will pay an agreed sum to each of the losers and that the winner will get the contract for the full-size stand.

In due course you should have in your office *three* beautiful little models, all satisfying your brief and all, surprisingly, quite different! Now you can choose the best of the three. Your stand is therefore likely to be better than many of your competitors.

It may be that to choose between the models is difficult. Make a careful assessment. Study the design. Are people attracted on to the stand? Can they see the whole exhibit without retracing their steps?

Once you have decided on the best of the three designs, ask the designers of the two losing designs to come to your office and tell them why you did not pick their design. This is not an enjoyable task but it is a courtesy you owe to the designer for the work he has put in on your behalf. He will naturally want to know why he has not been successful and if you explain this he will learn something and be grateful. If the runner-up is very close you can tell him that he will be asked again next time.

Next time, invite the successful designer, perhaps the runner-up and some new designers. In this way you will get to know designers and they will get to know you (500 words).

(LCC Private Secretary's Certificate)

7.   You are the secretary to an executive in a car-manufacturing firm. He asks you to prepare a brief summary of the changes in working conditions that Volvo have introduced, the reasons for such changes, and how far they have been successful. Read the following extract from the *New Statesman* and in not more than 150 words prepare the required summary.

They're building a new car factory at Kalmar in south-eastern Sweden to produce the successful Volvo saloons and station wagons. It is completely unlike any existing motor plant anywhere in the world: in fact, the Kalmar factory is something of a reaction against Henry Ford, against Detroit, against the moving line production system, the regimentation of workers, the soul-destroying monotony of industrial work. But it's not against productivity, profit-making, mass production. It is a gigantic Swedish compromise.

The idea is that workers cannot be expected nowadays to put up with Ford's concept that each step in the production of a motor-car should be broken down into its simplest form, taking the worker a few seconds to complete a tiny process before it passes along the conveyor belt to the next worker, who in turn adds his own diminutive but vital contribution to the whole. Workers need wider horizons and a greater involvement if they are to continue to produce good Volvos. So Kalmar has been constructed to reintroduce the small workshop concept of the early industrial era, to increase the amount of responsibility each worker has for the product, and to give him a much larger share in the production process — perhaps up to 30 minutes to complete a job assignment instead of 30 seconds. Swedish managers are certain it is all going to be an enormous success.

Each group of 25 to 50 workers will form an industrial team, with their own factory entrance, their own canteen area and their own sauna bath. And each will be responsible for the construction of a substantial amount of the car and be allowed to work at their own pace.

More than a thousand such job-enrichment projects are being tried out in a whole range of industries, though no one has gone as far as Volvo. Why Swedish management have brought in the psychiatrists, the sociologists and the behaviourists is simple: the increasingly better-educated Swedish working class is rebelling against factory life. Absenteeism — the 'silent strike' — is on the increase, recruitment is down and labour turnover is high. So job enrichment is a way of luring young workers into factory life or keeping them there.

The Swedish trade union movement takes a guarded view of the whole development. In many instances the unions are co-operating — but then, Swedish unions are accustomed to co-operating with management. But there are underlying tensions, which are seeking expressions in other ways than just the Kalmar method. Since 1928 Swedish workers have been virtually forbidden to strike except at three-yearly intervals when wage contracts are nationally negotiated — and even then, only when instructed to do so by their unions. The result is that workers are being alienated from trade unions as well as production line monotony. The Kalmar system may well solve the latter problem, but it does nothing to change the former.

Swedish employers resignedly assume that giving the workers more responsibility will eventually lead to a more insistent demand for workers' control of the whole firm. Meanwhile, the frustration at not being able to strike has been reduced by the increased satisfaction enjoyed by Volvo workers.

(LCC Private Secretary's Certificate)

8. Your employer does not have any fireproof cabinets for his important documents. You have read the following extract and decide to prepare a brief summary of the hazards of fire and how they can be overcome. Draft a suitable summary, giving it a title and taking not more than 150 words.

Do you keep thousands of pounds in your office? No, you probably don't. Like most offices, yours is likely to be full of correspondence files, order books, stock lists, financial records and so on. Nothing of interest to a thief.

Why is it, then, that leading firms of safe manufacturers supply so many security cabinets to offices? The answer is a single word: fire. No burglar could carry away tons of documents, even if he wanted to. But fire can completely destroy such documents within hours and often within minutes.

Businessmen often don't realise that, with their records destroyed, their entire business could be ruined overnight. Even if it is possible to compile a fresh set of records, the long delay can be disastrous. However, those who do realise their vulnerability to fire are wise enough to install security cabinets in which the most vital documents can be stored.

You may say, 'But surely most filing cabinets and sets of drawers are made of steel nowadays, and won't burn?' This is true, of course, but remember that steel is a good conductor of heat. In an office fire the furniture (if made of steel) will quickly become red-hot, and anything inside it will simply become roasted to ashes.

Some firms produce specially toughened and insulated equipment that can withstand very high temperatures for some hours. Naturally, any security cabinet would eventually get very hot inside if it were in a fire, but in normal circumstances an office fire will be detected fairly quickly and be put out in a few hours. During that time the precious documents inside the security cabinet will remain safe and unscorched.

There are other hazards associated with an office fire which these cabinets must withstand. Suppose the office is on an upper floor. If the building catches fire the floors (if made of wood) may burn through, causing furniture to fall heavily for some distance. If the cabinets were to burst open, the documents inside them would immediately spill out into the flames. A similar danger may arise if firemen direct their water hoses on to the cabinet, which is liable to split open just as a hot glass bottle can be cracked by being plunged into cold water. And then the documents would once again be exposed to the fire and flames.

The solution to these problems is to install proper security cabinets which will withstand fire safely, including heavy blows, falls, sudden cooling and so on. The cost is not low; but how much more expensive it is to have all one's vital records destroyed because of one careless match or dropped cigarette!

If a businessman does take the trouble to equip his office in this way, he might as well spend a little more on providing good fire extinguishers too. Then the dreaded fire might never happen (about 500 words).

(LCC Private Secretary's Certificate)

9. Read carefully the following extracts from an article in *The Times*. Then summarise, taking not more than 180 words, the problems which the Licensing Centre has faced and the ways in which it tries to deal with them and to cope with its work-load. There are 630 words in the passage.

The Driver and Vehicle Licensing Centre at Swansea, which handles the vast mass of paperwork necessary to keep the country on the road, has a bad reputation. It is criticised for delays and bungling. MPs are asked to sort out its mistakes, magistrates' clerks grumble that delays upset the flow of justice and the girls who answer the centre's telephones are hardened to the ripe language of fuming customers.

Delays and well publicised mistakes have made the centre a frequent target for abuse. Modernisation and centralisation, it is said bitterly, have led to bureaucratic chaos and a worse service.

Inside the 16-floor centre, however, the picture looks different. The 5,300 people who work there, many of them school-leavers and married women, reckon they provide an efficient service. They are, to quote one of them, 'absolutely fed up' with their bad press and they pin on their notice-boards the many letters of appreciation they receive.

One license application in every 20 has to be returned to sender because the form is wrongly or inadequately filled in, or is not accompanied by the fee. That is one of the roots of the delay. An MP who complained loudly of delays to his own documents had sent them to the wrong place. A writer who criticised dealys in getting a license had, it turned out, written his name wrongly on the form.

The centre, built as part of the Government's office-dispersal policy, is a data superbank with the largest computer complex of its kind in Europe. It is the apex of the new system of vehicle and driver documentation, replacing the licensing network formerly run by 183 local authorities. The disjointed nature of the old system and the burdens it imposed made modernisation urgent.

The centre sent out its first licence in 1973 and is now the sole issuing authority for driving licences. It holds 25 million drivers' records and issues about 900,000 new, amended or renewed licences every month. It expects to process a licence in 10 working days, so that a person sending an application to Swansea can expect to get his licence back about three weeks after posting.

The huge volume of work means that the centre will not, in the foreseeable future, be able to process applications in less than 10 working days. So the three-week round trip for a licence will remain standard. Overtime or weekend working would make the operation too costly. Fewer mistakes are being made with the steady improvement of the system as experience grows.

Computers, of course, are only as good as the information provided, and the mistakes have human causes. A keyboard operator can make a slip that will get through the net. The indistinct writing of an applicant can be misread; a bilingual licence, as issued in Wales, can go by mistake to England; and some motor dealers still use the wrong forms, which leads to someone being credited with a car he does not own.

Mismatching and discrepancies can compound delays. People grow anxious, sometimes angry, when they find their departure date for a motoring holiday abroad coming closer, with their licence still in the Swansea system. Magistrates' clerks are often badgered by convicted people whose licences have been sent to Swansea, and who find they need their licences in a hurry. Most police forces take a reasonable view in cases where a licence is 'held up in Swansea', and the centre has a unit to deal with complaints of delay and work with the police and the Home Office.

One complaint made about the centre is that callers sometimes cannot get through on the telephone. In the driving licence section there are 24 lines and 24 girls answering up to 2,500 inquiries a day, from 8 am to 5 pm.

(LCC Private Secretary's Certificate)

10. Your firm will shortly be sending to Japan a party of businessmen none of whom has been there before. Using the material in the following extract, prepare a short document which could be distributed among the businessmen giving them an idea of what modern Japan is like. The document is to be headed 'Fact-sheet on Modern Japan', and it should not exceed 200 words at the most.

Look out of the living-room window of even the most comfortable middle-class house in Japan and the next house is never more than a few feet away. Or the next factory. And beside the bamboo fence of the last house on the outskirts, beside the wall of the last factory, the rice paddy commences.

Four-fifths of Japan is uninhabitable mountain, so that 108 million people have to live, manufacture and grow their food in an area about the size of the Irish Republic. This dense civilisation must have thickened almost in front of the eyes during the last 120 years, ever since Japan — then an impoverished feudal society with a population limited by famine, of some 30 millions — was forcibly reopened to the world by the great imperial Powers.

And not only thickened, but changed, and changed again. Working in timber rather than stone or brick, the Japanese have never built to last. Then nearly half of Tokyo was reduced to ashes in the great earthquake of 1923 and well over half of it destroyed again by the Americans in 1945. My friend Ishiguro, who had been back to Japan for only two short visits in the last five years, was constantly astonished as she showed me round Tokyo by the sight of new buildings, and baffled by the miles of new subway line.

It has been difficult to build upwards for fear of earthquakes, though clumps of high-rise buildings are now appearing in Tokyo which are designed to resonate freely in time with the shock waves. In Osaka they have escaped downwards and have dug out a huge underground shopping centre two floors deep, with its own decorative subterranean river. (An earthquake expert I talked to was very gloomy about what would happen down there when a big quake shattered the exits and extinguished the lights.) The dense, low urban sprawl on the surface is dominated by towering wire cages like gigantic aviaries, inside which you can take out your frustrations on a golf-ball, to keep you sane while you work to become rich enough to hit it out in the open. (I saw advertisement offering up to £27,000 for membership of a real golf club.)

The roads are clogged with the nation's products; the rivers and seas with its waste products. Miss Ishiguro begged me to make great efforts not to write another article about pollution, but the subject was not possible to avoid. Entire pages of the English language papers were full of nothing but pollution news; conversation returned to it again and again (430 words).

(From 'Frayn's Japan' by Michael Frayn in the *Observer*)

(*LCC Private Secretary's Certificate*)

11. Read the following extracts from an unsuccessful interviewee's account of her experience in applying for the post of Personal Assistant advertised by a management consultancy. Summarise the shortcomings of the firm's recruitment, interviewing and selection techniques.

Q. *What position were you applying for?*

A. The advertisement was not very clear but I think one could definitely say it was a personal assistant I didn't think that the company had really clarified in their own minds what they expected from the applicant. It was not their intention to employ a secretary but rather someone in the nature of a co-ordinator.

Q. *What attracted you to the advertisement?*

A. The fact that it was a fairly senior position and did not entail short-hand. I understood that it was of an administrative nature. I applied for an appointment but did not hear from them for several months. Then out of the blue I received a letter. Naturally after all this time I had forgotten about the job and as I had not kept the ad cutting it was a case of putting two and two together. I rang and asked what the job entailed and was told that they had had more than 300 replies. They had whittled these down and had chosen four women for interview. I felt that this can't be bad so I duly went along.

[The interviewer] . . . asked me what I knew about management consultancy. I said that I assumed it had something to do with selection, amongst other functions. At this point he shoved a great pile of papers and files at me which I assumed he wanted me to look at. In the meantime people were coming in and going out and the telephone was constantly ringing. I had the feeling that the impression he was trying to create was that he was very high powered and I certainly was impressed.

We rambled from one topic to another. First I was told about management consultancy and how their business had grown, the changes they had made and the kinds of things they concentrated on. From this I began to realise what side of management consultancy he was talking about and gradually things became more clear in my mind. We finally got round to the question of what I was to do in the organisation, all of which had taken about three quarters of an hour with interruptions and cups of coffee. I was also told about his job in Australia and, most important of all, that the last girl he had employed had finished up with a nervous breakdown and had to be sent away for a month. Apparently they realised that to co-ordinate their various activities — what jobs were on hand and who was attending to them and also the different locations of the consultants at any time — a secretary was so much waste of time. At this stage he called in his partner and I gathered from what was said that I would be expected to work for him as well. I remember specifically saying 'Look, if I'm with you and with him, who is minding the store back here?' The reply was that this was something that was going to be worked out later.

Q. *Was the duration of the interview adequate?*

A. It went on for two hours and they seemed to think we all got on splendidly. I, on the other hand, came away feeling totally bemused. Of course I was told that no decisions about taking on new staff could be made without being vetted by their psychologist. The psychological tests were going to find out what sort of person I was. All he really wanted to do at that [first] interview was to find out if he personally liked me or not. Possibly also whether I liked him, but it looked very much as if assumed that this was so. As far as he was concerned, only two of the four short-listed applicants were chosen to go for the tests and I had given a thorough rundown of my experience in my letter of application.

He didn't go into my past history. Well, he really didn't ask any questions at all. He told me and it really seemed like a one-man band.

The impression I had when the question of my knowledge of management consultancy came up was that he had scored a point over me and that was fine with him. Of course this having scored a point over me did not seem the right attitude at all. I am sure an interviewer must always remain objective and I felt that he was very subjective, the subject being himself.

Q. *Did the interview end on a warm and friendly note?*

A. We were very good friends, indeed: in fact the switchboard girl remarked on my way out that he must have liked me, otherwise the whole thing would have been over in ten minutes.

Q. *What happened then?*

A. A call came through asking me to attend a second interview. I went along thinking that I was going to have an interview with their psychologist roughly on the lines of questions relevant to the job and personality, but nothing of the sort. I arrived at the place which was in a basement. The psychologist did not appear; his wife, who I think acted as his assistant, handed me the various papers. As far as I remember there were some timed tests at the beginning and then the major one which I think had something like two hundred and ninety questions. It took from about one o'clock to five. I believe one was the recognition test where one has to fill in the next line, where one gets circles and squares. I don't know the name. It was quite meaningless to me. I simply viewed all these with total disbelief when I realised what I had let myself in for.

As far as I can recall there were three [separate] tests. The first short one was timed and then we had this very long one. At the beginning of the questionnaire it said that there were various questions on sex, which you could leave out if you wished. For example, do I like to leave my desk tidy or do I like to kiss attractive men. I just ask you, which does one answer? There were so many that one just plodded on until they were finished. After that I took one more test in English and Arithmetric at which I probably failed, but by that time I couldn't sit upright any more and I really did not care anyway.

Q. *What happened after you had finished the tests?*

A. They said they would let me know. Later I had a letter of rejection.

I rang up the psychologist and spoke to his wife, asking for the test results but was told that as these belonged to the company they had no power to release them.

Q. *Why did you not refuse to take the tests at the beginning?*

A. I was in two minds about this but I was also at the time interested in getting the job, although the more I thought about it the less I wanted it. (1218 words.)

(From Eva Roman and Derek Gould, *Recruitment and Selection of Typists and Secretaries*)

12.   You are employed as a secretary by a firm which makes toys and a range of fireworks (firecrackers, rockets, sparklers, etc.). The firm is thinking of closing down its fireworks factory. For the benefit of one of the firm's executives, summarise, in not more than 160 words, the following correspondence which has been published in a national newspaper during the last few days. You need to write a short covering memo to the executive, explaining to him (or her) where you saw the correspondence and why you think it is significant.

Sir

My daughter Mary took part in a local fete at our village last week, and at the end of the day she joined in the firework celebrations. There were a number of children and young people roaming around, letting off fireworks. One of these hit Mary in the face. As a result, she is now blind in one eye and has a permanent burn scar on the left side of her face.

Isn't it time the government banned fireworks? How can manufacturers be so wicked as to sell these dangerous things?

Yours faithfully
(Mrs) Elizabeth Onslow

Sir

On behalf of my Association, may I reply to the letter from Mrs Onslow which you recently published?

I naturally sympathise deeply with the very great distress which her daughter's accident has caused. However, I am sure your correspondent would not wish to ban kitchen knives, or even building bricks. Yet these, if thrown indiscriminately by reckless persons, can be just as lethal as any firework.

Your readers will know that the sale of fireworks is strictly controlled, so that only responsible persons of a certain age can buy them. The solution to tragedies such as Mary Onslow's is better education and more stringent control. Fireworks bring enormous pleasure to many people, and it seems a pity to allow a very tiny irresponsible minority to deny this pleasure to the public.

Yours faithfully
Maurice Morgan
Secretary, Association of Chemical Processors

Sir
    How hypocritical can one be?
    Maurice Morgan is *paid*, I repeat *paid*, by his Association to utter platitudes defending his members. Fireworks are lethal — he admits it himself! I hope the government will take immediate action to put an end to this trade in death and disfigurement.

Yours disgustedly
Paul Simon

Sir
    As a plastic surgeon at one of London's biggest hospitals, I should like to comment on the correspondence which has recently appeared in your columns.
    Every year, I treat a large number of cases of firework burns. The majority of patients are children, often quite young children. The pain and suffering which these patients have to endure is very considerable, and although it is often possible to repair much of the damage by means of plastic surgery there is an inevitable legacy of disfigurement and impaired function. And, of course, plastic surgery is of no avail in the many cases where there has been an eye injury.
    My colleagues and I have pressed for many years for very strict controls on the sale of fireworks and your recent correspondents have convinced me that only a complete end to the manufacture of these dangerous toys will be effective.
    For professional reasons I prefer not to sign my name, and remain

Yours faithfully
London Surgeon

Sir
    'London Surgeon' makes a very good case, but like your other correspondents he is in danger of throwing the baby out with the bathwater.
    Fireworks do indeed give much pleasure. Why then should we allow an irresponsible group of people to deprive us of that pleasure?
    Mr Morgan writes that the sale of fireworks is strictly controlled, but your readers will all know that children can get hold of fireworks —

perhaps through contact with older children. The answer would be to prohibit the sale of all fireworks to the public, but to licence local authorities and other responsible bodies to hold firework displays under carefully controlled conditions.

We have done this locally for several years, and public support has been most encouraging.

Yours etc.
Jennie Staples
Youth and Recreation Officer,London Borough of Bridgenorth

Dear Mr Editor
My Mum won't let me have any fireworks for my birthday party because she had been reading your newspaper and I don't think it's fair.

Lisa Smith (aged 9)

NOTE: This correspondence is now closed — *Editor*

(LCC Private Secretary's Certificate)

7

COMPREHENSION

At work a secretary will have numerous incoming pieces of paper which have to be quickly assimilated and assessed. Practice in comprehension will help to develop this skill.

Comprehension questions are a most useful tool for examiners of communication, since they test the ability of students to read with understanding and to express themselves clearly. A methodical approach and an ability to recognise the implication of the questions are needed and the following suggestions may prove helpful.

METHOD

1. Read the passage through at least twice, or until you have understood it.
2. Read the questions very carefully.
3. Re-read the passage, searching for the answers to the questions. It may be helpful to mark the appropriate points of the passage with the question numbers in the margin.
4. Write your answers.
5. Check your work for omissions, unnecessary information and for accuracy.

GENERAL ADVICE

1. Number your answers accurately.
2. Avoid presenting your answers out of sequence if possible.
3. Set your answers out clearly. Look at the worked examples to see how this may best be done.
4. Write in complete sentences except, for example, in vocabulary questions or when you are asked to give a list.
5. Use your own words, not those of the passage, wherever possible.
6. Recognise the limits of each question. Resist the temptation to write at length. Some students use the 'shotgun' technique of including everything that may conceivably be relevant in the hope of somehow hitting the target. Such a technique will lose marks. Your answers must be as brief and to the point as possible.

7. Confine yourself to the information given in the passage **unless** you are asked a general knowledge type of question.
8. Your answers should rarely overlap. If you find yourself giving the same information in answer to more than one question, the chances are that at least one of your answers is wrong.

TYPES OF QUESTION

If you can recognise the different types of question you may be asked, it will be easier to produce an answer which is to the point and which conforms to the limits of the question. The main types of question are listed below and are included in the two worked examples which follow.

1   VOCABULARY

Typical questions may be phrased as shown in the following examples:

> *Explain the meaning of the following words as they are used in the passage:* ...
> *Explain, in context, the meaning of:* ...
> *Find an alternative word or phrase for* ...

(a)   Your answer must be set out to include the original word used and your own alternative, for example

> original word   your alternative
> *connotations*   *implications*

(b)   Your answer must use the same part of speech, or its equivalent, as the original. Test this by checking that your answer can replace the original word in the passage. For example, either (but not both) of these answers would be appropriate:

> *hurriedly — with haste, quickly*

(c)   Give one answer only. If you give more than one, the examiner will mark the first and ignore others. Do not give an answer like this example:

> *lure — attraction or enticement*

It is permissible, if there is no one synonym available, to give two words linked by the conjunction *and,* provided that your answer obeys rule (b) above, for example

> *anarchic flux — chaotic movement and change*

2   RE-EXPRESSION

The questions are similar to vocabulary questions but you are required to give the meaning of a phrase, or even a sentence, from the passage, rather than the meaning of one word only. Such questions may be expressed as follows:

> *What does the author mean by . . .?*
> *What do you understand by the following expressions . . .?*
> *Rewrite in your own words the following sentence: . . .*

(a)   Figures of speech should be changed into literal expressions, for example (see Exercise 1)

> *blue skies — free from problems*

(b)   Your answer may be written either as a phrase which could replace the original one in the passage (see Worked Example 2 (b)), or as a complete sentence.

3   INTERPRETATION

Such questions usually take the form of direct questions referring the student to the passage, for example

> *Why does the author contend that . . .?*
> *What reasons does the author give for . . .?*
> *What conclusions does the author draw . . .?*
> *Explain . . .*

The answers to these types of questions may be found in one sentence or even a single phrase in the passage. However, check carefully through the whole passage to ensure that you do not omit any relevant information.

4   SUMMARY

The questions are usually easily recognisable, for example

> *Suggest two abstract nouns to describe . . .*
> *Describe in two or three sentences . . .*
> *Describe in about forty of your own words . . .*
> *Summarise in your own words . . .*

Do not waste any words in your answer. Your ability to express yourself concisely is being tested. Always give your summary a heading if possible.

5   REASONING

These questions are among the most difficult to answer. They may take many forms, for example

> *Do you agree with the author when he states . . .?*
> *What are your views on . . .?*

The marks will be awarded to students who demonstrate a logical approach, even though the conclusions reached may vary. The reasoning in your answer should be supported by evidence and example wherever appropriate.

6   GENERAL KNOWLEDGE

Although comprehension exercises primarily test a student's understanding of a passage, some examinations include general-knowledge questions in the comprehension questions.

Two such questions are:

> *Name one or two Middle East nations* (see Exercise 13)
> *What do you understand by solvency?* (see Exercise 10)

Students who are well read and keep themselves informed on current events by regular reading of newspapers will not usually find difficulty with these questions. Do not waste too much time on trying to work out or guess the answer.

WORKED EXAMPLES

EXAMPLE 1

Read carefully the following extracts from the *Employer's Guide to Pay As You Earn,* issued by the Board of Inland Revenue:

The Pay As You Earn method of deducting income tax from salaries and wages applies to all income from offices or employements (except in a few isolated types of case for which the employers concerned will be given special instructions). Thus Pay As You Earn applies not only to wages and salaries but also to annual payments, bonuses, commissions, directors' fees, pensions, and any other income or emoluments.

Under Pay As You Earn the amount of tax which the employer has to deduct depends on the employee's total gross pay since the beginning of the income tax year.

Where an employer has an arrangement under which meal vouchers are issued to his employees, the value of the vouchers issued to an employee is not regarded as part of his taxable income provided the following conditions are satisfied:

(1) the vouchers are non-transferable and used for meals only;
(2) where any restriction is placed on their issue to employees they are available to the lower paid staff;
(3) the value of the vouchers issued to an employee does not exceed 15p for each full working day.

Where condition (3) is not satisfied the value in excess of 15p a day is regarded as taxable income and is to be shown in a return at the end of the tax year.

(a)   What difference is there between 'wages' and 'salaries'? Can you suggest any reasons why an employer or employee might have a preference for using one of these terms instead of the other?

(b)   What do you understand by 'offices'?

(c)   What, broadly speaking, is the difference between 'bonus' and 'commission'?

(d)   A company decides to issue meal vouchers to its senior staff only. Comment on the tax position.

(e)   What is 'gross pay'? When the tax has been deducted and the employee receives his pay, suggest an expression to replace 'gross pay'.

(f)   Your employer plans to issue meal vouchers worth 25p a day to all his staff. Prepare a short explanatory statement which can be printed on a slip of paper to be inserted into each employee's pay packet together with his weekly supply of vouchers. Use the relevant material from the the passage and make your answer roughly 50-60 words in length.

(g)   What is a 'return'?

(LCC Private Secretary's Certificate)

Comment

In (g) the word 'return' may refer either to employers or employees. Both possibilities are included in the answer in order to help students.

ANSWERS

(a)   Wages are usually paid weekly and based on an hourly rate of pay. Salaries are usually paid monthly and are based on an annual remuneration. Employees might well prefer the term 'salary' because it implies that their job carries a higher status than that of a wage-earner. Employers might prefer monthly payments because they would reduce the work of the accounts department.

(b)   Offices – appointments

(c)   Bonus – a payment additional to salary and often made to employees as a lump sum paid once a year; the amount may be related, for example, to the firm's profits, to productivity, or may be arbitrarily decided.
Commission – a payment additional to salary and paid to employees on the basis of their individual performance, usually a percentage of, for example, the value of sales they have made.

(d)   Meal vouchers paid to senior staff only will be regarded as taxable income because their issue does not conform with the second condition quoted in the passage, viz. 'where any restriction is placed on their issue to employees they are available to the lower paid staff'.

(e) 'Gross pay' is the total pay before any deductions have been made. A suitable term for the amount of pay an employee receives after deductions would be 'net pay'.

(f) *Meal vouchers*

In future you will receive, with your weekly pay, a supply of five meal vouchers worth 25p each. The first week's supply is enclosed. These vouchers are non-transferable and may be used for meals only. 10p of the value of each voucher is regarded by the Income Tax Commissioners as taxable income and should be declared on your annual tax return.

(g) A return is a form listing the amount of income, from all sources, which is completed annually by everyone in receipt of an income for the income tax inspectors. (A return is also made by employers to the income tax inspectors listing payments made to their employees.)

EXAMPLE 2

Read carefully the following extract from one of the scripts of *Civilisation*, a television series by Kenneth Clark, and then attempt the questions below it.

When I look at the world about me in the light of this series, I don't at all feel that we are entering a new period of barbarism. The things that made the Dark Ages so dark — the isolation, the lack of mobility, the lack of curiosity — don't *obtain* at all. When I have the good fortune to visit one of our new universities, it seems to me that the inheritors of all our catastrophes look cheerful enough — very different from the melancholy *late* Romans or pathetic Gauls whose likenesses have come down to us. In fact I should doubt if so many people have ever been as well-fed, as well-read, as bright-minded, as curious and as critical as the young are today.

Naturally these bright-minded young people think poorly of existing *institutions* and want to abolish them. Well, one doesn't need to be young to dislike institutions. But the dreary fact remains that, even in the darkest ages, it was institutions that made society work, and if civilisation is to survive, society must somehow be made to work.

At this point I reveal myself in my true colours: as a stick-in-the-mud. I hold a number of beliefs that have been repudiated by the liveliest intellects of our time. I believe that order is better than chaos, creation better than destruction. I prefer gentleness to violence, forgiveness to *vendetta*. On the whole I think that knowledge is preferable to ignorance, and I am sure that human sympathy is more valuable than *ideology*. I believe in courtesy, the ritual by which we avoid hurting other people's feelings by satisfying our own *egos*.

(a) Indicate clearly the meaning or force of the following words in the extract:

obtain
late

> *institutions*
> *vendetta*
> *ideology*
> *egos*

(b)   Lord Clark calls himself a *stick-in-the-mud.* From your reading of the extract suggest a better and fuller description of his views in not more than ten words.

(c)   Comment on any *unintentional* revelations about himself which Lord Clark communicates when he says one of the following:

> *'these bright-minded young people'*
> *'I believe . . .'* (last sentence)

(LCC Private Secretary's Certificate)

Comments

Question (c) required comment on only one of the two expressions given, but, to aid students, answers to both are given.

ANSWERS

(a)   obtain — prevail
      late — latter day
      institutions — established patterns of society
      vendetta — feud
      ideology — abstract theories
      egos — inner selves

(b)   Lord Clark's views are optimistic, conventional, humanist and compassionate.

(c)   *'these bright-minded young people'*
      The expression 'bright-minded' suggests admiration tinged with a little envy. The context suggests Lord Clark's disapproval of their wish for change.

      'I believe . . .'
      Lord Clark's expressed awareness of other people's vulnerability suggests that his own feelings are sentitive and easily hurt. However, the word 'ritual' suggests a rather cynical view of courtesy when it is not spontaneous consideration for others but is formalised behaviour that gives more satisfaction to the giver than to the recipient.

EXERCISES

1.   Read the following passage and answer the questions below:

The Flexible Time-Clock

Flexible working hours is a system which, by putting an end to the nine to five working day myth, brings a more human touch to the working situation, but forces nobody into another *straitjacket*. It does not demand, either, that the individual, who is set in his ways, should change his habits. With flexible working hours, the working day is split into three sections — one when everyone must be present (the core time) and two at either end of the day (the flexible bands when everyone can come and go as he pleases). Flexible working hours started in Germany and was developed by the personnel manager of Messerschmitt-Bolkow-Blohm GmbH, a large company in Munich in the aerospace industry. The staff problems with which he was faced were the same as in any large *conurbation*. The *commuting* problem, however, is different, since the offices, a large modern block with about 4,000 employees, are on the outskirts of Munich and are not well served by public transport.

The system was introduced in 1968, and quickly spread not only in his company but throughout Germany and to other parts of the Continent. It is now estimated that there are well over 2,000 applications of the system. It has been adopted in administrative organisations, insurance companies, and head offices, as well as in local and central government. One of the latest and most interesting applications is in a retail clothing store — although, given the varying traffic volumes and reliance on part-time assistants, it is surprising that the idea was not born in the retail environment.

In the system core times are set to coincide with the daily peak demands on the organisation — in an office from 10 a.m. until 4 p.m. — and flexible bands are added during which employees can be present or not at their will. In the office situation, these might well be between 8 a.m. and 10 a.m. and 4 p.m. and 6.30 p.m. The main restrictions, apart from presence during the core time, is that over a given *settlement period,* which can be a week or a fortnight, but more usually a month, employees have to work the total number of hours for which they have contracted, i.e. if the contracted time is seven hours per day, they have to be present in total for 140 hours in a month of 20 working days. There are refinements. Many companies have added an additional flexible band to cover the lunch break. Employees can take up to 1½ hours, but they must observe a minimum of half-an-hour. Most companies which have implemented this system allow a further concession; the possibility of a debit or credit carry forward of up to ten hours. Debit/credit hours should be made up, or taken, during the flexible bands of the following settlement period; but some companies allow a half day per month off in core time against accumulated credit hours.

It is not all *'blue skies'* however. But nor has the old adage that if you give a man enough rope he will hang himself proved true, either. At Messerschmidt-Bolkow-Blohm, for example, employees are almost always in credit to the tune of, on average, approximately four hours per employee. There are other advantages to the company, according to a survey carried out by the German Personnel Management Association.

Out of a total of thirty companies replying, improvement in working atmosphere was reported by 24; reduction of paid absence by 25; reduction of overtime worked by 15; increased productivity by individuals adjusting hours worked to their own best work rhythm by 17; improved recruitment success by 19; and reduced personnel turnover by 6.

(Management Today, January 1973)

(a) Summarise in not more than 100 words how the flexible work-hours system works.

(b) Give the meaning of the following expressions, as they are used in the passage:

> *straitjacket*
> *conurbation*
> *commuting*
> *settlement period*
> *'blue skies'*

(c) What advantages does the system have (i) for employers, (ii) for employees?

(d) What disadvantages can you forsee?

Read the passage and then answer the questions which follow.

The life cycle of the committee is so basic to our knowledge of current affairs that it is surprising more attention has not been paid to the science of comitology. The first and most elementary principle of this science is that a committee is *organic* rather than mechanical in its nature: it is not a structure but a plant. It takes root and grows, it flowers, wilts, and dies, scattering the seed from which other committees will bloom in their turn. Only those who bear this principle in mind can make real headway in understanding the structure and history of modern government.

Committees, it is nowadays accepted, fall broadly into two categories, those (a) from which the individual member has something to gain; and those (b) to which the individual member merely has something to contribute. Examples of the (b) group, however, are relatively unimportant for our purpose; indeed, some people doubt whether they are committees at all. It is from the more robust (a) group that we can learn most readily the principles which are common (with modifications) to all. Of the (a) group the most deeply rooted and luxuriant committees are those which confer the most power and prestige upon their members. In most parts of the world these committees are called 'cabinets'.

When first examined under the microscope, the ideal size of a cabinet council usually appears — to *comitologists,* historians, and even to the people who appoint cabinets — to be five. With that number the plant is *viable,* allowing for two members to be absent or sick at any one time. Five members are easy to collect, and when collected can act with competence, secrecy and speed. Of these original members four may be well versed, respectively, in finance, foreign policy, defence and the law. The fifth, who has failed to master any of these subjects, usually becomes the chairman or prime minister.

Whatever the apparent convenience might be of restricting membership to five, however, we discover by observation that the total number soon rises to seven or nine. The usual excuse given for this increase, which is almost invariable (exceptions being found, however in Luxembourg and Honduras) is the need for special knowledge on more than four topics. In fact, however, there is another and more *potent* reason for addition to the team. For in a cabinet of nine it will be found that policy is made by three, information supplied by two, and financial warning uttered by one. With the neutral chairman, that accounts for seven, the other two appearing at first glance to be merely ornamental. This allocation of duties was first noted in Britain in about 1639, but there can be no doubt that the folly of including more than three able and talkative men on one committee had been discovered long before that. We know little as yet about the function of the two silent members but we have good reason to believe that a cabinet, in this second stage of development, might be unworkable without them.

(C. Northcote Parkinson, *Parkinson's Law*)

(a)   Explain the meaning, in their context, of the following:

>   *organic*
>   *comitologists*
>   *viable*
>   *potent*

(b)   What is the implication of the statement 'The fifth . . . prime minister'?

(c)   Why might people doubt whether the (b) group are committees at all?

(d)   Why is it foolish to include more than three able and talkative men in one committee?

(e)   What is the purpose of the ironic reference to Luxembourg and Honduras?

(f)   Suggest the function of the two silent members.

3.   Read the passage and then answer the questions which follow.

Shoddy Goods and the Law

The Supply of Goods (Implied Terms) Act 1973 makes void any provision in a contract for the sale of goods, made on or after that date, which releases the retailer from his legal obligation to supply goods.

which are of merchantable quality
which meet the description applied to them and
which are fit for the purpose for which they were sold.

What does this mean in practice? Suppose that you bought a television set on 19 May and that it refused to give a picture on 25 May. With it came a manufacturer's guarantee, which said:

Should the equipment fail to operate satisfactorily it should be reported to the dealer from whom it was purchased who will normally be able to provide service and make any claim under guarantee on your behalf. The dealer or service agent will be entitled to make a charge to the purchaser for any labour, postage, packing, and transportation costs involved in diagnosis, removal and replacement of faulty component parts.

It is now certain that this guarantee has no adverse legal effect whatsoever on your rights against the retailer. You can go to him and insist that he repairs the television set — clearly faulty when you bought it — without any charge to you, and that he provides you with another set while he is doing so. If he refuses to do so, you are legally entitled to take your set elsewhere to be mended, to hire another one in the meantime, and to recover the cost of doing so from the shop which originally sold you the set.

Guarantees

You may still see exclusions of responsibility in guarantees for some time to come. Ignore them. The fact that a guarantee says that you must pay labour charges, for instance, has no legal effect on your rights against the retailer. The place where you bought it — whether it is a mail order firm, a discount store or your local high street shop — is still responsible for compensating you for any faults. And it doesn't matter whether you have paid cash or you are buying on credit. If you are buying on HP, any cost that you incur can be deducted from future instalments.

This doesn't mean that a guarantee is not a good thing to have. A good guarantee can still be very useful. In practice it may well be the quickest way of getting your faulty equipment put right without argument. A guarantee like this, for instance, adds to your normal legal rights, without taking anything away: 'We guarantee that should this Automatic Washing Machine prove to be defective by reason only of faulty workmanship or material within 12 months of the date of purchase or commencement of hire purchase, we will repair, or at our option, replace the defective part free of any charge for labour or for materials or for carriage'.

(From *Money Which?*)

(a)   Explain, in your own words, the meaning of *'makes void . . . to supply goods'*.
       In what way does the new law give additional protection to the consumer?

(c)   What advantages might a good guarantee still offer?

4.   Read the following extract from the instructions supplied with a small electronic pocket calculator and answer the questions below it. No special knowledge is required. Keep your answers brief.

Your calculator uses a standard nine-volt battery type PP3-P available at most camera shops. Do not use any other type. To operate calculator, turn power switch to 'ON' position. Switching off clears the machine.
    To use mains adaptor, remove battery from calculator. Plug adaptor into electric mains and connect to calculator using the lead provided.
    When battery weakens the display figures on calculator will go out. Always remove a worn battery to prevent damage.
    The calculator will work out your *VAT, trade discounts, tax rebates,* etc. To do this, use the percentage key. There is a memory key to enable you to store sub-totals.
    If an error is made when entering a figure the C/CE key should be pressed once. This will cancel the entry but leave the rest of the calculation intact. Pressing the C/CE key *twice* will clear the machine ready for a fresh calculation.
    The calculator is guaranteed for one year. For service, pack securely and return, *carriage paid,* to makers. No liability can be entertained for misuse or tampering.

(a)   Members of staff in your office are permitted to use the calculator. Prepare a short list of instructions telling them what to do (e.g. what checks to carry out) if they cannot get the machine to work.

(b)   What do you think is the point of using the mains adaptor?

(c)   Your employer decides not to buy a mains adaptor, saying 'It will limit the calculator's flexibility'. What do you think he has in mind?

(d)   Explain briefly what you understand by **two** of the following: *VAT, trade discounts, tax rebates, carriage paid.*

(e)   Rewrite the last sentence of the passage in your own words, paying special attention to the meaning of 'entertained' and 'tampering'.

(f)   The battery has run out. The calculator will not work because the battery has now leaked and damaged the machine. Your employer proposes to send the calculator back to the makers (it is only two months old). Comment on his intended action.

(20 marks)

(*LCC Private Secretary's Certificate*)

5.   Read the following extract from a leaflet published by a manufacturer of electric ovens and answer the questions which follow:

We have now perfected our Qualbest* fan oven. We consider this *well-tried, tested and proven* fan oven to be the greatest advance in domestic baking and roasting since the introduction of *thermostats* in the early thirties.

In this Qualbest fan oven, the element which provides the heat is at the back, leaving the whole of the width of the oven free for cooking without any fear of scorching from *elements* at the side. The heat is re-circulated by the fan throughout the oven, thus ensuring an even heat on all four shelves. The results are almost indistinguishable whether you put the food on the bottom or the top shelf!

Not only will you get the same results whichever shelf position you use, but you can fill every shelf from top to bottom of the oven; that means really large quantities of food cooking at the same time. Many slow-cooking foods like fruit cake are cooked as much as an hour faster. Food browns more evenly too, because the heat reaches all the surfaces of the food, not just those areas near the elements. This is a *classic* among ovens!

Improved sound insulation has been added to our latest fan ovens, too.

* Registered trade mark.

(a)   A housewife plans to cook several dishes for a meal. Some need to be placed in the cool part of an oven and some in the hot part. Comment on this in the light of the extract.

(b)   Next list fully but briefly all the advantages and disadvantages of a fan oven which you notice or infer from a close reading of the passage.

(c)   Briefly explain the purpose of the asterisk in the passage.

(d)   In your own words, briefly explain what you understand by **three** of the following: well-tried, tested and proven; thermostats; elements; classic; registered trade mark.

(20 marks)

(*LCC Private Secretary's Certificate*)

6.   In March 1976 the Department of Energy issued an explanatory supplement to its bulletin, *Energy Trends!* Read the following extract and answer the questions which follow it:

Gas (Tables 7-8)

Table 7: Natural gas supply is the total natural gas input (including imported natural gas) into the public supply system after stock changes at gas supply installations have been taken into account. *Indigenous supplies* consist almost entirely of purchases by the gas supply industry from operators on the UK part of the *Continental Shelf*. 'Gas sent out' covers town gas (that is, gas made from coal or oil) and natural gas for direct supply (including gas supplied for non-energy purposes).

Table 8: Gas sales are the quantities estimated to be sold and consumed during each period, and differ from 'Gas sent out' mainly because of losses in *transmission* and consumption in the offices and showrooms of the gas supply industry.

(a)   From what you read you should be able to make a confident guess as to the subject of Table 7 and Table 8 and hence their titles. Suggest a title for each table.

(b)   In a given period, which would normally record the *higher* figures and why — Table 7 or Table 8?

(c)   Explain in your own words what you understand by any **two** of the following: indigenous supplies; Continental Shelf; transmission.

(d)   If there is an increase in the supply of home-produced natural gas but no increase in the amount of natural gas supplied to the public, state in your own words the two possible reasons for this.

(LCC Private Secretary's Certificate)

7.   The following extract is taken with modifications from *Video and Audio-Visual Review,* vol. 1 (1975) no. 10:

For an industry whose prime concern is communication, the audio-visual aids business is remarkably ineffective at conveying its own image. Too many times we have attended demonstrations of new video recorders, tape systems, cine projectors, etc., where *paradoxically* anything but the equipment itself has been used to convey the sales message. One importer recently went so far as to use 16 mm cine film to portray its company identity, which would have been encouraging had the company not been launching a colour video tape machine.

Not that we are ourselves beyond criticism. The *logical media* for *Video and Audio-Visual Review* might arguably be video tapes, video disc, film-strip or *microfiche*. However, even in those days of rising publicising costs, cold print remains substantially cheaper than any plastic-based magnetic format.

(a)   Would it make any difference to the sense, and why, if the first sentence had spoken of 'primary concern' instead of 'prime concern'?

(b)   In your own words, say what you understand by the following words or phrases in the extract: paradoxically; the logical media; microfiche.

(c)   If someone suggested that the extract was taken from an editorial, explain briefly what he meant **and** say whether you agree, and why.

(d)   In a word or two, give an example from the extract of a 'plastic-based magnetic format'.

(e)   If a typewriter manufacturer sent out a beautifully designed sales letter written by a leading artist in superb italic script, what connection would this have with the ideas in the first paragraph of the extract?

In a few lines say how far you regard such ideas as valid or invalid.

(LCC Private Secretary's Certificate)

8.   Read the following extract from a British Rail brochure entitled *'The way to enjoy the great outdoors'* and then answer the questions below it:

Whether tent or caravan, taking your own home with you is the free and easy way to motor around Europe or Ireland. Not only are you free to go as you please, but you can stop for a day or a week whenever you see a place which takes your fancy — without the worry of looking for somewhere to stay every night or the inconvenience of making your plans fit in with hotel mealtimes. And, of course, camping or caravanning does allow you to have a marvellous holiday in Europe without spending a fortune. Your *itinerary* can be tailored to your needs.

On the Continent people take camping very seriously, and unless you particularly want a *spartan holiday* you'll find it can be very luxurious. Most camp sites have all the mod cons you would wish for. Washing and toilet facilities, hot and cold showers, electric razor sockets, ironing rooms, restaurants, bars, shops — even electricity sockets for lighting.

An all-inclusive scheme which gives you hire of a caravan, and ferry tickets for car and passengers, costs from about £26.50 per person. Caravans are collected in France or Ireland — so there's no need to tow it to the English port or pay for its ferry crossing.

(a)   An opponent of caravan holidays says: 'They are cheap but very inflexible'. How far does the extract support or contradict this statement?

(b)   Explain what you understand by any **two** of the following: the great outdoors; a spartan holiday; an all-inclusive scheme; itinerary.

(c)   Your employer is considering taking his family for a caravan holiday during the middle of the summer. Prepare a short informal memo to him, set out correctly, in which you explain the convenient or desirable features of such a holiday (using the extract for your information). As a thoughtful secretary, add any comments of your own about any possible drawbacks that occur to you.

(d)   Your employer has a wife and teenage son. Having looked at the brochure he decides that £100 should easily cover the cost of a three-week caravan holiday on the Continent, using the British Rail all-inclusive scheme. Can you make any comment on this?

(e)   The term 'British Rail' is a relatively new one. The earlier form was 'British Railways', another possible form would have been 'British Railroads'. Comment on the suitability of *rail, railways and rail roads* in this context. Which do you think is the best modern choice, and why?

(f)   Mention any two features of the style or language of the extract (quoting briefly if you wish) which indicate that it is designed to catch the attention of the casual reader and have a forceful sales impact.

(LCC Private Secretary's Certificate)

9.   The following passage is taken from *The Shell Guide to England*, a detailed guidebook about English towns.

In every English town much conforms with the *norm* of modernity. All traffic signs are the same everywhere. The fascias and window-dressing of the *chain stores* are the same. Advertisements are the same. The brands in the shops are the same. The citizens are also very much the same. All this is very convenient; all *urban* life flows together, and the approach to an unfamiliar town offers no problems. It might be added that all modern buildings are very nearly the same, or, if they are not, they very soon will be.

In fact, no English town would be better worth visiting than any other, were it not for the enormous legacy of the past. There is so much of it that even the most *affluent* and rapidly developing town cannot entirely wipe out its old self. This is what gives each town its special 'character'.

(a)   Explain what you understand by **two** of the following: norm; chain stores; urban; affluent.

(b)   The opening of the extract sounds very boring. Suggest how the writer will probably continue his chapter (do not write a continuation of the extract but merely indicate what you expect he will say). Do you think it is ever wise business practice to begin an article in such a negative and dissatisfied way? Give your reasons in a line or two.

(c)   The writer may, later on, comment on the effect of petrol stations and garages on the English town and country scene. Do you expect he will think their effect is good or bad? State clearly what evidence you base your answer on.

(d) Express the opening sentence in your own words.

(e) How far do you think the argument in the second paragraph is valid? For example, how would it apply to towns built in a developing country or in a newly discovered part of the world?

(LCC Private Secretary's Certificate)

10. Read the following extract from an advertisement for a large insurance company and answer the questions which follow it:

Since we started in business it's been one disaster after another

Even in the best run businesses, the occasional setback is only to be expected.

Now if you're thinking that we appear to have had more than our fair share, we would point out that we've been in the insurance business for close on 255 years.

So it's not really surprising that we've been involved in some monumental disasters.

Yet in each instance, we're happy to say, we paid up without quibbling or delay.

And this fact has undoubtedly helped us become one of the largest insurers in Britain today.

Because nothing does more to enhance the reputation of an insurance company than a demonstration of its ability to pay up when things go wrong.

After all, that's what insurance is all about, isn't it?

(a) The title of the advertisement seems alarming. In 5 to 10 lines say why you think it is a good or bad title.

(b) For the benefit of a junior colleague, pick out the major features of layout and style in this advertisement which you think are not particularly suitable for business writing and explain why. Do not exceed 10 lines.

(c) An advertising executive remarks: 'Every firm must close down *eventually*. Therefore, the longer a firm has existed, the closer it is to its eventual closure. Therefore it is foolish to boast that you have been in business for 255 years'. Do you accept this argument as valid? Give reasons for your answer.

(d) Another executive remarks: 'This advertisement merely stresses the company's solvency'. Firstly, what do you understand by solvency? Secondly, do you agree with him? Thirdly, do you think that, if he is right, this is a sound basis for an advertisement?

(LCC Private Secretary's Certificate)

11.   Read the following extract from an article about women drivers and answer the questions which follow:

Why is it that women are such bad drivers? They often hesitate for so long at a busy road junction that there will be a whole queue of cars sounding their horns. If you see a car travelling at 20 miles an hour along a main road, keeping so far away from the kerb that no one can overtake, you can be sure the driver is a woman!

Perhaps women drivers suffer from a *built-in inferiority complex*, because we men just won't believe that a woman can drive well. And yet there are far more men involved in motor accidents than women — and women seldom drink alcohol — unlike some men. Of course, women tend to be inexperienced drivers (whereas their husbands probably drive to work every day) and this makes them more nervous. But at least a nervous women driver will go carefully. She doesn't try to show off, or, like a man, assert her masculinity (if that isn't a contradiction in terms).

I'm surprised that the motor insurance market does not offer favourable rates to women drivers. If the actuaries got to work they would doubtless find that motor claims from women drivers are far fewer than those for men but that the number of women drivers is NOT lower pro rata.

(a)   What, briefly, do you think are the reader's expectations after he or she has read the first few lines of this extract? To what extent are those expectations borne out by the rest of the extract?

(b)   List as many good points about women drivers as you can, using the material in the extract.

(c)   What do you understand by 'a built-in inferiority complex'? If you like, give an example to help to explain.

(d)   Explain briefly in your own words the meaning of **two** of the following: assert masculinity; a contradiction in terms; actuaries; pro rata.

(e)   Would you agree or not that the article is an example of anti-feminism? Give your reasons in a few lines.

(20 marks)

(LCC Private Secretary's Certificate)

12.   Read the following extract from *Britain 1973: An Official Handbook* and answer the questions below it.

The pattern of machine tool production is highly cyclical; deliveries in 1971 were valued at £190 million, including numerically controlled tools worth £19 million. Exports of complete machines in 1971 had a value of £97 million, 11 per cent up on 1970. Of the orders on hand at the end of 1971 (£96 million), 56 per cent were for export; Australia

(£9 million), the Federal Republic of Germany (£8 million), France (£7 million) and Italy (£6 million) were the main overseas markets in 1971.

Seven of the industry's 200 or so companies provide over half of total deliveries, although because of the high degree of specialisation small firms are numerically predominant.

(a)   What do you understand by the pattern of machine-tool production is highly cyclical'?

(b)   Explain in your own words **one** of the following:
       'the high degree of specialisation'
       'small firms are numerically predominant'.

(c)   Would you say that machine-tool manufacturers are all firms of much the same size? Give reasons for your answer.

(d)   Estimate (as nearly as you can) the average annual exports of an average small machine-tool firm in 1970 or 1971.

(20 marks)

(LCC Private Secretary's Certificate)

NOTE: You should study Section 13 'Visual Communication' before attempting the following two questions.

13.   Read carefully the following extract from an article by Roger Eglin in *The Observer* in 1972, and then attempt the questions below it:

Anyone who believes the North Sea is a huge find in world terms ought to bear in mind that so far recoverable reserves of some four million barrels of oil have been proved against 270 billion barrels in the Middle East.

No amount of worrying can gloss over the fact that for the next twenty years or more the world as a whole will be hugely dependent on the Middle East and Africa for its fuel.

Europe alone will rely on imported oil for 60% of its fuel needs. By 1985, the United States Department of the Interior forecasts that America will be importing 44% of her oil requirements. Much of this will have to come from the Middle East; in 1985 America may have to draw from the Middle East as much crude oil as that region produces today. To add to American fears, domestic oil production fell last year for the first time in history.

For Britain, the picture is more optimistic. In 1970, out of the total energy consumption, coal accounted for 43%, oil for 48%, natural gas for 6%, hydro-electricity for 0.5% and nuclear power for 2.5%.

By 1980, British total energy consumption will probably be up to 209 million metric tons at present; and oil, with 54% of the total, will be playing a still bigger role. Nuclear power will have tripled its share to 7.5%; hydro-electricity will be much the same, and coal will be down to

17%. Natural gas will have improved most, with a 22% share of the market.

In national strategic terms, the reality behind these figures is that during 1970-1980 Britain's fuel imports will be declining — despite the anticipated growth in consumption.

(a)   You have been asked to prepare two large wallcharts to show very clearly the comparative importance of coal, oil, natural gas, hydro-electric power and nuclear energy for the British economy in 1972 and 1980 respectively. Using the data in the extract, sketch out the two charts in sufficient detail for a firm's poster department to prepare full-size wallcharts.

You may use any method you consider appropriate. Supply any instructions, captions and other necessary details.

(b)   State briefly the predicted pattern for American and British fuel imports during the next ten or fifteen years.

(c)   What do you understand by 'billion'? Is there any chance of ambiguity in this?

(d)   Name one or two Middle East nations.

(e)   In the second paragraph of the extract the word 'depcndent' occurs. When would you use the word 'dependent'?

(LCC Private Secretary's Certificate)

14.   Study the following table and then answer the questions below it.

Public Expenditure in 1976-7

	£ million	Proposed cuts
Defence	3,818	110
Overseas services	741	12
Agriculture, fisheries and forestry	853	152
Trade, industry and employment	1,421	3
Nationalised industries	2,394	100
Roads and transport	1,781	91
Housing	3,583	115
Other environmental services	1,558	85
Law, order and protective services	1,156	27
Education and libraries, science and arts	4,753	86
Health and personal social services	4,093	75
Social security	7,625	—
Other public services	507	17
Common services	563	12
Northern Ireland	1,019	16
	35,865	901

Source: *Economic Progress Report*, 1975.

(a)　What approximate percentage of the total public expenditure is accounted for by 'social security'?

(b)　By what percentage approximately is it proposed to cut expenditure on 'education and libraries, science and arts'?

(c)　Which one of the areas of public expenditure listed above has suffered the greatest proportional cut?

(d)　What benefits are included under the heading 'social security'?

(e)　Use the information in the table to draw a suitable statistical diagram to be published in a newspaper under the heading 'Public Expenditure in 1976-7'. Before drawing the diagram you are to simplify the information by reclassifying the areas of expenditure given in the table under no more than six appropriate headings.

15.　The following extract was taken from *Focus on Malaysia* published by Progress International. Read the passage and then answer the questions below.

Wherever one looks in the world, there is the threat of *confrontation,* guerrilla or urban warfare, clashing ideologies. It is so in Africa, or in the Middle East, even in Europe, and in South East Asia. But in those same regions there are always the countries of strength, stability and progress. Malaysia is certainly one such.

Few countries with racial or religious divisions can boast of so steady a progress towards national unity and one has only to visit Malaysia to *appreciate* that, though there is no under-estimating of the situation, it is well under control and that confidence in the country's future, far from being diminished, is stronger than ever.

It is in fact business as usual. And what a business it is proving to be. Last year, the real growth of the economy was around 3.5 per cent, remarkable in a year of painful international depression — especially when one considers that in the US and the leading countries of Europe real output actually declined.

What has to be borne in mind is that though Malaysia is regarded as a developing country, its economy is controlled in a *sophisticated* way. The major product sectors, such as rubber, tin, timber, palm oil, are controlled as efficiently as anywhere in the world.

This is a well-blessed country, with its considerable range of raw materials and its rapidly growing manufacturing and construction sectors. On top of all else, Malaysia has the benefit of oil reserves. The final figure of reserves and the *optimum* contribution to the economy remain to be seen, but what is unarguable is that Malaysia's oil is going to save it a lot of money.

(a)　Explain the meaning, as used in the passage, of the following expressions: *confrontation; appreciate; sophisticated; optimum.*

(b)　What reasons are given in the passage for the author's confidence in the country's future?

(c)   What two possible political difficulties does the author imply that Malaysia may have to face?

(d)   The author's style of writing might be described as 'journalistic'. Comment on any **two** features of his writing which might justify such a description.

16.   Inflation Accounting is becoming more widespread. Show your ability to understand the subject by answering the questions printed below:

Accounts generally record actual historical market transactions rather than estimated current values. They do not try to reflect the 'true worth' of a company. Although accounts have traditionally been prepared on an historical cost basis there is now an increasing desire to allow for the falling value of money over time. A generally conservative approach is a feature of accounting treatment, although companies are increasingly inclined to become more 'realistic'?

(a)   Why are the market transactions called 'historical'?

(b)   In what way do conventional accounts not reflect 'true worth'?

(c)   Why should there be any need to allow for the falling value of money?

(d)   What is the implication of the word 'realistic'?

(20 marks)

(LCC Private Secretary's Diploma)

17.   Wage statistics have become part of everyday conversation. Show your understanding of the following passage by answering the questions printed below:

Wage rate figures for August 1975, and total wage and salary earnings figures for July 1975 were released by the Department of Employment on Wednesday. The rate of increase of total earnings (which include overtime and shift bonuses) had been running significantly below that of hourly wage rates for some time, due to reductions in overtime working and to increases in rates which simply consolidate earlier gains in bonuses. In the year to July total wage and salary earnings rose by 27½% — up from a year-on-year rate of 25½% in June but down from a 28½% in May.

(a)   Name two factors in total earnings which do not affect hourly wage rates.

(b)   Why did the consolidation of bonuses affect the two sets of figures?

(c)   In what way did early gains in bonuses affect more recent increases in hourly rates?

(d)   In your own words — what happened to wage inflation during the period discussed in this passage?

(20 marks)

(LCC Private Secretary's Diploma)

18.   Read the following passage and answer the questions which follow it.

It seems that noise, among other things, is a problem to today's office workers. It lowers their efficiency and the stress conditions can cause headaches leading to frequent absences.

Many of the girls whom I meet tell me that conditions in the offices in which they work are far from ideal, and that not only have they become a race of 'working wounded' because of the noise to which they are continually subjected, but that they also suffer from backache and eyestrain because of the unsatisfactory office furniture and bad lighting. Some of these girls are audio-typists, but the majority of them are machine operators. The machine operators it seems are really very unhappy with their lot. The business machines they operate leave much to be desired. Regular servicing is the exception rather than the rule so that the operator is continually struggling with an accounting machine which, while not broken down, is faulty and needs very careful handling.

A great percentage of the girls I spoke to were very dissatisfied with their working conditions. They had not found themselves in pleasant, modern offices, but in dingy surroundings with out-of-date furniture — chairs and desks at inconvenient heights, resulting in backache for the user, and with badly sited fluorescent lighting which again resulted in headaches for the worker. The management, in many cases, were not interested in these complaints.

Many of the girls I am concerned with are particularly anxious to become audio-typists, and for this we train them but once in the job it seems to me that the concentration that is necessary, together with the volume of work they are expected to produce, is too much for them. The wearing of headphones for long periods bothers them; they feel that the constant use of an electric typewriter puts them in a stress condition, and the whole situation worries them. I suggest that they could have a much greater variety of tasks in the beginning with shorter periods of heavy concentration. I am sure that many firms work on this principle, but it is certainly not the case with all of them.

In the past few months I have come across several cases where an office junior was required to type, deal with callers and take charge of a small switchboard. These girls all said that they had left their employment on account of attacks of migraine. I think that their employers were totally unaware that on coming straight from college to their first job the girls required a period of *adjustment*. It is very important that a girl feels part of the firm in which she works. How else can employers hope for loyalty and productivity? Yet, many of the employers do not take any steps to help a girl settle in her job, or to make her feel happy so that they (the employers) may benefit by better productivity and less turnover of staff.

Boredom was one of the chief complaints I received from girls who

had originally looked forward very much to becoming machine oper-
atives and who had chosen this job because they felt they would prefer
it to secretarial duties. I realise that this must be a great problem for the
employer — it is difficult to *infuse* romance and excitement into an
accounting machine. I did manage to assist one of these disappointed
girls to obtain a position in a university where the various machines are
kept in a large department and the girls and trained to work each one of
them and their duties are rotated to *obviate* boredom.

Training for secretarial work seems to be much more *prevalent* than
training for the machine operator. It is sometimes assument that
machine operators can be taught 'on the job' and this, I think, is quite
wrong. Reputable companies such as NCR, SWEDA, etc., the Compto-
meter Schools, and the local Technical Colleges all run courses to examination level in Machine Accounting, Office Practice and so on. Day-
release in available and most employers take advantage of this opportunity, but there are still those who do not.

Imagine that the passage accurately describes working conditions at
your place of employment, and that staff have held a meeting to discuss
their grievances. At this meeting you were asked to act as secretary and
to keep an informal record of the proceedings:

(a) (i)   List the complaints that were made.   (15 marks)
(b)   Draft a memo for submission to your Personnel Officer making
          recommendations that would result in a much improved working
          environment for the aggrieved employees.
(c) (i)   What do you understand by: (20 marks)
                'stress conditions'
                'better productivity'
                'turnover of staff'
                'their duties are rotated'?
    (ii) Which of the groups of girls mentioned in the passage has greater
          justification for feeling a sense of grievance? Give reasons for
          your choice.
    (iii) Give another word or phrase similar in meaning to each of the
          following words as it is used in the passage:
                adjustment
                infuse
                obviate
                prevalent   (30 marks)

                          (*LCC Secretarial Studies Certificate*)

19. Read carefully the following extract from *Home and Garden* (June
     1973).

Setting up a house or flat with *period furniture* in mind frequently results in the mood that everything must be done 'in period'. This is, of course, ridiculous. Anyone overloaded with that kind of passion for historical accuracy should give up sound plumbing, central heating and refrigeration and carry on with oil lamps, open fires and an ice-house in the garden.

Far better to use judgement. The only worthwhile reason for choosing period furniture is not that *it will appreciate* in time (although that's a pleasant side-thought) but, first, that you like it to look at and, second, that it's useful.

The reasons why we like looking at period furniture would probably need a highly trained *psychiatrist* to work out. A sense of *modest permanence* in our increasingly impermanent world comes into it, no doubt, as does pride of ownership. On the visual plane, things are easier to explain. That patina* for example can never be equalled in a modern piece.

(a) Do you think this extract was written mainly for people who dislike period furniture, like it, or know nothing about it? What would you say is the author's attitude to it? Give your reasons in roughly 10 to 20 lines.

(b) What do you think the writer of the extract would say to people who express regret for the 'good old days' of two or three hundred years ago, when life was more peaceful and simple?

(c) Explain in your own words what you understand by the following words and phrases as used and italicised in the extract: *period furniture; it will appreciate; psychiatrist; modest permanence.*

(d) Imagine that you are the editor of *Home and Garden.* Make any comments to the author of the extract that you feel are relevant. You may be favourable or unfavourable, depending on your personal reaction. There is no 'right' answer; you are merely asked to consider the style, the English, the presentation of the subject.

*patina = richly shining surface

(30 marks)

(LCC Private Secretary's Certificate)

8

MISCELLANY

This section contains other aspects of written communication with which the secretary should be familiar. The following topics are included:

> press releases
> advertising
> forms
> telegrams, cables and telex.

PRESS RELEASES

Most large firms nowadays demonstrate their recognition of the importance of good publicity by having Public Relations or Publicity Departments. However, in smaller firms, or firms which have few contacts with the public or with the community, no such specific organisation is needed and it can be part of a secretary's job occasionally to prepare material for publication in the press.

Articles in the press can benefit a firm greatly both internally and externally. In an age of advertising (and almost a third of the price of a packet of soap powder is spent on advertising) such articles provide free publicity. Within a firm they not only help to boost staff morale but can also assist recruitment.

It may seem, indeed it is, a relatively simple matter to produce a short informative report on some event within your organisation for publication outside. But there are other implications. If the topic is of sufficient interest, it may well be followed by further enquiries from the press. To avoid misunderstandings and misreporting it is essential that press enquiries, in person or on the telephone, should only be answered by someone authorised and competent to do so.

When reporters and perhaps photographers arrive to cover an event they should be given every assistance. Someone should be detailed to escort and inform them and some basic written information is often presented as a press kit in a folder. For example, the kit prepared for the visit of a Minister for Transport Industries to the Bristol Omnibus Company might contain the following information sheets:

The Minister's programme
A bus ride for the Minister
Minister sees Bristol Omnibus Company's computer terminal in action
Computerised schedule planning possible in future
Grants save many rural bus services
Bristol Omnibus Company modernise single-deck buses
B-line — the Bristol/Marconi bus location system.

Photographers will be greatly helped by having someone appointed to escort them, to help in the setting up of groups or scenes for the photographs and to give them particular details, such as names for the captions of their pictures.

Another method of briefing reporters is the embargo press release. This contains information released to the press on the understanding that it will not be published before the date specified. Such a release has two objects. First, it enables newspaper editors to plan ahead and helps to ensure that they have space to publish the information on the most appropriate date. Second, it can brief reporters covering the event so that they know what further information to seek.

If your firm produces a regular newsletter or magazine it can be helpful to send copies to your local newspaper. The editor can then extract and publish suitable news items. It is important to choose appropriate media for press releases. The content may be suitable for local newspapers and/or for trade and technical journals, or an important item may be more suitable for wider publication. For publication in the national press, use may well be made of a news agency.

One such agency, for example, is Universal News Services, which especially serves business and trade associations. It disseminates information from its subscribers over a teleprinter network to the national and provincial newspapers, to radio and television stations and to the London bureaux of international news agencies. Additionally it provides a mailing service for the world's trade and technical journals, has a special Enternews unit handling arts, entertainment and leisure industries and offers a shorthand reporting service to cover, for example, company meetings.

The following is an example of a basic press release sent out by teleprinter service:

UNS MOTEL
£230,000 MOTORWAY MOTEL CONTRACT

A £230,000 CONTRACT HAS BEEN AWARDED TO MARPLES RIDGWAY BY THE TRUST HOUSE FORTE GROUP FOR THE CONSTRUCTION OF A 100-BEDROOM MOTEL AT THE SCRATCHWOOD SERVICE AREA ON THE M1 AT HENDON.
WORK ON THE TWO-FLOOR MOTEL AND CAR-PARKING AREA WILL START THIS MONTH AND LAST FOR 40 WEEKS.
IT WILL BE THE FIFTH CONTRACT MARPLES RIDGWAY HAS

CARRIED OUT ON THE SITE, AS THE COMPANY HAS BUILT THE ORIGINAL SERVICE AREA, INCLUDING DRAINAGE, CAR PARK, RESTAURANT AND POLICE POST AND EXTENSION.

UNS

CONTACT: KENNETH MATTHEWS OF ERIC BUSTON AND ASSOCIATES

BRISTOL (0272) 27666

0914 AUG 19

Such a basic press release is likely to be followed by enquiries for more detailed information for publication in, say, the trade press.

CONTENT

Since your article may have to be cut it should be written so that it may be 'pruned' from the last sentence upwards. This makes it easy for the sub-editor to fit into the space available without having to rewrite. Thus the essence of the story should be contained in the first paragraph, with the next most important information in the second paragraph, and so on.

If you include photographs, you must write a condensed version of the article as a caption. The caption should be firmly attached to the photograph, preferably pasted on the reverse. Never send a photograph without this information.

Your article should be factual without literary embellishments. A press release for the national press will be shorter and less detailed than for the local paper. Articles for technical and trade journals should be checked for accuracy by an expert.

If your article is sent to more than one newspaper remember to alter the story slightly for each. No paper, literally or figuratively, likes to have a carbon-copy story.

People's names must be spelled correctly and forenames, or at least initials, should be used, not just 'Mr'. For local papers it is helpful to give the addresses of persons mentioned and possibly some personal details about their hobbies or children, for example.

Finally, always include a name and telephone number of someone the press can contact for further information.

PRESENTATION

The following points should be observed.

1. Leave plenty of space at the top of the sheet (headlines are the editor's prerogative, but give a factual heading).
2. Leave wide margins (for the sub-editor's use).
3. Use double spacing (for ease of correction and alteration).
4. Type on one side of the paper only (this saves the typesetter's time).
5. If you use more than one sheet of paper, write one of the following at the bottom of the sheet:

> *more follows*
> *m.f.*
> *more*

6. Each continuation sheet should have a catch line; that is, the last few words of the previous sheet should be repeated, for example

> *the Chairman concluded*

7. Finish your article as follows:

> *– ends –*

An example of a press release is given in Figure 21.

EXERCISES

1. As Personal Assistant to the Managing Director, write a press release of 100-200 words on the official opening of the Oriental Tools Factory by the Minister of Commerce on Friday, 26 November 19——.

   either   Assume that the factory is on a new industrial estate in an area of high unemployment. Jobs will be available for unskilled and semi-skilled production workers (men and women), office workers and canteen staff. Some vacancies will exist for skilled engineers, research chemists and managers.

   or   The factory will bring light-engineering work to a rural area in a country where there is little tradition of factory work. Training schemes will be essential. Stress the advantages of improving the standard of living and the benefits to the economy of the country.

2. Write an embargo press release in about 300 words on:

   either   a new company product which is to go on sale shortly and which is an important technological development;

   or   a fashion house's new Autumn designs (this will be accompanied by sketches, which, however, you do not have to draw).

3. In about 500 words prepare a press release for a large firm, locally situated, which is having difficulty in attracting good-quality school-leavers as trainees in administrative and technical jobs. The firm already advertises vacancies through the usual media but hopes for wider publicity in the local press in order to improve recruitment.

(RSA Diploma for Personal Assistants)

Embargo: Please do not publish before 12
           noon, Thursday, 13 February

£55,000 WILL BRING IN THE STARS

The leading international figures in men's
tennis will return to Torquay this summer
for one of the world's leading competitions
- the £55,000 Torquay Tennis Tournament.
The Lawn Tennis Association have confirmed
that the tournament, the most valuable in
Britain after Wimbledon, will take place
from June 16th to 21st.

The event will be the only one in Britain
to be graded an AA men's competition in
the Commercial Union Grand Prix series.
The singles winner collects £9000, the
runner-up £4500 and the losing semi-
finalists £2250 each. The winning doubles
pair share £2400.

With the Wimbledon fortnight to follow, the
world's top men will be playing for three
weeks in front of British spectators.

Torquay made tennis history last year by
making a five-year agreement with the
Association of Tennis Professionals to
stage a major tournament annually. ATP
agreed not to support any other top-flight
competition anywhere in the world during
the same week as the Torquay event.

more

Figure 21   Embargo press release

the Torquay event.

It was the first time such a long-term
arrangement had been made between a
sponsor and the ATP, with the full
approval of the LTA.

Ronald Lewis, Torquay's Special Events
Manager, said:

'With so many sponsors having to withdraw
their support from tennis, the borough is
particularly pleased to continue with such
a first-rate international event. The
extra prize money should bring out the best
in the competitors.

'This is the tenth consecutive year in
which we've run a tournament in Torquay,'
added Mr Lewis. 'It's always been important in the British Calendar. Now it's
one of the elite handful of the world's top
events.'

                    - ends -

11 February 19--

Embargo: <u>Please do not publish before 12</u>
          <u>noon, Thursday, 13 February</u>

THE TORQUAY TENNIS TOURNAMENT
Contact: Brian Bryans, Martin Martins
0803 711111

Figure 21   *(continued)*

ST. HILDA INDUSTRIAL ESTATE

GREAT HARTLEMOUTH

★ In the fast-growing East Anglian Region

★ In the centre of the Town

★ Close to the Docks with good Port facilities for Export/Import to/from Europe

★ Ample male and female labour

Industrial and Warehouse Units
Immediately Available

From 3,000 to 60,000 square feet and upwards

Another project being undertaken by

United Building Enterprises Limited

Apply to Agents: Barnes and Shacks
                     26 Fore Street
                     Great Hartlemouth GH3 4BR
                     Telephone: (061) 2233

Figure 22   Display advertisement

ADVERTISING

Writing advertising copy is a highly skilled business about which many books have been written. In their examinations students may be asked to write relatively straightforward advertising copy, for example for classified advertisements, for job advertisements, for appeals for funds for charity, or for 'sales' advertisements.

Advertisements ('adverts') in the press are often divided into two kinds — *classified* and *display*.

Classified advertisements appear under main headings which group together the type of product or service for sale or wanted, such as the following example:

> BEAUTIFUL UPRIGHT PIANO; perfect
> working order; £170; Tel. 01 380
> 6040

The information in these advertisements is run on from line to line, often all in the same type face, with no special layout.

Display adverts, on the other hand, will have a variety of type faces and sizes (see Figure 22) and will frequently be illustrated. In magazines, and sometimes in newspapers, use is made of colour.

BORROWED MONEY

COSTS MONEY

BORROWED MONEY

COSTS LESS

WHEN YOU DEAL WITH

M O N E Y M A K E R S

65 Ferry Road
Witheridge   WT5 4DG
019 423 6781

We have lower overheads and
lower margins. You reap the
benefit in many ways - by
paying less or having extra
money to spend.

Figure 23   Displayed classified advertisement

Some advertisements in the classified section also make use of special layouts, such as the advertisement shown in Figure 23. These are called *displayed classified* or *semi-display.*

Why do people advertise? Briefly, in order to sell something, seek something they wish to buy, give away something, exchange it or seek donations. This is a very much simplified explanation — advertising men could give many specific reasons for using advertising which would show its versatility.

Adverts have to be persuasive. Attention must be attracted and then interest held by the message of the advert. Often information must be given which will not necessarily result in an immediate purchase. Perhaps there will be an eventual purchase of an expensive item, such as a car; perhaps the products and services of a group of firms will be stressed.

Some very famous advertising campaigns have been a combination of press and other advertising, of the 'hard sell' and the less dramatic but still interesting and convincing informative kind. The various advertisements suggesting that we buy more cheese are a good example.

CONTENT

Short and classified advertisements must be almost telegram-like, with an opening which catches the reader's attention and then as much abbreviated copy as possible contained in as few lines as possible. Classified adverts are charged for by the line, with a minimum charge for probably three or four lines.

Semi-display and display adverts are charged for by column centimetres with a minimum size, often of three centimetres. Although they will be bigger than classified adverts, they should not necessarily contain more words or the value of the display in catching the eye may be lost.

Informative adverts, however, are often more successful if they are long but informal. Tests have suggested that long copy outsells short copy by 90 per cent.

Look at Figure 24. It is far more effective than Figure 25 would be because it tells us far more about a *person* (and the personal touch is very important in advertisements). It also tells us what 'Help the Aged' can do and what even a small donation can mean.

Some of the points to bear in mind when writing advertising copy are as follows.

1. Know exactly what type of product or service is being advertised, for example mass product, luxury product, industrial (not for general public) product or service, charities, tourism, public service.
2. Consider the type of campaign, for example image-building, direct sales, prestige.
3. Decide on the classes of market (these are usually divided into six groups, ranging from 'upper management' to 'pensioners, widows and lowest-paid groups', and based on income).

Woman living alone
in a cold, wet flat

Mrs Thriscott is 68 years old. She used to live alone on the top floor of an old house. Her flat was cold, wet and full of draughts; there was no hot water, and it was virtually impossible for her to keep warm. When she wanted to go out, she faced climbing up and down a hundred steps in all.

Then she applied to Help the Aged for a new flat. Since she moved into the new place which Help the Aged have provided, Mrs Thriscott is a changed woman. "My great thrill, of course, is hot baths every day. I've never been cold since I've been here. My health is wonderful, perfect! People tell me I look years younger."

Help the Aged also help provide Day centres where old people find care and companionship.

Because of loans available to Help the Aged every £2 you give provides £40 of housing.

£150 donation names a flat in memory of happy times with someone dear to you. £250 names a double flat. £450 names a common room.

Every day matters to old people in need. Tear out this advertisement and send with your gift as quickly as possible to:

Hon. Treasurer, Rt Hon. Lord Maybray-King
Help the Aged, Room G1,
8 Denman Street, London W1A 2AP

Figure 24   Display advertisement

4. Remember the importance of headlines both as attention-catchers and, for those who will read no further, as containing the essence of your message.
5. Achieve the correct copy progression, first directly involving the reader, then developing the 'selling' proposition, suggesting the reader's action and finally repeating the benefits.

DIRECT MAIL ADVERTISING

We are all familiar with the letters, leaflets, brochures and coupons which drop in a seemingly never-ending stream through out letterboxes. Many go

```
┌─────────────────────────────────────────┐
│                                         │
│  Woman living alone in cold wet flat    │
│                                         │
│                                         │
│       Elderly People need               │
│   companionship and good homes          │
│                                         │
│  Send your donation to:                 │
│     Hon. Treasurer,                     │
│     Rt  Hon. Lord Maybray-King          │
│     Help the Aged, Room G1,             │
│     8 Denman Street,                    │
│     London W1A 2AP                      │
│                                         │
└─────────────────────────────────────────┘
```

Figure 25   Short display advertisement

straight into our wastepaper baskets but at least some catch our attention. The sales letter, which with modern techniques can now be addressed directly to individuals by name and can even have their names in the body of the letter, is a favourite ploy of advertisers.

Figure 26 shows an example (students should also refer to Section 4 'Letter Writing').

EXERCISES

1.   Prepare a classified advertisement for **one** of the following situations, and include all the information that would appear in a real-life advertisement:
      (a) the sale of a house
      (b) the sale of a car.

(SCCAPE Advanced Secretarial Certificate)

2.   Prepare a display advertisement, to take up not more than a 12 centimetre double column, for a summer sale.

3.   Write a display classified advertisement in not more than 100 words appealing for funds for a charity to help old people. The advertisement is to appear in your local paper.

4.   Rewrite the following to produce a concise display advertisement suitable for the press:

Kirktown Corporation invites applications from registered medical practitioners for the appointment of Deputy Medical Officer of Health and Deputy Port Medical Officer at a salary of £5,500 per annum, in-

MAGNUM AND MAGNUM LTD

Steam House

Walsall Street

Manchester MN4 1BR

18 June 19--

Mrs K N Opus
16 Point Road
Beechwood
Cheshire CH4 9AZ

Dear Mrs Opus

WE HAVE A 'MAGNUM' THAT REALLY BUBBLES!

No, we are not about to sell you a bottle of 1878
vintage champagne - the liquid we have in mind is
just plain, ordinary water; a liquid that combines
very well with our latest product. It is:

The MAGNUM Electric Kettle

made in stainless steel. The heat-resistant handle is
cool to the touch and a choice of fresh exciting colours
will enhance the decor of your kitchen.

It boils two pints of cold water in just ONE minute and
the automatic cut out means that you can be elsewhere
when the 'MAGNUM' bubbles!

That kind husband won't need a second mortgage in order
to buy it for you - - - - - - - - - - - - - -

Do come and see it today in your local showroom.

Yours sincerely

J R Magnum
Sales Director

Figure 26 Sales letter

creasing by £175 per annum to £6,500 per annum. Applicants should possess a Diploma in Public Health and have wide experience in public health administration, including epidemiology, and should be capable of assuming full responsibility for the supervision of the Public Health Department in the absence of the Medical Officer of Health. Previous experience of Port Health duties is desirable. The person appointed will be required to devote his whole time to the duties of the office. He will also be required to pass a medical examination and to reside within the city. Applications, on forms to be obtained from this office, accompanied by three recent testimonials, must be addressed to the Director of Personnel (and endorsed Deputy Medical Officer of Health) and be received on or before 4th July, 19——.

(SCCAPE Advanced Secretarial Certificate)

5.   Your company is trying to promote a range of inexpensive kitchen aids. Write a sales letter to housewives in your area informing them about the products and telling them about special displays and offers at local stores during the next month.

FORMS

Large companies frequently have specialists who are concerned with the design and content of forms throughout the company, for example in an Organisation and Methods Department. In many other companies, however, forms are designed as and when needed within individual departments. The secretary may be concerned with the design of forms; she will almost certainly be concerned at some time or other with filling them in or seeing them when they have been completed by other people. Because of this, any book on communication would be incomplete without mention of the principles of form design, although it should be said that what follows is no more than a brief introduction.

Figure 27 shows the first page of a job-application form. It looks a fairly standard document. Now look at Figure 28, the same form, but this time it has been completed by an applicant. It becomes apparent that the form has been designed with too much space in places and not enough elsewhere. It was badly designed, with not enough thought being given to its purpose and to the information that would be entered on it.

From this it can be deduced that the first principles of form design are:

1. to determine the purpose of the form and what information is required
2. to prepare the layout of the form so that the appropriate space is allowed for each item.

A third rule must be added:

3. to determine who will need the form and how it will be used.

Based on these principles the following steps should be followed in considering the design of any form.

1. Establish whether or not a form is needed. Forms are an advantageous method of obtaining information in an orderly way but they tend to proliferate, so the introduction of yet another must be viewed with suspicion.
2. Determine what information the form is designed to produce. Guard against the form that asks for information that is not needed but 'would be interesting to know', or 'might come in useful some time'.
3. Assess how the form will be used, including the amount of handling and filing requirements. This will affect size and type of paper or card.
4. Decide on a logical order in which information will be requested.
5. Prepare the wording for the form so that it is concise and unambiguous. Give the form a title.
6. Design the layout of the form to allow appropriate space for the answers. Remember that too little space may lead to omission, too much to verbosity.
7. Consider the number of forms needed and the cost of duplicating or printing the copies.

Above all, forms should have a clear, neat appearance and should be as simple as possible so that no confusion arises.

EXERCISES

1. Design an accident-report form that could be used to report the following accident. The letter was written by a bricklayer in Barbados to the firm he worked for. It is taken from the *Master Builders' Journal,* which reprinted it from the *Bulletin of the Federation of Civil Engineering Contractors.*

Respected Sir,
    When I got to the building, I found that the hurricane had knocked some bricks off the top. So I rigged up a beam with a pulley at the top of the building and hoisted up a couple of barrels full of bricks. When I had fixed the building there was a lot of bricks left over. I hoisted the barrel back up again and secured the line at the bottom, and then went up and filled the barrel with extra bricks. Then I went to the bottom and cast off the line. Unfortunately the barrel of bricks was heavier than I was, so before I knew what was happening the barrel started down, jerking me off the ground. I decided to hang on and half-way up I met the barrel coming down and received a severe blow on the shoulder. I then continued to the top, banging my head against the

ANY COMPANY
APPLICATION FOR EMPLOYMENT

FULL NAME (SURNAME FIRST) .... MR/MRS/MISS
IN BLOCK LETTERS

DATE OF BIRTH .... AGE ....

NATIONALITY ...., MAIDEN NAME ....

HOME ADDRESS...

.... TEL. NO. ....

PRESENT ADDRESS...
(if different from
above) .... TEL. NO. ....

SECONDARY EDUCATION

| SCHOOLS ATTENDED | YEARS | | QUALIFICATIONS ATTAINED |
	FROM	TO	
....	....	....	....
....	....	....	....
....	....	....	....
....	....	....	....
....	....	....	....
....	....	....	....
....	....	....	....
....	....	....	....

FURTHER AND HIGHER EDUCATION

| COLLEGE | YEARS | | QUALIFICATIONS ATTAINED |
	FROM	TO	
....	....	....	....
....	....	....	....
....	....	....	....
....	....	....	....
....	....	....	....

Figure 27   Application form

ANY COMPANY

APPLICATION FOR EMPLOYMENT

FULL NAME (SURNAME FIRST) WATKINSON ~~MR/MRS~~/MISS
IN BLOCK LETTERS ... MARGARET MILLICENT ....

DATE OF BIRTH .. 9 th Oct 19- AGE ..... 34 ....

NATIONALITY ..... British ..... MAIDEN NAME ....

HOME ADDRESS .... 'Rose Leigh' 16 Gardenia Gardens .....

Buckingham Palace Road ,... TEL. NO. Weston-super-Mare 65431
Weston-Super-Mare, Somerset. WS1 2FP
PRESENT ADDRESS ....
(if different from
above) .... TEL. NO. ....

SECONDARY EDUCATION

SCHOOLS ATTENDED	YEARS FROM	TO	QUALIFICATIONS ATTAINED
Scotch Comprehensive	19-	19-	
School			
Welsh Grammar School			
For Girls	19-	19-	
English Grammar School	19-	19-	
Irish Grammar School	19-	19-	O' level Eng Lang,
			Eng Lit, Maths, French,
			RI DomSci ......
			A' English, History, French.

FURTHER AND HIGHER EDUCATION

COLLEGE	YEARS FROM	TO	QUALIFICATIONS ATTAINED
County University	19-	19-	B.A. History (2nd
			Class Hons.) .....
Urban Technical College	19-	19-	'O' level Law LCC
			Adv.Typ. 100 wpm
			Shorthand PSC
LCC Elem. Spanish, LCC Higher	French ,	Pitman's 12	0 wpm shorthand

Figure 28   Completed application form

beam and getting my fingers jammed in the pulley. When the barrel hit the ground it bursted its bottom, allowing all the bricks to spill out. I was now heavier than the barrel and started down again at high speed. Half-way down I met the barrel coming up and received severe injuries to my shins. When I hit the ground I landed on the bricks, getting several painful cuts from sharp edges.

At this point I must have lost my presence of mind, because I let go of the line. The barrel then came down giving me another heavy blow on the head and putting me in hospital. I respectfully request sick leave.

2.   Design a suitable application form which could be used by all applicants for clerical or secretarial posts in the offices of a road-haulage contractor (see also Section 12).

(Scottish HND in Secretarial Studies)

3.   Design a Stationery Stores Requisition Form to be used for drawing out materials for use in the offices of a company. The form should allow for recording the name of the department, name of person requisitioning, date, quantity and description of items, and spaces for entries by the stores clerk supplying the goods. Invent any other relevant points. The form must not be larger than A5.

4.   Design a form to be used to monitor the progress of engineering apprentices throughout four years' training on the job. They will move through different factory departments on a six-monthly basis and must show satisfactory progress.

5.   Draw up an interview assessment form (see Section 12) for applicants for clerical and typing posts.

TELEGRAMS AND TELEX

Messages sent by any of these means must be kept concise because the cost of a telegram is calculated on the basis of the number of words used. With telex the transmitting time and the distance are considered in calculating the cost.

The letter in Figure 29 might have been sent in an abbreviated form for speed. A telegram or telex would have been much shorter, such as the following:

```
Dear Mr Masters

There is now some urgency to finalise the Paish
Limited contract.  I shall be at Heathrow airport
for a short while on Wednesday 16th November
during the stopover of my flight from Rome to
New York.  Will you please meet me there so that
we can conclude this business?  My Alitalia flight
627 is due to arrive at 16.50 hours.

Please let me know whether or not you will be able
to meet me.  I very much hope that it will be
possible.

Yours sincerely


Robert Walters
```

Figure 29   Letter to be condensed to telegram

1. URGENT WE FINALISE DETAILS PAISH LIMITED CONTRACT STOP ARRIVING HEATHROW ALITALIA FLIGHT 627 SIXTEEN FIFTY HOURS WEDNESDAY SIXTEENTH NOVEMBER STOP PLEASE CONFIRM THAT YOU CAN MEET ME STOP THERE DURING STOPOVER ONLY
(33 words)   WALTERS

No doubt you will have already noticed some points in the message that you feel could be omitted or condensed. Before looking at a rewritten version let us see what information needs to be included.

1. Reason for meeting — urgent finalisation of Paish Limited contract
2. Where — Heathrow
3. When — 16.50 hours, 16 November
4. Flight — Alitalia 627
5. For how long — stopover
6. Can it be arranged — confirmation needed.

The first message had all this in it, but expressed in too long a form. Certain words could have been omitted, for instance 'Wednesday' (the date is sufficient), 'Limited' (the recipient could identify the contract from the word 'Paish'). Some of the phrases could also be condensed, for example 'Please confirm that you can meet me' is far too long. There are three 'stops', each of which counts as one word in a telegram. The message should be rewritten to avoid some of these.

Now consider this version:

2. URGENT YOU MEET ME TO FINALISE PAISH CONTRACT DURING STOPOVER FLIGHT ALITALIA 627 HEATHROW SIXTEEN FIFTY HOURS SIXTEENTH NOVEMBER STOP PLEASE CONFIRM
(22 words)   WALTERS

It is possible to condense this even further, as with the following:

3. URGENT SEE YOU SIXTEENTH NOVEMBER STOP ARRIVING ALITALIA FLIGHT 627

(10 words)

WALTERS

Unfortunately some of the essential information has now been left out. The message omits all except two of the points on our check-list and gives only part of one of the remaining ones, that is, it stresses the urgency but does not give the reason for the meeting. It would be likely to lead to the following on the part of the recipient:

1. wondering why Walters wants to see him (there might be several reasons)
2. wondering where they are supposed to meet. He might assume that Walters would come to him from the airport (and which airport anyway?)
3. puzzling over the possible time of arrival
4. taking no action to get out the relevant papers and consider them before the meeting
5. sending no confirmation to Walters.

The second message therefore emerges as the most suitable. It is clear and yet relatively concise and contains all the relevant information.

The following information may be a useful guide to follow in the writing of any abbreviated message to be sent:

1. select only essential points
2. arrange them so that they are clear and convey the information accurately and as concisely as possible
3. use as few additional words as possible, substituting single words for phrases, for example

    'please confirm that you can meet me' — 'please confirm meeting possible'
4. avoid very long words — they may be counted as two words
5. do not abbreviate where this could cause confusion
6. avoid using 'stop' where possible (or 'comma' and other punctuation marks which each count as one word in telegrams — note that in telexes punctuation is shown as in normal writing)
7. use words rather than figures where there might be confusion
8. remember that parts of the address count in the number of words in a telegram.

EXERCISES

1. Your Personnel Officer, Miss B. Shaw, is at present attending an EEC conference but can be reached through your Brussels office. In view of the unrest among junior staff it is felt that her early return is imperative. Draft a telex message asking her to contact Head Office as soon as possible.

   (LCC Secretarial Studies Certificate)

2. Your firm's main warehouse and records have been damaged by fire. Draft a telex to your supplies asking them to:
   - (a) inform you of any orders delivered within the last week or *en route*
   - (b) hold any deliveries due to be made during the next ten days
   - (c) send a full list of all your orders
   - (d) be prepared to deliver to an alternative address:

3. Write an overseas telegram not exceeding twenty words in length (excluding names and addresses) to your employer, who is abroad on holiday, informing him of the following circumstances.

   You are the first to arrive at your office one morning, to find the caretaker waiting for you. He is in a state of great agitation. He tells you that he saw a man in a raincoat, with no hat or gloves, and carrying a briefcase, running down the stairs of your building. The caretaker thought the circumstances suspicious, and he had tried the doors of several offices, to find that yours had been forced. When he entered the room he found papers thrown all over the floor, a vase of flowers broken, ink on the carpet, desk drawers open and the safe door open. You go with the caretaker and see that the safe is empty. You know that when you left last night it contained £150 in cash and £50 worth of stamps. You ask him if he has telephoned the police, find that he has not done so, and do so yourself. The police arrive, examine the room and take statements from other members of the staff.

   (RSA Secretarial Duties II)

4. While on holiday abroad you are involved in a serious car accident a few days before you are due to return. The driver of the car in which you were travelling is seriously injured and your injuries will keep you in hospital for a week. Send an overseas telegram to your employer and follow this up with a letter. The overseas cable is to be set out in the correct form.

   (LCC Private Secretary's Certificate)

5.   'I have had more trouble than enough from secretaries trying to abbreviate my telegrams' was a remark made by a Company Secretary the other day.

(a) When should you not try to shorten telegrams?
(b) Why are telegrams now falling into disuse?

(LCC Private Secretary's Certificate)

9

MEETINGS AND COMMITTEES

How often does one telephone a businessman only to be told 'He is at a meeting'? It seems to happen more and more as meetings increase in popularity as a means of communication.

Many harsh criticisms are directed at this increasing use made of meetings. Some of the criticisms have resulted in humorous definitions of what a meeting is, for example

1. 'A committee comprises a bunch of the unfit, appointed by the unwilling, to do the unnecessary'
2. 'Meetings are composed of people who individually can do nothing and who collectively decide that nothing can be done'.

Unfortunately it is true that meetings do often have certain disadvantages, and these will be looked at in more detail later. However, they are useful tools in any large business as an aid to management because they ease the increasingly difficult task of co-ordinating the activities of large and diversified organisations, whether public or private.

WHAT IS A MEETING?

Legally a meeting is 'the coming together of at least two people for any lawful purpose' (Sharp *v.* Dawes, 1876), but under some circumstances one person can constitute a valid meeting, for example where one person holds all the shares of a particular class in the company (East *v.* Bennett Bros, 1911). Meetings can, of course, range in size from small to large numbers and can have very many purposes, such as meetings of shareholders of a company or joint consultation between employers and unions. Where a fairly small group of people meet on a regular basis, the meeting is often referred to as a 'committee' meeting.

COMMITTEES

There is sometimes some confusion about which meetings are 'committee' meetings. A true committee is a body of people who are:

1. collectively responsible for their decisions and actions to a higher authority, and
2. authorised to come to a decision by a majority vote and normally bound by that vote.

There are many meetings of groups of people to discuss matters of common interest, or to act in an advisory capacity, where the members have no collective responsibility. Such meetings should not be called 'committee' meetings. However, many of them are given this title. As a result there can be some misunderstanding by the members, who think that they are participating in a democratic, and often policy-making body. They are subsequently aggrieved when their majority decisions are not interpreted as being binding on their superiors. Such 'non-committees' may be found in the Civil Service, in education and in industry in the guise of management committees and staff conferences — which act in a consultative capacity only.

PURPOSES OF MEETINGS

Meetings have all or some of the following purposes:

1. to give information
2. to obtain information
3. to bring together knowledge and experience to solve a problem
4. to develop co-operation and influence attitudes
5. to air grievances
6. to take decisions, within their sphere of authority.

ADVANTAGES

Here are some of the positive advantages of meetings.

1. Members have the opportunity to devote their time to affairs either for which they have an aptitude or in which they have a particular interest.
2. More knowledge and experience can be brought together and more information be made available than one man could collect in the same time.
3. Discussion is often profitable because ideas are developed or new solutions proposed through the medium of the meeting itself.
4. Job satisfaction can be increased if people feel that they are making a worth-while contribution to their organisation.
5. Management can be kept informed of the feelings and reactions of their employees and thus possible causes of trouble can be avoided.
6. The flow of communication downward and upward is improved, and (as was suggested in Section 1) horizontal communication can be helped by the establishment of regular meetings of line managers.

DISADVANTAGES

The main disadvantage of meetings may be summed up in two words: 'delay' and 'personality'. Delay can occur in three ways.

1. Decision-taking may be unduly postponed because of long or irrelevant discussion. One man acting on his own might come to a decision much more quickly.
2. There is often some delay in the calling of a meeting because it is difficult to assemble people at short notice. Where a decision is needed instantly, delay can be serious.
3. Irrelevant discussion, besides delaying decision-taking, can cause annoyance and frustration. The effects of this on a meeting where attendance is optional can be startling.

One of the authors of this book attended one committee meeting, of some twenty-five people, where a single individual was determined to have his say, no matter what effect this had on the business of the meeting. The chairman was new to his task and Mr 'I-want-to-talk' succeeded only too well in his purpose, to the extent that, after about an hour, one by one the other members started to murmur apologies and slip away. After two hours the chairman closed the meeting. Only twelve people were still present.

Attendance at the meeting was voluntary. In consequence, when the next meeting was convened, of the twenty-five present on the previous occasion, only ten attended, together with a few others who had not suffered previously.

The personalities at a meeting can delay proceedings in the ways mentioned above, but there are other ways in which a meeting can be ruined through human failings. For instance, a dominant chairman or secretary can so take command of a meeting that it become nothing more than a rubber-stamp for already decided policies. Equally a weak chairman can allow strong personalities in the meeting to bend the proceeding to suit their own purpose.

Size is an important factor in the regular meetings which are called 'committees'. The group should be large enough for all views to be represented, but it is often considered that the effectiveness of a committee varies in inverse proportion to its size. Some authorities suggest that no committee should exceed ten members and that six is an ideal number.

TYPES OF MEETINGS

Meeting vary from the very formal to the very informal, just as they vary in size from the mass meeting of 5000 or more people to the discussion between two people.

FORMAL

The very formal meeting will follow rigidly defined procedures and rules and the conduct of the meeting will be governed by a chairman. The most formal meetings in this country (despite the hubbub that radio transmission leads us to think takes place daily) are the meetings of Parliament. The procedure and rules are stated in the 'bible' of Parliament, *Erskine May,* and are interpreted by two chairmen: the Speaker in the House of Commons and the Lord Chancellor in the House of Lords.

Other formal meetings are Annual General, and General, Meetings of companies, meetings of Boards of Directors and Boards of nationalised industries, local government councils and committees, committees of professional associations, trade unions, works councils and joint consultative committees.

INFORMAL

The less formal the meeting, the fewer the rules governing its conduct and procedure. Most meetings do have someone 'in charge', even if that someone is not called the chairman. However, some meetings are simply informal discussion, perhaps following casual encounters. These will have scarcely any recognised procedure.

Meetings may be deliberately organised to remove formality so that the meeting will achieve its objective. Examples of such meetings are brainstorming and problem-solving sessions. There will be no chairman, no agenda, no rules of debate, no resolutions and no minutes (although some written record is likely).

Meetings not only vary in formality according to the written rules, Articles of Association, Standing Orders, Constitutions, that govern them, but also according to the business of the meeting. Some of the different kinds of business are identified for you below. It should be remembered that in any one meeting there might be a combination of several types of business considered and that, within a generally accepted procedure, the formality of a meeting should alter to allow for effective discussion and decision-making as required.

1   EXECUTIVE

The people at these meetings will be discussing and deciding matters but will have the additional task of implementing decisions. A Board of Directors is an example of an Executive Committee.

2   DECISION-MAKING

Some meetings have the power to make collective decisions on action to be taken. Such authority will have been given to them by a parent body or electorate and, as long as the meeting acts within its powers, its decisions are absolute. All true committees hold decision-making meetings.

3   DISCUSSION AND ADVICE

Discussion takes place in most meetings but there are many where it is the function of members to discuss questions and proffer advice to other people or bodies. Joint consultation meetings come within this category.

Many of these meetings, when held on a regular basis, are called (mistakenly) committee meetings. The members do not have any decision-making powers except in deciding what advice to give. An 'advisory committee' is a contradiction in terms.

4 PROBLEM-SOLVING

Any item of special business on an agenda may be a problem which the meeting has to solve. Also, special meetings may be held for the purpose of solving one problem. Much of the business of Residents' Associations is concerned with problem-solving. For example, such an organisation might set up an *ad hoc* committee to plan the best use and means of equipping a piece of land donated as a play space.

5 INFORMATION-GIVING

Meetings held for the purpose of giving information are frequently called 'briefings'. The prepared brief will be read to the meeting, and it is common for questions to be answered. The meeting is not intended as a forum for discussion and debate. That would take place on another occasion.

Briefings are given by companies and official bodies to the press and also many organisations now hold regular briefing sessions for their employees, from senior executives to the office junior or production worker. At each level of the organisation the staff will be split into groups of up to twenty, each to be briefed by the immediate manager. This can be a valuable addition to the formal systems of communication.

6 NEGOTIATION

Trade-union representatives and employers most commonly form the two sides in the battle that is joined in these meetings, where details of pay rises, fringe benefits and other changes in conditions of work, or redundancy payments and arrangements are worked out.

Such groups hope to reach agreement, even if only after a series of meetings, but their agreements will then have to be ratified by the bodies that they represent, for instance by the Engineering Employers' Federation and by the Executive of the AUEW or even by a ballot of its members.

Meetings between one person and another or one person and a group of other people for such purposes as employment, performance, appraisal, reprimands and discussion of grievances are considered in Section 12, 'Interviews'.

PROCEDURE AT MEETINGS

The pattern followed at meetings is a well-established one. It comes from rules and conventions that have been codified, considered, adjudged in courts of law and generally accepted as fair and reasonable.

Some of the procedure is mandatory, found in statutes such as the Public Order Acts and the Companies Acts. There are Common Law and judicial precedents to guide us and written codes found in Articles of Association, Standing Orders and Constitutions. Meetings themselves can take some decisions on their procedure and the chairman also has some say.

Many of the procedures are very old and not only are the traditional ways still followed but also the traditional terms are still used. Some of these are English words and phrases used in a special way, such as a *rider*, others are Latin terms, for example, *sine die.* Students need to learn these terms for examination purposes and so that they may understand how meetings work. A glossary of the most common terms is given in Appendix 3.

WHAT THE RULES COVER

These directives will frequently include some or all of the following:

1. membership, namely those people entitled to attend the meetings and vote
2. proxies, that is, the procedure when a member cannot attend and wishes another person to speak and vote in his place
3. arrangements which must be made for the election of officers
4. remuneration of, for example, directors
5. the frequency at which meetings must be held
6. the length of notice required when a meeting is called
7. regulations governing submission of motions
8. the duties and privileges of officers
9. the rules governing the recording of proceedings, for example, minutes.

The less formal meeting may be conducted in a somewhat similar way, with a chairman and with minutes being taken. However, there will be no set constitution or any liability to follow legal regulations.

TAKING DECISIONS

In a formal meeting the method of taking decisions has the following pattern.

1   MOTIONS

Each item to be discussed will have a proposal, normally called a *motion*, to which members will speak. It may be submitted in writing before the meeting or may be proposed during the discussion of an item of business. The procedure followed will be governed by the rules of the organisation.

Each motion will have a proposer and seconder. (NOTE: in Common Law no seconder is needed but one is usually required either by the rules or by convention.) A motion may be *dropped* if no seconder is found or when the meeting agrees that it may be withdrawn.

2   CHANGES

Motions may be changed, before they are voted upon, by *amendment* or *addendum.*

Amendments

An amendment alters a motion by inserting, deleting or changing the words of the original but it is not permitted to negate the motion or completely change it. Amendments should be duly proposed and seconded and the Chairman should call for all amendments to the motion before allowing discussion

The amendments should then be taken in the order in which the words of the original motion are affected.

Addendum

An addendum is the addition of words to a motion and is treated in the same way as an amendment.

3   SUBSTANTIVE MOTION/RESOLUTION

The motion as amended and added to then becomes the *substantive motion.* When voted upon and carried it is termed the *resolution.* This can be further altered by the addition of a *rider,* yet another phrase or clause.

It is the final resolution (including any rider) that appears in minutes and is the decision upon which action is based. Figure 30 shows the way in which a motion becomes a resolution and an example is given below:

Original Motion
'THAT there shall be a promise of an additional three days' holiday made to all salaried staff.'

Proposed Amendment 1
'That the word "not" be inserted between "shall" and "be".'
       NOT ACCEPTABLE — negates the proposal

Proposed Amendment 2
'That the words "an additional three days' holiday" be deleted and "a bonus payment of two per cent of salary" be inserted.'
       NOT ACCEPTABLE —changes the nature of the proposal

Amendment 1
'That the word "three" be deleted and the word "two" inserted.'
Amendment 2
'That the words "and weekly paid" be inserted between "salaried" and "staff".'
Amendment 3
'That the words "a promise" be replaced by the words "an offer".'

Amendments are voted upon in order in which the wording of the original motion is affected. Thus, in this case, the order would be:

Amendment 3
Amendment 1
Amendment 2

If we suppose that amendments 3 and 1 are carried and amendment 2 is defeated, we should then have a SUBSTANTIVE MOTION which reads:

'THAT there shall be an offer of an additional two days' holiday made to all salaried staff.'

Addendum

It may be that it is now proposed: 'That the words "who have completed one

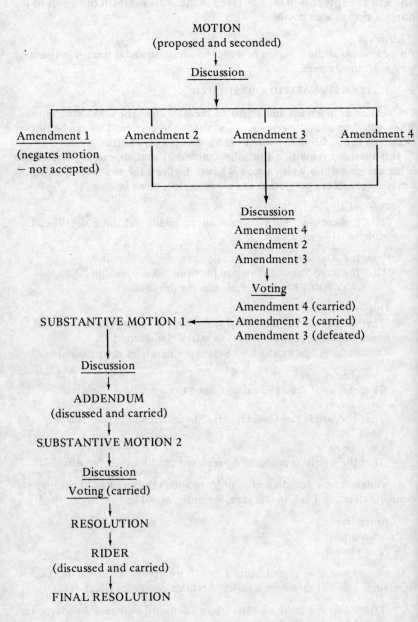

MOTION
(proposed and seconded)

↓

Discussion

Amendment 1   Amendment 2   Amendment 3   Amendment 4
(negates motion
– not accepted)

Discussion
Amendment 4
Amendment 2
Amendment 3

↓

Voting
Amendment 4 (carried)
SUBSTANTIVE MOTION 1 ←———— Amendment 2 (carried)
Amendment 3 (defeated)

↓

Discussion

↓

ADDENDUM
(discussed and carried)

↓

SUBSTANTIVE MOTION 2

↓

Discussion

↓

Voting (carried)

↓

RESOLUTION

↓

RIDER
(discussed and carried)

↓

FINAL RESOLUTION

Figure 30   From motion to resolution

year's service" be added to the motion.' If this is agreed the SUBSTANTIVE MOTION becomes:

> 'THAT there shall be an offer of an additional two days' holiday made to all salaried staff who have completed one year's service.'

The motion is then voted upon and becomes the RESOLUTION if it is carried. A further addition to the resolution would be a rider, for example

> 'That the words "The offer will be effective for this holiday year" be added.'
>
> Rider carried

The final RESOLUTION will thus be:

> 'THAT there shall be an offer of an additional two days' holiday made to all salaried staff who have completed one year's service. The offer will be effective for this holiday year.'

4   FORMAL MOTIONS

A formal motion is one that is concerned with the procedure of a meeting rather than with the business being discussed. These motions are aimed at assisting the business, particularly to end or prevent unhelpful or useless discussion.

Formal motions include the following:

(a)   that the question be now put (often referred to as the *closure* and meaning to close the discussion on the motion)

(b)   that the question be not now put (commonly called the *previous question*, that is, the original motion)

(c)   that the meeting leave the matter on the table, that is, takes note, but does not discuss it

(d) that the discussion (or the meeting) be adjourned

(e)   that the meeting proceeds to the next item of business

(f)   that the meeting be adjourned *sine die*, that is, indefinitely.

VOTING

Voting on motions and amendments in a formal meeting will usually be done by show of hands or by secret ballot. On less formal occasions the chairman sometimes assesses the sense of the meeting and there is then no need for a formal vote.

THE ROLE OF THE CHAIRMAN

The Chairman of a meeting is, as has already been suggested, an extremely important person. Upon his capabilities often depends much of the success or otherwise of the meeting. He needs to have strength of character, without being dogmatic or wishing to impress his own views on the meeting. He must have the ability to express himself fluently without making speeches. He must be able to maintain control over the meeting, but should not prevent useful exchanges of views. He must earn the respect of the members, but respect the opinions of others. He must ensure that he is always impartial in his conduct of the meeting even when he strongly disagrees with decisions taken.

His duties include the following:

1. ensuring that his own appointment and that of other officers is in accordance with the rules
2. making certain that the meeting has been properly convened, is correctly constituted and that a quorum is present
3. maintaining order and ensuring that the meeting is conducted correctly
4. taking items of business in the correct order
5. preventing irrelevant discussion and allowing adequate opportunity for those who wish to speak to do so
6. ascertaining the 'sense of the meeting' when a vote is not taken; or putting motions and amendments to the meeting in proper order
7. making, or having made, a record of the proceedings
8. communicating decisions to other people who will be affected by them.

The chairman usually has certain powers to assist him in the performance of his duties. They include the power to:

1. maintain order and have disorderly persons removed from the meeting
2. give rulings on points of order
3. decide points of procedure
4. adjourn the meeting if it is impossible to maintain order
5. conduct the business so that results and decisions are made known to the meeting
6. use a casting vote when the meeting is deadlocked. (NOTE: the chairman has an additional vote only if it has been conferred by the rules of the organisation. There is no casting vote in Common Law.)

The chairman can help the meeting by careful prior study of the agenda and any accompanying papers. He will then be briefed before he attends the meeting. His approach to the meeting may well follow a pattern similar to the following:

1. welcome members, particularly new ones
2. state the purpose of the meeting (if members do not already know this)
3. promote discussion (This can be done by addressing general statements or questions to the group or by addressing more specific enquiries to an individual.)
4. sum up at various stages
5. reiterate the arguments for and against any proposal just before any decision is taken
6. state the conclusion and action decided upon
7. bring the meeting to a close at an appropriate time.

THE ROLE OF THE SECRETARY

The secretary is the servant of the meeting. The extent of his (or her) role will depend on the meeting, but normally he is responsible for the following:

1. convening the meeting and preparing the requisite documents
2. all correspondence
3. general administrative work
4. any legal business (the secretary to a large organisation will have considerable responsibilities in this field, for instance all the legal work connected with the transfer of shares and the annual return to the Registrar of Companies)
5. the financial work of the organisation (except where there is an officer separately appointed to carry out this work, for example a Treasurer of a society or a Chief Accountant of a company).

In many voluntary concerns the secretary is often the work-horse of the committee structure and sometimes carries a disproportionate share of the work burden.

COMMITTEE MEMBERS

Members of committees are often recognisable types. Figure 31 shows some who are attending the Board meetings of Noah's Ark Limited. Starting from the left we have:

MR HARRY HIPPOPOTAMUS. He came up the hard way and covers his insecurity with roaring ill-temper when crossed, particularly if by the young upstart on his left.

MR CHESHIRE CAT. A keen young director with high-level paper qualifications. Thinks he knows it all.

LORD THOROUGH-BRED EQUINE. Sits on a multitude of Boards — his title lends prestige. Covers his ignorance with irrelevant social chatter. Anxious for the meeting to finish (going to the races?).

SIR LEO LION. Chairman and Managing Director. Autocratic figure who wants to maintain his sovereign power.

MR D.O.Z. DORMOUSE. Not really interested. It's all 'a bit of a bore'. He's much too tired anyway.

MR BASKERVILLE BLOODHOUND. A thorough, tenacious type with a good nose for trouble and a direct approach to problems.

MR SILAS SHEEP. Follows the crowd — afraid of expressing his own opinions. The perfect 'yes-man'.

Figure 31   The Board of Noah's Ark meets

One feels that this firm is not going to have too much useful direction of its activities from the Directors.

We know from Section 1 how people's relationships with each other change according to the group they may be in at any one time. Nowhere does this show up more clearly than in meetings.

In *The Social Psychology of Industry*, J. A. C. Brown states: 'Reason, however important a part it may play in society, does not play a major part in most people's lives'. Thus much of the time spent in meetings will be concerned with the expression of feelings and emotions.

This is not to say that in every meeting the discussion will be accompanied by fierce argument, displays of petulance or by a dozy dormouse falling asleep, though each of these can happen. What frequently occurs is time-wasting or, in a belated attempt to save time, hurried and unsuitable decisions are made.

Since the complexities of most organisations demand that meetings be held and because there is often a genuine desire to inform, consult and involve as many people as possible, it is increasingly important that all those who attend meetings develop a positive approach to them and a determination to make them work. The attitude that a meeting will be a waste of time 'because we always spend hours talking about stupid things and don't get anything done', or 'because there's never an agenda and we don't know what we're supposed to discuss', must go.

It is the responsibility of the Chairman to encourage useful contribution from all attending the meeting, but he cannot always choose members for their usefulness and co-operativeness. Members should take certain responsibilities. They should, for example, make themselves familiar with the work of the committee and make sure they have read the information provided for them by the Secretary. They have a duty to take a full part of the working of the group and to assist the Chairman in the performance of his duties. They should not expect the Secretary to take on duties that are outside his normal responsibilities and should be willing to accept other such duties as the committee sees fit to give them, always provided that they have the time and capacity to perform them.

Just as the Chairman and Secretary should not use the meeting as a forum for their own views, so should the members avoid this also, remembering that other people deserve the opportunity to express their opinions. Finally, the views having been expressed and a majority decision arrived at, the individual member either should be prepared to help carry this decision into effect or he should seriously consider his position as a member of the committee.

This section closes with notes for an outline answer to an examination question on committee organisation and some questions on meetings and committees. The next section covers in some detail the arrangements that have to be made for meetings and the recording of proceedings.

NOTES FOR AN OUTLINE ANSWER

QUESTION

'The camel has been described as a horse designed by a committee.' State the advantages and disadvantages of committee organisation and give an example, with reasons, of the circumstances in which:

(a)   a committee would be well-employed
(b)   it would be unsuitable.

(LCC Private Secretary's Certificate)

NOTES

Advantages of Committees
1. People can become experts in certain fields and can sometimes devote attention to affairs for which they have aptitude.
2. Greater variety of experience. More useful information can be pooled.
3. Ideas are brought to light by discussion.
4. Personnel have the chance to make a worth-while contribution to the organisation.
5. The feelings and reactions of employees can be made known to management.
6. Lines of communication are improved.

Disadvantages of Committees
1. Delay — postponement of decision-taking.
2. Delay — irrelevant discussion.
3. Delay — notice of meetings.
4. Dominant chairman or secretary can have too much power.
5. Weak chairman cannot control meeting.

Size is an important factor; on the one hand, it should be sufficient to enable all views to be represented but, on the other, it should be kept to a minimum.

The first part of the question is straightforward and should cause little difficulty. The second part, however, requires *an example* of each of the situations outlined. Students will not gain marks if they do not give *one specific example of each.* Areas from which examples might be chosen are suggested below, but this is not intended as a comprehensive list:

(a)   (i)   joint consultation
      (ii) specialist co-ordination
      (iii) problem-solving
(b)   (i)   imposition of policy
      (ii) forum for chairman
      (iii) need for speed.

There are, of course, many other areas which could be chosen. It must again be emphasised that the question asks for one example only of *each* of (a) and (b).

EXERCISES

1. How does voting take place on motions and amendments in a formal meeting?

2. Distinguish between formal and informal meetings. What are their respective advantages and disadvantages?

   (LCC Private Secretary's Certificate)

3. Explain the following terms used in procedure at meetings:
   - (a) motion
   - (b) amendment
   - (c) resolution
   - (d) rider
   - (e) right of reply.

   (LCC Private Secretary's Certificate)

4. What do you understand by the following terms used in connection with the conduct of meetings?
   - (a) agenda
   - (b) minutes
   - (c) quorum
   - (d) motion
   - (e) proxy
   - (f) ex officio

   (Scottish HND in Secretarial Studies)

5. Explain the meaning and implications of the following terms used in connection with meetings:
   - (a) meeting adjourned
   - (b) co-option
   - (c) sine die
   - (d) nem. con.
   - (e) closure
   - (f) substantive motion.

6. Comment on the essential difference between:
   - (a) a General Meeting **and** a Committee Meeting
   - (b) an Annual General Meeting **and** an Extraordinary General Meeting
   - (c) a Standing Committee and an Ad Hoc Committee
   - (d) an Executive Committee **and** an Advisory Committee.

   (LCC Private Secretary's Certificate)

7. You have been asked to suggest a new organisation for the local Ambulance Service. You have to choose between controlling the service by (a) a Committee, or (b) a Director with full operating authority. Discuss the 'pros' and 'cons' of each possibility and decide which would be the better choice.

(LCC Private Secretary's Certificate)

8. Committees are more prevalent in local government and voluntary organisations than in general business and commerce. What are the features of committees which seem to make them more suitable to the one and less attractive to the other?

(LCC Private Secretary's Certificate)

9. What is the role and purpose of a committee? Explain what you consider to be the essential requisites of good chairmanship.

(LCC Private Secretary's Diploma)

10. Meetings can be an exciting and rewarding element in business life. Why then is frustration, boredom and a low level of accomplishment the outcome of many meetings?

(LCC Private Secretary's Diploma)

11. What are the merits and demerits of committees as part of the organisational structure of a business?

(Scottish HND in Secretarial Studies)

12. What are the purposes of a procedural motion? Explain **five** such motions and their effect, if carried.

(RSA Diploma for Personal Assistants)

10

MEETINGS – ARRANGEMENTS AND DOCUMENTS

The secretary may be called upon to act as Secretary to a committee in her own right or to fulfil many of the duties of a Meetings Secretary for her employer. She should be aware of all the arrangements that may have to be made for a meeting and be able to prepare the relevant papers.

The most complex meeting with which the Secretary may be concerned will probably be a Company Meeting, either an Annual General Meeting of shareholders or a meeting of the Board of Directors. Fortunately, there is a procedure for such meetings for a limited liability company, a procedure detailed in the legal documents prepared when the company was formed.

These details are to be found in the Memorandum and Articles of Association of the company. They will cover such things as the length of notice that has to be given before meetings are held, the number of people required to form a quorum, elections, proxy voting, submission of resolutions. An example taken from a company's articles is given in Appendix 2. For most meetings, however, the Secretary will need to follow a procedure similar to that outlined below.

CHOICE OF DATE, TIME AND VENUE

The Secretary may be responsible for suggesting an appropriate date and time. On other occasions this will be decided at the previous meeting of a committee or there may be a regular calendar of meetings, for instance on the first Thursday of each month at 2.30 p.m.

The choice of venue may be straightforward, but the Secretary must check that accommodation is available. She must also ensure that the accommodation is suitable and make arrangements for the provision of such items as stationery, ashtrays or refreshments, if these are required.

NOTICE OF MEETINGS

Statutory requirements about notice of meetings must be observed, but otherwise it is advisable to send out notices of meetings about two weeks before the date of the meeting. If the date of the meeting was fixed at the previous meeting, then the notice is merely a reminder and could be sent out as late as one week before the next meeting. It is to be hoped that members who did not attend the previous meeting will already have been sent copies of the minutes, which include the date of the next meeting.

The notice of meeting itself is usually a very simple letter or memorandum (see Section 5), on the lines of Figure 32.

```
                               TRADERS  LIMITED
                               BURNTHOUSE  ROAD
                               LONDON    WC4  3BJ


RJL/TW                                 17th March, 19--


        ┌─────────────┐
        │  Name and   │
        │  Address    │
        └─────────────┘


Dear Sir,

The next meeting of the Board of Directors of
the above Company will be held on Tuesday,
6th April, 19--, at 11.30 a.m. in the Board
Room.

Yours faithfully,
for Traders Limited



R.J. Light
Company Secretary
```

Figure 32   Notice of meeting

AGENDA

The agenda of a meeting is the list, or programme, of the items of business to be discussed at a meeting in the order in which they are to be taken. It is an important document which can influence the discussion and decisions taken at a meeting.

Although in theory it is the Chairman of a committee who should be responsible for the agenda, it is in practice the Secretary who draws it up. However, it should be agreed by the Chairman before it is sent out to members.

In drawing up the agenda the Secretary should refer to some or all of the following:

1. minutes of the previous meeting
2. propositions received
3. correspondence
4. action taken following the previous meeting.

From these sources she will derive the main items of business for the agenda. Depending on the kind of meeting, certain other items will appear regularly on the agenda. For instance, Annual General Meetings have agenda items which always appear. The following list indicates the most common (not necessarily always in the order given).

Annual General Meetings — Agenda Items

A Limited Liability Company	*A Club or Society*
Directors' report	Chairman's and Secretary's reports
Annual accounts	Annual accounts
Auditors' report	Auditor's report
Election of auditors	Election/appointment of auditors
Remuneration of auditors	
Declaration of dividend	Subscriptions
Election of directors	Election of committee and officers

There will then follow any particular business to be discussed.

Other meetings will have certain alternatives which will appear regularly on the agenda. The following are fairly constant items:

Item 1   *Apologies for absence* (included in minutes, but sometimes omitted from the agenda)

Item 2   *Minutes of the previous meeting* (if these have been circulated, then this will be indicated; if they are enclosed, then this will likewise be noted)

Item 3   *Matters arising from the minutes* (there are some who regard this item as a time-waster and suggest that, as major matters arising should appear as separate items, this category should be omitted)

(Then follow the main items for discussion: items 4, 5, 6, and so on)

Next item   *Correspondence (optional)*
then   *Date of next meeting*
and
finally   *Any other business* (in Scotland this item would be *Any other competent business*).

Agenda items should be described in sufficient detail for their purpose to be clear to members attending the meeting. Relevant additional papers should accompany the agenda and should be clearly referred to in the agenda, as is shown in Figure 33. The agenda itself should be kept as short as possible, should be consistent and unambiguous, and it is advisable to consider:

1. what information can be presented in the form of appendices, or agenda papers, and

2. how much the committee can reasonably be expected to discuss at the meeting.

It is useless to overload the agenda. The Secretary may have to exercise some judgement in deciding which matters can be included and which should be left for a future occasion. In this way the Secretary can influence the work of the meeting. The order of items on an agenda usually determines the order in which they are to be discussed at a meeting. Here, too, the Secretary brings influence to bear and must exercise a degree of judgement when drafting the document. An example of an agenda is shown in Figure 33.

```
                  TRADERS LIMITED STAFF ASSOCIATION

          Committee meeting to be held on Friday, 20th May, 19--,
          at 5.30 p.m. in the Board Room.

                              AGENDA

          1.  Apologies for absence

          2.  Minutes of the meeting held on Friday, 22nd April,
              19--, (copies previously circulated)

          3.  Matters arising from the Minutes

              (a)  Minute No. 4 should be amended as follows:
                   for 'Mr R. Garnett' read 'Mr P. Garratt'.

              (b)  Minute No. 7 - Annual General Meeting.  The
                   firm has given permission for the Annual
                   General Meeting to be held on 6th July, 19--.

          4.  Subscriptions

              The following proposal has been received from
              Mr G. Heard, seconded by Miss R. Field:

                   'THAT this Committee recommends to the
                   Association at the Annual General
                   Meeting that the annual subscription
                   for the year beginning 1st August, 19--,
                   shall be £1'.

Paper A.  5.  Forthcoming events

              A draft programme of events has been prepared by the
              Social Sub-Committee for the consideration of the
              meeting (copy enclosed).

          6.  Correspondence

              The following correspondence has been received:

              (a)  copy of the Annual Report and Accounts of the
                   Company

              (b)  Memo from the Personnel Department about the
                   proposed introduction of a clock system for
                   all staff.

          7.  Date of next meeting

          8.  Any other business
```

Figure 33   Agenda

Combined Notice of Meeting and Agenda

It is common to send the notice and agenda out as one document. This saves time and postage. Figure 34 is an example of a combined notice. The remainder of the agenda follows, as illustrated in the previous example.

```
                        TRADERS LIMITED

                          MEMORANDUM

     To:  Members of Staff   From:  Staff Association
          Association                Secretary
          Committee
                            Date:  12th May 19--

          STAFF ASSOCIATION COMMITTEE MEETING

     The next meeting of the above Committee will
     take place on Friday, 20th May, 19--, at
     5.30 p.m. in the Board Room.  The agenda is
     given below and the relevant papers are
     enclosed.


                          P. Briggs

                           AGENDA

     1.   Apologies for Absence
```

Figure 34   Notice of meeting and agenda

The notice and agenda for a General Meeting of a company will be more formal, usually not contained in a letter. An example is given in Figure 35.

CHAIRMAN'S AGENDA

The efficient Meetings Secretary will endeavour to provide her Chairman with as much information as possible before a meeting. This is usually done by drawing up a Chairman's agenda, or notes. Such documentation will follow the pattern of the agenda for the meeting, giving full details about all the items and advice where relevant. There are several ways of setting out a Chairman's agenda. One for the meeting of the Traders Limited Staff Association (see Figure 33) might start as shown in Figure 36. Sometimes the agenda for the meeting is typed on the left of the page, with the notes for the Chairman on the right. Room must be left for the Chairman to write his own notes. This is usually done by leaving a column on the right-hand side. A copy of the notes should be sent to the Chairman several days before the meeting, preferably with the general agenda. The Meetings Secretary should retain three additional copies, which will serve as follows:

1. for use by the Chairman at the meeting if he should forget his copy, or for use by the Vice-Chairman in the absence of the Chairman
2. for use by the Secretary herself
3. for the file.

TRADERS LIMITED
BURNTHOUSE ROAD
LONDON WC4 3BJ

26th May, 19--

ANNUAL GENERAL MEETING

NOTICE IS HEREBY GIVEN that the Annual General
Meeting of the Company will be held in the
Burnthouse Rooms, Burnthouse Road, London
WC4 3BJ on Thursday, 30th May, 19-- at 12 noon
to transact the following business:

1. To receive the report of the directors
    and the accounts for the year ended
    31st March, 19-- and the report of
    the auditors.

(The remainder of the agenda would then follow.)

By order of the Board

K. Brown
Secretary

Figure 35 Notice of Annual General Meeting

SUGGESTED APPROACH TO AN EXAMINATION QUESTION

The following question, for which notes for an answer are suggested, includes
points from this section and from Section 9.

QUESTION

You are asked to make preparations for a small committee meeting which is
to take place in two weeks' time. How would you ensure that a quorum
would be present? What other matters will require attention up to the commencement of the meeting?

(LCC Private Secretary's Certificate)

TRADERS LIMITED STAFF ASSOCIATION

Committee meeting to be held on Friday, 20th May,
19--, at 5.30 p.m. in the Board Room.

CHAIRMAN'S AGENDA

NOTES

1. <u>Apologies for</u>   An apology has been
   <u>absence</u>   received from
                      Mr L. Partridge. He
                      will be on holiday.

2. <u>Minutes of the</u>   A spare copy is en-
   <u>meeting held on</u>   closed
   <u>22nd April, 19--</u>

3. <u>Matters arising</u>   Minute 4 should be
                      amended as follows:
                      for 'Mr R. Garnett'
                      read 'Mr P. Garratt'.
                      This was a typing error.

4. <u>Subscriptions</u>   The proposal detailed
                      in the attached agenda
                      follows the discussion,
                      under Minute 7 of the
                      last meeting, about
                      existing funds. Ex-
                      penses estimated are
                      £63. Balance in hand
                      is £86.32.

Figure 36   Chairman's agenda

ANSWER

This is a two-part question.

Part 1 (Note the use of the word 'ensure' in the question)
The following procedure is suggested:

1. check the number needed at the meeting for a quorum to be present
2. decide the time and place of the meeting (the question gives you the date)
3. check list of members
4. contact Chairman, either in person or by telephone. If he is unable to be present, contact Vice-Chairman
5. make personal contact, or telephone members until you have firm promises of attendance from the number required to form a quorum plus two. This should allow for unavoidable absence at the last moment
6. if you cannot arrange for a quorum to be present, you should refer back to your Chairman or Vice-Chairman to arrange a change of date or time. Then follow the same procedure again

7. confirm your conversations by letter as soon as possible, preferably sending out the notice of meeting and agenda at the same time
8. check two days before the meeting with members who have promised to attend
9. remind members or their secretaries of the meeting on the actual day.

Part II
The following action will be necessary before the commencement of the meeting:

1. prepare or answer any correspondence arising from Part I of this answer
2. book venues
3. draft the agenda and confirm with the Chairman
4. send out notice of meeting, agreed agenda and agenda papers
5. prepare and send Chairman's agenda
6. prepare attendance sheet
7. gather spare copies of all papers, including minutes of the last meeting
8. check availability of room on day before meeting and arrange minor details such as chairs and stationery
9. on day of meeting put up notice indicating venue and inform switchboard
10. take minutes, spare copies of all papers and correspondence to meeting.

NOTE: It is assumed that you are the Meetings Secretary. If you make the assumption that you are not, then you must arrange for a Minutes Secretary.

EXERCISES

Some of the following questions include points based on Section 9.

1. (a) As Secretary to the Company Secretary, draft the notice of meeting and agenda for the next Annual General Meeting of the Company for which you work.
   (b) Prepare a chairman's agenda on the assumption that your present chairman will be re-elected.

2. (a) As Secretary to your firm's Sports and Social Club, prepare the notice and agenda for the Annual General Meeting on 29 September.
   (b) To whom will you send copies and why?

(LCC Private Secretary's Certificate)

3. (a) As Secretary to the Wintergate Horticultural Society, draft an agenda for a meeting of the Management Committee. Supply your own details which should include, in addition to matters of formal business, five special items.
   (b) What is a chairman's agenda? Illustrate your answer by giving

chairman's agenda versions of two of the five special items you have devised in answer to (a).

(RSA Diploma for Personal Assistants)

4.   Draw up a chairman's agenda for a meeting of the Staff Canteen Committee. The Committee last met on Wednesday, 13 March. The meeting is to discuss the quality of meals served in the canteen, a possible rise in the prices of the meals, the installation of a coffee-vending machine and suggestions from the employees' suggestion box.

(LCC Private Secretary's Certificate)

5.   Your management is keen on maintaining morale amongst the staff and provides good social amenities at the firm's social and sports club. There are five sports sections, a dramatic society, a music society and a discussion group. The club is run by a Committee whose members are elected by the employees and the General Manager is Chairman.
Draft an agenda for the Annual General Meeting of this club and prepare a work sheet showing what steps you would take to ensure that all the necessary arrangements for this meeting are made.

(LCC Private Secretary's Certificate)

6.   Your employer has left the following note on your desk. Describe, with details, the action you would take and draw up the relevant documents.

Miss Jones,
     Joe Brown, the Chairman of my kid's school's Parents' Association, rang me. He wants a Committee meeting next Tues. week. The Secretary's away. Can you do the agenda, etc?
     The file's with this note. It's got minutes, circulation list, etc. with it. There are also two important letters, the one about the swimming pool and from the Director of Education.
     The meeting's usually in the school staff room at 7.30 p.m. The caretaker hasn't been contacted. The meeting's mainly to discuss the social evening, but I expect they'll also want to talk about the proposed extension.
     I must remember to bring up the question of a school trip abroad — thought we might 'twin' with a French town.
     Hope you can sort this out. There are eight on the committee, with me.

R. P. Knight

7.   What preparations must be made before a committee meeting is held?

MINUTES

1 PURPOSE

One of the principal functions of the secretary at a meeting is normally that of taking the minutes.

Minutes can be said to have three purposes.

(a) *Constitutional.* They serve as a record of the proceedings and are often legally required.
(b) *Executive.* Minutes often provide the basis for action.
(c) *Progressive.* They can serve as a basis for evolving policy.

It is very important that minutes should provide a comprehensive and meaningful account of the proceedings at a meeting. The term 'proceedings', however, means only the discussion that was relevant and, thus, minute-writing has been said to be the 'art of omission'.

One striking example of this art arose early in 1972 in the House of Commons, where the minutes of the proceedings are taken down verbatim by a bevy of shorthand writers. It can best be illustrated by quoting from the published accounts of the time. In *The Times* of 1 February 1972 Miss Bernadette Devlin, the Member of Parliament for Mid-Ulster, is quoted thus:

My only regret is that I didn't seize Mr Maudling by the throat while I had the chance. I was not allowed to have my say on the brutal murder of thirteen people yesterday. I walked up to Mr Maudling and hit him across the face as hard as I could with my fist. I was cold and calm and the blow was a calculated one. I did not lose my temper.

However, *The Times* parliamentary correspondent, Hugh Noyes, described it in the following terms:

Miss Bernadette Devlin, arms flailing and fists flying, launched herself across the House of Commons today in an attack on the Home Secretary, Mr Maudling, as that normally unflappable minister was answering questions on the events in Northern Ireland at the weekend.

Mr Maudling's glasses were sent flying as the diminutive mini-skirted M.P. for Mid-Ulster threw herself at the government front bench. The Home Secretary had already been called a liar several times by Miss Devlin, but words, for once, appeared to fail her as she was about to embark on another verbal attack. 'That murdering hypocrite' was all that could be heard above the uproar as she took off from her seat on the Opposition back benches. . . .

As she leapt on the Home Secretary, one flying elbow caught Mr Heath who was sitting beside Mr Maudling. The latter seemed to make little attempt to defend himself except to throw up his arms to protect his face . . . .

Finally, Miss Devlin, her long dark tresses flying, was carried from the

Chamber by M.P.s. To the astonishment of all, she returned a few minutes later and defiantly resumed her seat.

However, the official record, *Hansard*, gives us a very different picture of the affair:

MISS DEVLIN: On a point of order, Mr Speaker.
MR SPEAKER: At the end of the statement, please, I should like the Right Hon. Gentleman to finish his statement.
MISS DEVLIN: Is it in order for the Minister to lie to this House?
MR SPEAKER: Order . . . .
MISS DEVLIN: On a point of order, Mr Speaker. That is the second time the Minister has stood up and lied to the House. Nobody shot at the paratroops, but somebody will shortly.
MR SPEAKER: That is not a point of order . . . .
MISS DEVLIN: On a point of order, I am the only person in this House who was present yesterday when, whatever the facts of the situation might be said — (*Interruption*) Shut up! I have a right, as the only representative of this House who was an eye-witness, to ask a question of this murdering hypocrite —
HON MEMBERS: Order!
MISS DEVLIN: I will ask him a question —
MR SPEAKER: Order. The Hon. Lady has no such right. She has that right only if she is called by me.
MISS DEVLIN rose — (*Interruption*)

In this particular instance the words spoken were all recorded except when there was a confused blur of sound. Few secretaries are required to record meetings verbatim, however, and there are not many secretaries with a sufficiently high speed of shorthand to take down verbatim minutes.

Some items must be very fully recorded; these include decisions and directions about actions to be taken. The recording of resolutions must be verbatim. Such minutes are called 'minutes of resolution'.

'Minutes of narration' require the Secretary to summarise what is being said as it is being said. This is not easy at times. for the Secretary may well not be sure about the value of the discussion. The following may help:

(a) the minutes must be impartial and balanced, so record differing points of view
(b) keep your notes as short as possible, but remember that you will need to be able to read them at a later date
(c) record the names of the persons speaking — they will not normally be included in the minutes, but are useful as a reference point
(d) make sure a list is made of all present
(e) relate your minute items to the agenda items — if your agenda is a good one, it should help you

(f)　distinguish between items under 'Any Other Business'

(g)　draft the minutes as soon as possible so that you have a clear recollection of the meeting (but do not rely on your memory!)

(h)　keep your notes until the minutes have been signed.

Comprehension and interpretation are an integral part of minute-taking, particularly for a formal policy-making committee. The Secretary must always be prepared to ask for clarification at a meeting and must avoid ambiguous drafting.

2　PRESENTATION

(a) *Style*

The sole purpose of minutes is a factual one. The style of writing should be concise and accurate.

(b) *Use of names*

In the general body of the minutes, names are normally omitted. However, there are occasions when they should be included, as follows:

(i) LIST OF MEMBERS PRESENT

Such a list is usually headed by the Chairman's name, with the other names following in alphabetical order, for example:

Present: W. N. White (Chairman)	Miss T. S. Green
U. R. Black	P. M. Orange
V. Z. Brown	Dr N. L. Red

(ii) APOLOGIES FOR ABSENCE

These are listed in a similar way:

Apologies for absence were received from C. Cherry, E. Hall, Mrs B. Williams and H. Wood.

(iii) ELECTIONS

Names of persons elected to office are recorded.

(iv) RESOLUTIONS

Names of proposers and seconders of resolutions are often included:

It was proposed by Mr V. Z. Brown, seconded by Mr P. M. Orange, that: 'the meeting should adopt the Secretary's report without amendment'. The motion was carried unanimously.

NOTE: This might as easily be found expressed as follows:

The Secretary's report was received and unanimously adopted without amendment.

(v) ACTION

The names of people who have agreed to perform duties or who are required to take action will either be minuted or included in a separate action column.

(c) *Resolutions*

Resolutions often have a formal layout. Examples may be seen in (b) (iv) above and in Figure 33.

(d) *Layout*

The layout of minutes follows closely that suggested for reports. The minutes should have a heading, which will be followed by details of time, date and venue of the meeting.

The lists of people present and apologies will then be given, followed by the other items on the agenda, each numbered and with an appropriate heading. An example is given in Figure 33. The same pattern within the minutes should be adopted for all formal resolutions.

(e) *Numbering*

Numbering of minutes normally takes one of the following forms:

(i) the minutes are numbered consecutively, starting with number 1 for the first item of each set of minutes

(ii) the first set of minutes is numbered, as described above. If it is supposed that the last item on this set is numbered 9, then the first item on the minutes of the next meeting would become number 10, and so on. Thus no two minutes of the meetings of this committee would bear the same number.

(iii) a similar system is used here, but the numbers run through one year, calendar or financial, only. At the beginning of a new year the minutes will once again start with number 1.

The order of the minute items is often very similar to that used for the agenda of the meeting. The minutes of the Traders Limited Staff Association Committee meeting, for example, for which the agenda is given in Figure 33, might start as shown in Figure 37.

It will be noted that minutes do not exactly follow the agenda where 'Matters Arising' are concerned. This would also have happened had there been no matters arising, or no apologies. The items would then have been omitted from the minutes entirely.

(f) *Recording any other business (AOB)*

This item would be dispensed with if there were no discussion under that heading. Indeed, the heading itself should never appear in minutes. Any discussion under it at the meeting will be given an appropriate place in the minutes but as a separate and distinct item (or items).

The following shows how a Secretary's note on AOB might look when turned into minutes.

Secretary's notes	**Minutes**
7. *AOB*	7. CANTEEN PRICES
MR BROWN *Complaints re canteen prices. Up 20% in 18 months. Beyond a joke.*	The attention of the meeting was drawn to the further increase in canteen prices. Although subsidised, they were now 20 per cent dearer

MR GREEN	*Still subsidised.*
MISS PINK	*Should complain. Disgraceful.*
CHAIRMAN	*Do you want us to complain formally?*
	AGREED
MR GREEN	*Tennis in summer. Can we use local courts again? Plenty of people would like to.*
CHAIRMAN	*Hope so. Ask Sec. to enquire. Are we going to hire as an Association again?*
	YES
CHAIRMAN	*How many nights a week? Which months?*
MISS PINK	*Two. May-Sep inc.*
MR BROWN	*One enough — didn't use two most of last year.*
MR GREEN	*Yes we did — except for August.*
CHAIRMAN	*Shall we try for two then?*
	YES
	No O.B. Closure 4.45

than eighteen months ago. The meeting agreed that a formal complaint should be made.

8. USE OF TENNIS COURTS
The Secretary was asked to enquire about the possibility of the Association hiring the Park tennis courts for two nights a week for months of May to September inclusive.

There being no other business, the Chairman declared the meeting closed at 4.45 p.m.

(g) *Repetition*
The Minutes Secretary often finds that discussion at a meeting sways backwards and forwards between agenda items. She will have to note this as it occurs but, in writing the minutes, she must omit repetitive matter and re-arrange the discussion to fit logically under the appropriate heading, again usually following the order in the agenda.

(h) *Signature*
One copy, or the minute book copy, of the minutes is put before the Chairman at the next meeting. Once the meeting has agreed that the minutes are a correct record, the Chairman is authorised to sign them.

(i) *Minutes book*
Minutes may either be kept in a loose-leaf binder or may be written in a bound minutes book. They are compulsorily required for companies under the Companies Act.

There are advantages in having a loose-leaf book:

(i) minutes may be typed and duplicated easily for circulation
(ii) copies of past minutes may be made easily
(iii) if required, relevant reports and other data can be filed with the minutes
(iv) corrections that are too long to be made on the existing minute sheet can be inserted easily.

However, adequate precautions must be taken against the minutes being removed deliberately, or, having been removed for copying, being lost. Such precautions are specified in the Companies Act and will include having lockable binders and numbered minute forms.

```
                    TRADERS LIMITED STAFF ASSOCIATION

Minutes of the 64th Committee meeting of the Staff Association
held on Friday, 20th May, 19--, at 5.30 p.m. in the Board Room.

Present:   R. Right (Chairman)
           Miss B. Able
           P. Briggs
           Miss R. Field
           G. Heard
           Mrs Q. Mudd
           C. A. Risk


                                                             ACTION

1.  APOLOGIES FOR ABSENCE
           Apologies for absence were received from G. D. Fish
           and T. Mann.

2.  MINUTES
           The Minutes of the meeting of 22nd April, 19--, were
           taken as read.  The following amendment was made:

             Minute No. 4.  The name of Mr R. Garnett was incorrect
             and was changed to read 'Mr P. Garratt'.

           The minutes were then approved as a correct record and
           signed by the Chairman.

3.  MATTERS ARISING

           Minute No. 7.  The meeting was informed that permission    Secretary to
           has been received from the Managing Director for the       acknowledge
           Annual General Meeting to be held on 6th July, 19--, in
           the canteen.

4.  SUBSCRIPTIONS
           The meeting considered a proposal from Mr G. Heard,
           seconded by Miss R. Field, for a change in the annual
           subscription.  It was pointed out that the present
           subscription had not been raised for five years and it
           was inadequate for the Association's present expenses.

           It was unanimously resolved

             'THAT this Committee recommend to the Association at
             the Annual General Meeting that the annual subscription
             for the year beginning 1st August, 19-- shall be £1.
```

Figure 37   Minutes

(j) *Indexing*

As minutes of meetings accumulate from year to year it is often difficult to identify quickly when a subject under discussion at a meeting was considered previously. An index is necessary to show when subjects have been discussed (and what decisions were made, if possible).

This will be done most easily by giving each minute sheet an indexing title and number. Then a visible index binder in alphabetical and date order or a separate alphabetical card index can be kept. The former would be most convenient for use at meetings.

Minute-writing has been considered in some detail because, although it is not often included in examinations, it is frequently an important part of the Secretary's work and is a prime example of the practical use of the techniques of summarising.

```
             BLANKSHIRE COLLEGE STUDENTS' UNION

                   Annual General Meeting

                 16th May, 19--, 5.30 p.m.


                          AGENDA

        1.  Minutes of the Annual General Meeting of
            14th May, 19--

        2.  Matters arising from the Minutes

        3.  Chairman's Report

        4.  Treasurer's Report

        5.  Election of Officers

            The following nominations have been received:

            Chairman      Mr D. Whittle
            Proposed by:  Mr R. Longstaff
            Seconded by:  Miss N. Prince

            Treasurer  1. Mr P.R. Stoke    2. Mr G.O. Owen
            Proposed by:  Mr D. Whittle       Miss T. Winn
            Seconded by:  Mr S. Derry         Mr C. Old

            Secretary     Miss N. Prince
            Proposed by:  Miss T. Winn
            Seconded by:  Mr G.O. Owen

        6.  Affiliation to the National Union of Students

        7.  Annual Subscription

        8.  Any other business
```

Figure 38 Exercise 1 — agenda

EXERCISES

MINUTES

1. Draft the minutes for a meeting for which the agenda is given in Figure 38. Invent all necessary detail.
2. Write out the minutes of the Comlon Ltd Staff Club Committee meeting, suitably expanding the rough notes written on the agenda in Figure 39.

(LCC Private Secretary's Certificate)

A meeting of the Staff Club Committee of Comlon will be held in Room 10 at 1700 hours on 22 June, 19——.

Present: McBee (chair) *
Renshaw (Hon. Sec.)
Davies (Treasurer)
Kerr (Sports Sec.) Britton,
Court, Cooper, Turner

AGENDA

APOLOGIES FOR ABSENCE Hurst Roberts Bolton

MINUTES OF PREVIOUS MEETING OK

MATTERS ARISING FROM MINUTES Nil

CORRESPONDENCE Letters of thanks (re hospital visiting + gifts) received from P. O'Grady, M. Daniels, H. Francis

HON. TREASURER'S REPORT Pleased with balance in hand of £150 but this will be eaten into as expensive barbecue coming up.

ARRANGEMENTS FOR BARBECUE 8 Sept. – evening. Appointed sub-committee to work out details – viz. White, Mason, Parks, Patel.

PROPOSED BADMINTON TOURNAMENT This was sports highlight of '77, so agreed to repeat it between early Sept. and end Oct.

ANY OTHER BUSINESS Proposals for changes to Constitution to be discussed next time (for members' approval at next AGM)

DATE OF NEXT MEETING Fortnight's time – same time + place.

Figure 39 Exercise 2 — agenda and minute notes

3. The following is an extract from the notes made by a Secretary at a meeting. Draft the appropriate minute items with an action column.

4. RESEARCH AND DEVELOPMENT EXTENSION

Chair	Now have architects' plans and costings.
Jones	Copies?
Chair	Costings — distribution next week. Smith, will you arrange?
Smith	Yes. How many and to whom?

Chair	Sec will let you have list. Plans and model on view — foyer — from next week.
Smith	When can we finalise?
Chair	Suggest at next month's meeting.
Frost	Building to commence?
Chair	Hope next Jan, completion Aug.
	Always dependent on weather. But going to USA Sep and want opening ceremony first.
Frost	Who to open? Suggest royalty — after all very important export possibilities.
Smith	What about TUC? Unions very helpful and want to keep good ind. rel.
Jones	Why not someone in the Co.? From grass roots? Must be innovative — why someone well known?
Frost	Publicity.
Jones	Might get more if do something different.
Chair	Much too soon to talk about. Suggest on agenda about 3 months before completion.
Frost	Too late to get anyone.
Chair	OK. Will put on earlier. Satis? Let's move on. Time getting short.

AGREED

5.		Date of next meeting
		Thurs 9 Mar 10.30 Brd Rm
6.		AOB
Jones		New computer. When payroll going on?
Chair		Soon.
Frost		2 months' time but problems in programming.
Jones		Always are! Months behind already. Disgraceful. Someone incompetent.
Frost		Resent that accusation. Not the programmers' fault.
Jones		Not A/cs Dept either. We've not been given necessary help. Want to have a firm date so that can train my people for new system.
Chair		Is firm date possible?
Frost		No.
Chair		When can we have one?
Frost		Next month. By the way — have looked at the ancillary equip. you suggested at last meeting. It's OK. We'll need to spend an extra £5000 on software.
Smith		Propose that authorised expenditure on the agreed additional equipment be increased by £5000. Let's get on with it — we've been here for hours!
Frost		Second.

Chair	Agreed?
Jones	No — abstain — not convinced but not against.

CARRIED NEM. CON.

Smith	How's new advert. camp. going?
Chair	Told it's going well. Only in S of Eng until next month then all over country.
Frost	My wife likes TV commercial.
Jones	What about costs?
Chair	Reasonable consid. coverage getting.

CLOSURE 12.15

4. How would you minute the following?

   (a) a resolution
   (b) an amendment to the minutes of the previous meeting
   (c) a request by one committee member that his dissent be recorded
   (d) the taking of the chair by the Vice-Chairman in the Chairman's absence.

5. The following items appear on the agenda of a meeting to be attended by your chief:

   (a) absences
   (b) minutes of previous meetings
   (c) finance
   (d) contract with Jones and Co.

   Expand each item to show how it might appear in the Minute Book, inventing any details you think necessary.

   (LCC Private Secretary's Certificate)

6. Some organisations tape record the proceedings of their meetings instead of having a shorthand writer present. Unless such tape recording is done professionally, this method can have many disadvantages. What difficulties have to be overcome both in recording a meeting on tape and in subsequently transcribing from that tape?

   (LCC Private Secretary's Diploma)

GENERAL QUESTIONS

The following questions require knowledge of matters discussed in Section 9 as well as in this section, and require also some common sense and initiative.

7. At the Annual General Meeting of the Chilbury Tennis Club the chair-

man put forward a motion to recommend the adoption of the club accounts for the preceding year together with the report of the Away-
Fixtures Committee.

Mr *W*, a member, moved 'as an amendment' that the accounts and
report be not adopted. The chairman asked those voting against this
amendment to raise their hands and declared that the amendment had
been defeated. He then asked those in favour of the motion to adopt
the accounts and report to raise their hands. He then declared the
motion carried.

The next item on the agenda was the increase of the auditor's fees to
£50. Mr *X* moved that this be approved. Mr *Y* seconded the motion.
Mr *Z*, a member, moved an amendment to substitute £40 for £50. A
discussion followed during which some speakers supported the motion
and some the amendment. Mr *Z* then rose and decided to withdraw his
amendment. The chairman thereupon asked those in favour of the
motion to raise their hands and declared the motion carried.

(a) Explain the errors in procedure, if any, at the above meeting.
(b) Assuming that the correct procedure had been followed, draft
minutes covering these two items of business.

(RSA Diploma for Personal Assistants)

8. In connection with the minutes of meetings:

(a) Describe two methods of indicating who was present at a
meeting.
(b) Explain the meaning of 'in attendance'.
(c) Describe two ways of displaying item headings.
(d) Distinguish between minutes of resolution and minutes of narration.
(e) Explain the procedure for signing minutes.

(LCC Private Secretary's Certificate)

9. Prepare the agenda, showing at least eight items, of the Annual General
Meeting of a social club. Assuming that you have attended this meeting
and taken the minutes, write up the first three items.

(Scottish HND in Secretarial Studies)

10. As Secretary dealing with the work of an important Committee:

(a) Explain how you could find out quickly the date of the meeting on which a certain topic was first discussed.
(b) Discuss the advantages and disadvantages of a loose-leaf
minute book compared with a bound one.
(c) An item in the minutes of the last meeting (already recorded

in the minute book) is inaccurate. Explain how it can be put right and under which item on the agenda the matter should be raised.

(d) Comment on the difference between 'postponing' and 'adjourning' a meeting.

(LCC Private Secretary's Certificate)

11. You work for an executive who acts as Secretary to a committee. You help him to prepare for and follow-up the monthly meetings, and attend to take the minutes.

(a) How will you ensure that each agenda you draft for his consideration is as accurate and complete as you can make it?

(b) A letter arrives raising an urgent matter which should be discussed by the committee. However, it is August and no meeting is scheduled for that month. Your employer is ill and cannot be consulted. What would you do, and why?

(LCC Private Secretary's Certificate)

12. As a Secretary you may be concerned with arranging, attending and recording proceedings of meetings. How would the degree of formality or informality of a meeting affect these duties?

(LCC Private Secretary's Certificate)

13. At a meeting shortly to be held by your company many visitors who are not eligible to vote have been invited. Suggest a procedure to be followed on the day of the meeting to ensure that a separate record is obtained of members and visitors present and that those voting on a show of hands are in fact members entitled to vote and not visitors.

(LCC Private Secretary's Certificate)

14. A works consultative committee has been set up in your firm and you are appointed Secretary. Describe the correct procedure for calling a meeting, the duties of the secretary before and during the meeting and state the points you would bear in mind in writing up the minutes afterwards.

(RSA Diploma for Personal Assistants)

15. Explain the usual duties that the Secretary of any organisation has in connection with meetings.

(RSA Diploma for Personal Assistants)

11

ORAL COMMUNICATION

Oral communication is a unique method of giving information because, except for telephone conversations, it is direct — that is, face to face. The speaker has more means of conveying information than the writer. Both use words, though the speaker will use more of them: but she can also use indications of tone, facial expression and gesture to add layers of meaning to, or even to change the meaning of, the words pronounced.

A reprimand, for example, will be reinforced by a stern tone and serious facial expression, or it may be softened if given in a less formal manner. Such a remark as *Drop in and see us sometime* may convey that literal meaning. It may also be spoken in a manner which conveys the opposite: *Don't come near us again!*

Oral communication has several advantages over the written word. Most important is its immediacy. If the listener's response is negative, whether by spoken disapproval or a look of boredom or incomprehension, then the speaker can immediately elaborate on the information given or correct any mistakes. There is thus a better chance of understanding (which is not the same thing as agreement) being more quickly reached than if written communication had been used. Going along and talking to someone rather than writing to him may well make agreement over a problem easier to reach. The advantages of meetings have been discussed in earlier sections.

The enormous use made of the telephone in business emphasises its advantages of speed and also of economy. Nowadays even a long-distance telephone call is likely to be cheaper than sending a letter.

There are some disadvantages, however, in the use of oral communication, principally because a conversation has no permanent record and memories are notoriously inaccurate. Inaccuracy may occur for a variety of reasons, including some of the following:

1. the listener may not be receptive to the views being expressed by the speaker
2. the speaker may be using a language which, either because it is imprecise or too specialised, will be lacking in meaning to the listener
3. the listener may not have sufficient background knowledge of the subject under discussion, that is, the frame of reference may not be adequate.

In addition oral communication is often less carefully prepared in the speaker's mind than a written message would be. It is often less concise and nearly always less precise.

SPEAKING

The disadvantages mentioned above lead to a consideration of the value of clear speech. However well one's thoughts are expressed in terms of language used, and however well-chosen words may be to appeal to the particular listener, the ability to speak clearly is imperative. Little emphasis is placed nowadays upon the necessity to suppress all traces of accent, provided that the clarity of what is being said is not obscured. Indeed, many people would say that they welcome the shades of expression and intonation heard in the voices of people who come from different parts of the United Kingdom or elsewhere. What is necessary, however, is that one should not allow one's voice to jar on the ear of the recipient. A pleasant voice is an asset. So, too, is the ability to articulate clearly and to talk at a speed that is neither too fast to obscure comprehension nor too slow to induce in the listener a desire to fall asleep.

Anyone who has had elocution or singing lessons will know that the voice is an instrument that can be played, just as a violin can be played, and that its pitch can be altered and modulation introduced to make it more pleasant.

The effective speaker needs to understand how to gain, and hold, the attention of the audience, large or small. To gain attention appropriate use of loudness or softness of voice, of movement and gesture and of the intensity and forcefulness with which the words are delivered will be required. In retaining the listener's attention sensitivity to the listener's reactions, adjustment to that reaction, the uses of pauses, repetition and a systematic arrangement of content are important.

The need to plan written communication is easily recognised. The need to plan what one wishes to say (except on the most formal occasions) is often overlooked. Even a short five-minute presentation, giving perhaps a brief report, is likely to be more comprehensible and persuasive if it is structured carefully.

It is wise to make the most important and interesting points early in one's presentation to attract and retain the listener's attention. The speaker should indicate his plan by outlining briefly the scope of his topic. He should use sign-posts during his talk, such as: *First, I shall explain . . .; Next . . .; Finally . . . .* At the end of his talk he will repeat himself by a brief recap of what he has said.

LISTENING

It has already been said that communication is a two-way process and the role of the listener is not a passive one. Considering how much time we spend listening, it is surprising that most people do it so ineffectively.

Studies into efficient listening have revealed the remarkable fact that re-call of facts and understanding of principles described by speakers in ten-minute periods is very low. Immediately after the speaker has finished, recall is only 50 per cent. Two weeks later it will be only 25 per cent.

Learning to listen effectively requires a recognition of some of the causes of inattentive listening, and how to overcome them.

1   UNINTERESTING SUBJECT

If a subject appears superficially uninteresting or irrelevant, the listener often 'switches off' and thinks of something else. A good listener will decide that he can learn something worth while or useful and concentrate on discovering it. Remember that G. K. Chesterton once said 'there is no such thing as an un-interesting subject. There are only uninterested people'.

2   DISTRACTIONS

The ineffective listener is easily distracted by bad delivery or by a speaker's irritating mannerisms and fails to notice the significance of what is being said. The hum of background noise, and the state of the weather observed through the window, are sufficient to distract some listeners.

3   DIFFICULTY

Technical or difficult subject-matter or terminology, instead of acting as a challenge, cause many listeners to 'opt out'.

The good listener will try to avoid these, and other, pitfalls and take a more positive approach. Looking at the speaker will help you to concentrate and will assist the speaker by showing him that he has your full attention. Con-centrate on listening to only one speaker, for example when answering the telephone in a busy room, or at an interview. Try to develop the ability to identify the real information among the padding.

WORDS

Having ascertained that you are speaking pleasantly, you should then move on to considering your use of language and additionally to considering your listener. Provided that the listener is in a fairly receptive frame of mind, he should be asking himself three questions as he listens to you:

(a)   What does the speaker mean, that is, what is she trying to say?
(b)   What basis has she for her communication, for example, what are the facts that have led her to this conclusion?
(c)   What may she be leaving out (either deliberately or accidentally)?

1   DIFFERENT MEANINGS

Our concern is not merely for the words used by the speaker. The same word will mean a different thing to different people, because we all have varied lives and experience and we attach different values to the same word. Our 'frames of reference' vary. Even the common words of the English language have very many meanings. In fact, the 500 most common words in our language have a total of some 14,000 meanings listed in the *Oxford English Dictionary*. Here is one example of a very simple word, the word *run*, which has a multitude of meanings, only sixteen of which are given here.

RUN

to move the legs quickly
a single spell or act of running
a small stream or watercourse
a continuous stretch of something
a regular track made by certain animals
the part of a ship's bottom which rises from the keel and narrows
   towards the stern
to unravel
to coagulate — of milk
to come to the end of a period of time
to be played continuously — of a play
to issue a writ, for example, the Bow Runners
a landing of illicitly imported goods
a sudden fall of earth
a sudden rush on a bank
an enclosure for domestic animals

Some of these meanings are common and would probably cause very little difficulty, but others have very specialist purposes.

2   IMPRECISION

It is a common failing to use language which is imprecise. An example of the problem can be seen in the use of an apparently simple word, *event*. To most of us an event is, quite plainly, something that happens. The dictionary definition is *the fact of a thing's happening; a thing that happens, especially an important thing*. To a specialist in operational research, drawing up a critical path analysis to find out the minimum time that it will take to complete a complex task, an *event* means the end of one activity and the beginning of another. An event will be shown on a critical path diagram by a circle but nothing is actually happening at that time. Imprecise language comes also in the use of words and phrases such as *vast, like, pretty, fairly often*, and *a lot of*. These are vague and indefinite.

3   THOU SHALT NOT KILL: THOU SHALT NOT STEAL

An effective example of the use of simple words comes in the Bible, where the art of verbal presentation is superbly illustrated. Although this is a book, and therefore is written rather than oral communication, much of the material was originally handed on by word of mouth so that it is an appropriate example of the spoken word. The Ten Commmandments take 284 words, of which 217 words are of one syllable and of which only ten are more than two. We may have to admit that each and every one of us often breaks one or more of the Ten Commandments, but we may also have to admit that we are unlikely to misunderstand them. The language is precise in the extreme.

Such precision is the exception rather than the rule unfortunately. There are many imprecise terms and they are more commonly found in oral communication than when information is written.

4   SPECIALISED VOCABULARY

Perhaps the most difficult area of language, and the one where the greatest problems in the use of words arise, is the area of specialised language. We now have psychologists, technologists, computer men, administration men and others who are building up their own empires. Many of these people have by necessity had to establish special terms to describe special processes. However, we now find that it is becoming increasingly difficult for the specialist to talk to the layman, because so many of the words he uses are unintelligible to the ordinary person. Other jargon words that one meets are found more often in written communication, such as the commercialese mentioned in the section on letter writing.

5   EMOTIVE TERMS

A further instance of our inability to use clear language occurs when we become emotional. There are many words in our language that now have a very definite air of prejudice about them, for instance, *red, coloured, teenager*. The angry man will also use terms and epithets that he would not be tempted to use in the cold clear light of reason. (This is incidentally a compelling reason for restraining oneself from the discussion of issues with another person at a time when one is annoyed with that person.)

OTHER BARRIERS

1   FEAR AND DISLIKE

Oral communication can fail when either the imparter or the recipient of the information is governed by fear, whether it be of giving a wrong impression to the boss or of being thought a fool. Communication is affected by the fact that we like some people and dislike others and so allow our feelings about the sender or receiver to influence us.

Similarly we can be affected by the knowledge that we have acted in a way which annoyed someone else. We subconsciously expect the other person to feel some hostility towards us (which may or may not be true). Thus we may adopt a defensive posture in future communication and set up yet another barrier.

2   UNINTENTIONAL COMMUNICATION

Unconscious communication is the, often small, *extra* gestures which we add to the words that we are speaking or by which we betray our thoughts when we are listening. These extras can be expression in the voice, such as the sarcastic tone or the laugh, or they may be the look on the face: the smile, the downturned mouth or the twitch of the nostrils. Finally, it may be our gestures that give us away: the glance at the watch, the doodling on a piece of paper or the playing with a pencil.

3   TOO MUCH INFORMATION, TOO EARLY

The total content or timing of a communication affects its success. If we try to communicate too many facts or ideas at a time then communication will probably fail. People can only absorb so much at any one time. If the communication is too long, then the earlier parts of the message will be forgotten as later items are imparted. Additionally, information given at too early a stage will sometimes be forgotten before the time comes for it to be used.

4   LINKS IN THE CHAIN

The more hands a message passes through, the less likely it is to arrive at its final destination without being radically altered. You will no doubt remember the children's party game where a whisper is started at one end of the room and repeated by each person in turn to her neighbour until it reaches the last child. By this time it is inevitably much shorter and often totally different in context.

This, of course, is what happens to rumours — the 'grapevine' — but it can also happen to other oral communication unless great care is taken to keep the number of links in the chain as short as possible.

5   CRY 'WOLF'

A message repeated too often may lose its impact rather like the old story of the boy who cried 'Wolf'. After a time, people stop listening. They may *hear* the message, but they do not assimilate it and act upon it.

A LOGICAL APPROACH

Most of us find talking easier than writing, probably because we feel that when we talk we can use phrases that would not be acceptable in a written communication, slang for instance. It is unfortunately not true that good oral communication is the easier medium. Equally it is a mistake to assume that written communication of any length deserves planning, but that talking does not require it. Few people, even if expert in their subjects, would wish to give an hour's lecture totally unprepared, while the same people might enter into an important discussion having given very little thought to their subject, their approach to it or to their listeners. Planning what you are going to say is just as important as planning what you are going to write.

From this it should not be assumed that oral communication should be so rigidly planned that it cannot be changed. The flexibility that one enjoys in talking must be maintained, but the approach must be as thorough as with the other media.

TELEPHONE TECHNIQUES

A neglected area of secretarial training is that of the use of the telephone. Secretaries, even when experienced, may find themselves in difficulties when dealing with relatively routine calls, let alone those that require tact.

Consider the following script of a telephone conversation. In it there are ten major errors. Write these down and compare your answers with those given in Appendix 4.

The scene is the Sales Manager's office. He is out. The telphone rings and his secretary answers it.

SECRETARY:	Hello.
CALLER:	Can I speak to the Sales Manager, please?
SECRETARY:	No, I'm sorry, he is out.
CALLER:	Who is that speaking, please?
SECRETARY:	His secretary.
CALLER:	Oh! Well, I wonder if you can help me.
SECRETARY :	Yes?
CALLER:	I put in an order for six gross of your BX45 six weeks ago and I have not yet received them. The order number is 456940 and your invoice number is 005746.
SECRETARY:	Just a sec. I'll have to get a pencil and paper. *(She puts the receiver on the desk and fetches a pencil and a piece of scrap paper)*
SECRETARY:	Hello, I've got something to write on now. Give me the information again.
CALLER:	Six gross BX45 ordered six weeks ago. Order number 456940; your invoice number 005746. *(Secretary scribbles furiously)*
SECRETARY:	Just a moment. What was the order number?
CALLER:	456940.
SECRETARY:	And the invoice number was 5746?
CALLER:	No!! 005746.
SECRETARY:	O.K. I've got that. *(knock on the door)*
SECRETARY:	Come in. *(Jane enters)* Hello, Jane! *(To caller)* Hang on, please. *(To Jane)* Shan't be long, but Mr James is out and I've got to deal with his calls. *(To caller)* Was there anything else?
CALLER:	Well, I want to know when I can expect delivery. Can you get Mr James to ring me?
SECRETARY:	All right, but he won't be in till late this afternoon.
CALLER:	I shall be in until 5.30.
SECRETARY:	I'll ask him to ring, then. Good-bye.

(She notes something on the paper)
(She replaces the receiver, leaves the paper on her boss's desk and goes out of the room with Jane)
The message reads:
'6 gross BX not sent. Their order 456940.
Invoice 005746. Please ring today re delivery.'

You may have found it relatively easy to spot the mistakes, but if you watch and listen to some telephone conversations you will soon find that there are many common errors.

The overriding impression that any firm wishes to convey to the outside world will be that of a progressive, efficient organisation, anxious to give good service. Telephone calls play a major role in creating the image of the company. Callers will tend to attribute to the organisation the personality characteristics of the secretary to whom they talk on the telephone. If the recipient is indifferent, inaudible, inattentive, inane, incompetent or inconsiderate, the firm's public image will indubitably suffer.

The poor impression given by many people during a telephone call may be partly accounted for by the failure to realise the difference between this kind of oral communication and face-to-face communication. Expression, gestures and appearance cannot help the telephone caller. The smile has to be in the voice and smiling when you speak does help to give your voice a pleasant tone. You should aim at being polite, friendly, helpful and considerate.

Here is a check-list of dos and don'ts which should help you to assess your effectiveness when you answer a telephone call.

DO YOU?

1. Answer promptly?
2. Always have pencil and message pad handy.
3. Answer with the appropriate information, for example,
   'Good morning. Extension 340. Miss Smith speaking.'
4. Speak into the mouthpiece.
5. Speak pleasantly and distinctly.
6. Try to recognise the voices of people you should know and use their names.
7. Assure people who may have to wait for information that they have not been forgotten.
8. Take messages correctly, write them out so that the recipient will be able to read them easily and put them where he will see them.
9. Exercise self-control when callers are annoyed or impatient.
10. Know enough about the company, for instance to reroute calls that have been put through to you in error.
11. Exercise discretion.
12. Have the same manners and consideration for everyone, from your Managing Director to the stupid customer making a frivolous complaint.

13. Admit it when you do not know the answer to a query.
14. Leave instructions when you are expecting a call and have to go out of the office.

IT IS HOPED THAT YOU DON'T

1. Misuse the instrument.
2. Use slang or clumsy phrases.
3. Sound curt or rude.
4. Ask first 'who is speaking?' before saying first that the person required is out.
5. Carry on a conversation with someone else in the room.
6. Call across the room to someone who is wanted on the telephone.
7. Lose your temper.

MESSAGES

The taking of messages combines oral and written communication. The efficient secretary will ensure that by both her own telephone and that of her boss stands message pads, such as that shown below:

TELEPHONE MESSAGE

Date.. . . . . .Time. . . . .
For. . . . .
From: Name . . . .
Company. . . . .
(and address) . . . .
. . . .
Telephone No. . . . .
(and extension)
Message. . . . .
. . . .
. . . .
. . . .
Taken by. . . . .

Had such a pad been available at the time of the telephone conversation given earlier, the secretary might have left a coherent message, such as this:

TELEPHONE MESSAGE

Date . . . .*23rd March 19—* . . . . Time. . . .   *10.45*. . . .
For. . . . . *Mr R. James*. . . . .
From: Name . . . . *Mr W. Brown* . . . .
Company. . . . . *Fosters Limited*. . . . .

(and address) . . . . *26 Green Lane, Reading* . . . .

. . . .

Telephone No. . . . . *Reading 46641 Ext. 344.* . . . .

(and extension)

Message. . . . .

. . . . *Mr Brown wants to know when he can expect delivery* . . . .

. . . . *of the six gross BX45 ordered six weeks ago. Their* . . . . . .

. . . . *order no. 456940; our invoice no. 005746. Please* . . . .

. . . . *ring him before 5.30 p.m. today.* . . . .

Taken by . . . . *Miss Jones* . . . .

EXERCISES

1. Suggest, with reasons, two occasions when you would consider it more appropriate to use oral communication in business rather than any other media.
2. What barriers to communication can affect oral communication and how may they be overcome?
3. Why is the meaningful use of language so important in achieving good communication?
4. Planning is as important with oral as it is with written communication. Why is this so? Illustrate your answer with some specific examples.
5. What are the advantages of an oral communication over a written communication?

(SCCAPE Advanced Secretarial Certificate)

6. (a) Write briefly on the disadvantages in general of an oral communication.
   (b) Indicate, with reasons, whether a telephone communication has advantages over a face-to-face situation.

(SCCAPE Advanced Secretarial Certificate)

7. Suggest a set of rules for the efficient use of the telephone in a business organisation.

(LCC Private Secretary's Certificate)

8. (a) What information should appear on any record of a telephone message?
   (b) How should you answer the telephone:
       (i) when an external call is transmitted to you from the switchboard?
       (ii) when an external call comes directly to you?

(iii) when a call which your employer requested comes through from the switchboard, but he has meanwhile gone out of the room?

(LCC Private Secretary's Certificate)

9.   Prepare a list of instructions to staff on the use of the telephone, bearing in mind the need for economy and efficiency in the firm.

(RSA Diploma for Personal Assistants)

10.   What in your opinion are the main defects that occur in the use of the telephone in business and how do you think they could be avoided?

12

INTERVIEWS

So, you are looking for a job? Perhaps it will be your first. Perhaps you have been a 'glamorous temp' for six months and the glamour has rubbed off. Perhaps you are looking for promotion and this means moving to a new firm. Whatever the reasons, when you apply for a job you are likely to be interviewed.

Interviews can take as many forms as can the interviewers themselves. Some secretaries will claim that they have never, in the course of several jobs, had to face a proper interview. The supply of qualified secretaries in big cities particularly has fallen so far short of demand over recent years that an employer would greet with glee the young, personable girl who could produce even minimal proof of ability to type and take shorthand. He would not have dreamt of subjecting her to the indignity of a barrage of questions or a selection test; indeed, he probably would not have dared to do so. He had a vacancy that had to be filled.

The picture is changing, however, particularly with 'top jobs'. Secretaries leave colleges with high-level qualifications, not only in the skill subjects but also in Secretarial Duties, Communication and Structure of Business. They demand work which offers them opportunities to use their skill and knowledge. They also demand, and get, high salaries. The employer, in turn, is becoming more and more selective as he realises what an asset a good secretary can be, and what havoc a bad one can wreak!

The application form, selection test and interview routine are being adopted more widely and it should therefore be of interest to the secretarial student to know something of what she might face. It is also useful to have some inkling of what employers seek and why they ask particular questions.

THE PAPER WORK

THE ADVERTISEMENT

Your first impression of a possible future employer will often come from the advertisement that you answer. This can sometimes reveal considerable information, not just about the job, but also about the employer. Study the two examples in Figure 40. Both refer to a similar type of job.

1.   Secretary wanted for Sales Manager. Must
      have good speeds. Minimum age 25. Good
      salary and holidays.

      Apply to:
                        Box 10
                        The Morning Clarion

2.   THE A.V.A. GOE COMPANY

                        requires

      a senior Secretary to the Sales Manager. The
      Company is a long established one, specialising
      in the manufacture of plastic containers, and
      has a wide home and overseas market.

      We are seeking to recruit an experienced
      secretary to join a vigorous and expanding
      sales team.

      Candidates should preferably be in the age
      range 25–40 with shorthand and typewriting
      speeds of 120/50 w.p.m. respectively.

      Salary by negotiation. Good working conditions.
      Three weeks annual holiday. Luncheon vouchers.
      Pension scheme.

      Apply in writing, giving details of background,
      qualifications, experience and salary required
      to:
                        Personnel Officer
                        Xford Trading Estate
                        Xford   XY3 2ZA

Figure 40   Job advertisements

The first tells you very little about the firm or the job, but the second gives you considerable information. Obviously much more thought has been given to the second in terms both of the information in which you may be interested and of setting out with some degree of precision what the company wants. This indicates that the second firm is a well-organised firm which has made some effort to define the jobs within it.

If the advertisement had asked, as some do, that interested people should write for further information and an application form, then here would be further evidence that the process of selecting new employees was carefully considered.

THE APPLICATION FORM

A well-designed application form will elicit much information about a candidate for employment. Personal data, such as age, sex, nationality, are usually requested. There will also be questions about educational and other qualifications and previous jobs. There should be space to note down any other relevant experience, which is particularly useful for those applying for their first secretarial posts. References will also be asked for at this stage.

THE JOB SPECIFICATION

The 'further information' sent out by a firm with the application form is based on a job specification, which will also have been used in drafting the advertisement. To arrive at the job specification the job itself must have been analysed and carefully described. Then the type of person who would be needed for this particular job will be described and requirements laid down for qualifications, skill and experience. For instance, a Sales Manager's secretary might have to take minutes of meetings as part of her job. It might therefore be decided that she should have a minimum shorthand speed of 120 w.p.m.

Some firms will have detailed and current job descriptions and specifications. Others will write them only when a vacancy arises. Many more will have them only for top management posts or not at all. However, the practice of analysing jobs is increasing, so it is more and more likely that the secretary will find that future jobs for which she applies will have been studied in this way.

The system has many advantages. It can, for instance, show clearly where a secretary's job allows ample time for knitting or painting finger-nails and can enable employers to introduce more productive tasks (or decide that the secretary is not needed at all, of course). It also enables the applicant to acquire full and precise details of the job. Selecting people for interview is also made easier. The candidates' letters and/or application forms will be compared with the job specification and the most likely applicants will then be shortlisted for interview.

The interview may also be preceded by:

1 SELECTION TESTING

Candidates may be asked to take a test to establish, for instance, their level of intelligence, numerical ability, or shorthand and typewriting skills.

2 TAKING UP REFERENCES

Where the applicant has been asked to give names of people to whom reference can be made (as opposed to testimonials) then these references can well be taken up before interview. This gives the interviewer yet more information.

So, even before the interview itself, much knowledge about the candidate is already available. The date and time of the interview is set and the candidate duly arrives.

THE INTERVIEWER

Who does the interviewing? This varies considerably from firm to firm. In small companies it may be the 'boss' who does all the hiring and firing and thus the interviewing.

Companies with specialist Personnel Departments often use a member of this department for at least part of the interviewing process. Sometimes the main interview will be with the Personnel Officer or his assistant, with merely a brief chat with the prospective boss. In other organisations the main interview will be with the man who needs the secretary and the Personnel Department will cover only the practical details such as salary, holidays, hours of work and contract of employment.

The applicant for a secretarial post will usually be interviewed by one person (or one at a time) but interviewing panels are common in some jobs. They are considered in more detail later in this section.

THE INTERVIEW

The nervous interviewee, who has walked the length of the room and is now seated in front of an imposing desk, confronted by a poker-faced individual, is scarcely likely to do herself justice. If the interview is to be effective, the interviewer must establish a *rapport* with the candidate. It is possible to achieve this in a fairly normal way, though some interviews are conducted more as seemingly casual chats, with the interviewer and candidate seated side by side in easy chairs in an informal setting.

The object of the interview is to elicit information from the candidate that will allow the interviewer to build up a picture of her, compare it both with the job specification and with his assessment of other applicants and make some prediction of likely future performance. Interviewers use various methods to do this. The interview may be conducted in one or a combination of the following ways.

1. *In depth*, with the interviewer having worked out in advance what main areas must be covered.
2. *Standardised*, often with a very comprehensive questionnaire, which the interviewer will go through with the candidate.
3. *Under stress*. Here the interviewer will deliberately seek to put the candidate on the defensive, to embarrass or annoy her, in order to discover how she can stand up to working under strain. This technique should only be used by a well-trained interviewer.

The interviewer will be trying to use the limited period of time to make as accurate an assessment as he can of the candidate's potential. Many efforts have been made to draw up a general plan which would help an interviewer in his task. One of the most widely accepted has been the Seven-Point Plan of the National Institute of Industrial Psychology. This plan has been amended over the years, as with the modification given below, which was developed by Elizabeth Sidney and Margaret Brown.

1.   *Personal data:* age, sex, home circumstances, marital status
2.   *Physique:* health, speech, manner and appearance
3.   *Education and technical qualifications and experience*

4. *Work or other experience*
5. *Mental abilities:* intelligence, verbal ability, speech and writing, mathematical ability
6. *Social roles:* gregarious/solitary, leader/follower, persuasive/organising
7. *Initiative:* self-starter/dependent, ability to work without supervision
8. *Emotional stability:* ability to tolerate stress, maturity
9. *Motivation:* goals and objectives, strength (drive)

The information under 1, 2 and 3 can be partly obtained from the letter or form of application and item 5 can be partially assessed through selection tests. Items 7, 8 and 9 are the most difficult to assess and it is here that the interviewer must be most skilful.

ASSESSMENT

When the interview is competed the interviewer will make a written assessment of the candidate so that he can eventually make his choice. Assessment forms are frequently used for this purpose, with the interviewer either filling in spaces with short comments or ranking candidates on a scale, such as that shown in Figure 41.

THE CANDIDATE

We have looked at the purposes of the interview and how it may be conducted. Now let us turn to the interviewee. The first priority is to be well prepared for the interview. This would include the following.

1. Study the advertisement and any further information carefully.
2. Write a good letter of application (see Section 4) and fill in any form very carefully and neatly.
3. Think about the interview and about the questions you may have to answer. It is useful to obtain some background information about the company prior to the interview.
4. Be prepared to talk fully about yourself, your past and your ambitions for the future (the interviewer will certainly not be impressed with monosyllabic answers).
5. Be ready with any queries you may have.
6. Remember that the initial impact is of importance so wear an outfit in which you feel smart, but which will also appeal to an interviewer who will possibly be much older and more conservative.
7. Remember the 'little things' about your appearance such as:
   (a) shining clean and tidy hair
   (b) discreet make-up
   (c) discreet perfume (he may not like his office smelling like a hothouse)

CANDIDATES FOR SECRETARIAL POST

Grade candidates on the following scale:

A. highly suitable for the post
B. suitable
C. suitable only if she receives, for example, further training or is relieved of some responsibility (please specify any reservations in the section headed 'Comments')
D. unsuitable

	A	B	C	D

EDUCATION
  1. General Education
    e.g. 'O' and 'A' levels, PSC, OND
  2. Skills				

JOB EXPERIENCE
  1. General Secretarial experience
  2. Other relevant experience				

BACKGROUND AND INTERESTS
  1. Stable personal background
  2. Interests and pursuits				

PERSONALITY
  1. Stable and mature
  2. Shows qualities of leadership
  3. Shows qualities of initiative
  4. Integrity and loyalty
  5. A warm and friendly personality				

MOTIVATION
  1. Ambition
  2. Realism of goal
  3. Degree of determination				

PHYSICAL IMPRESSION
  1. Health
  2. Physical appearance
  3. Dress and turnout
  4. Speech and manner				

COMMENTS				

Figure 41 Interview assessment form

(d)   clean (preferably unbitten) finger-nails
(e)   clothes that are clean, well-ironed or pressed and brushed
(f)   unladdered tights (take a spare pair)
(g)   clean shoes (including the backs of the heels) that are not in need of mending.

Be aware that, if you are good enough to be called for interview, then you are already, on paper, a possible for the job. So have confidence in yourself and do not allow the prospect of the interview to give you nightmares.

THE FIRST MINUTES

First impressions *are* important and not only to the interviewer. If you feel that you have not made a good start to the interview, it may inhibit your performance throughout.

1   ENTERING

The interview starts as soon as you walk through the door of the interview room. You are not required to make a 'grand entrance' like a star of one of the American musical extravaganzas of the 1930s, but it is important to walk in looking confident and carrying yourself well. Close the door firmly (but do not bang it) and move to the chair which seems obviously placed for you.

2   SITTING

Usually you will be asked to sit down. If you are not, pause briefly and then take the seat. Should anyone ever try on you the trick of placing *two* chairs and requiring you to make a choice, do not let it worry you. Choose the one which is in the position that *you* prefer.

When you sit down, try to do so with grace. Settle yourself comfortably in the chair, not on the edge, or in a lazy, slumped position. The feet should be firmly placed on the ground so that uncontrolled nerves cannot give you away. Your handbag should go on the floor beside you or on your lap. Resist the temptation to wriggle.

3   HANDS

What to do with one's hands is often a problem. Suddenly they seem large and awkward and have an uncontrollable tendency to tremble or twitch. Try placing one on top of the other, loosely, on your lap, resisting the temptation to twist them together. A determined effort to relax the hands can help in establishing a feeling of confidence. Never sit on your hands, twist a handkerchief between your fingers or play with a lock of hair or jewellery.

4   THE OPENING QUESTIONS

The first question should be answered especially clearly and distinctly as the interviewer will not have heard your voice before. Often the first few questions are fairly straighforward ones, designed to put you at your ease. They may have little or nothing to do with the job itself, for instance

> *Did you have a good journey?*

Interviewers do, however, sometimes ask a difficult question at the beginning, designed purposely to see how you react before you have had time to relax. Do not rush into your answer. Take a (not too obvious) deep breath and answer calmly and deliberately. One favourite question that sometimes seems to upset candidates is: 'Why have you applied for this job?' You should be able to answer this, particularly if you have followed the suggestions for interview preparation made earlier. Remember, however, that the interviewer is not likely to be impressed with answers such as:

> *I'm bored with the job I've got*
> *It looked interesting*
> *I should like to work with people*
> *The money is better.*

The interviewer's impression of you would probably be more satisfactory if the answers were more positive, for example

> *My present position offers less opportunity for me to use my qualifications than the position you are offering seems to do. It has been very useful and necessary experience for a first job, but I should now prefer something with better prospects.*

> *I have been in my present post for three years and there are no prospects for promotion. The post you advertised seems to offer the opportunity for varied and interesting work, with some responsibility and the possibility of advancement.*

FACING THE PANEL

As was mentioned earlier, interviews by a panel are held for some jobs. The following hints on panel interviews may be helpful.

1   THE SIZE

The panel may be of only two people or may consist of as many as seven or eight. One person will normally be the chairman or leader of the panel and will carry out the role of welcoming the candidate and putting the first question.

2   THE ROLES

Sometimes different members of the panel will adopt different roles with, perhaps, one specialising in asking technical questions while another asks questions about home background or about general interests. On other occasions one panel member will put rather piercing or aggressive questions while another will appear to be much more friendly. This is often a deliberate approach to assess how the candidate reacts to the change of mood. Where these two people are seated to the right and left of the panel respectively, the candidate has to cope not only with the abrupt switch of pace, but also with a switch of direction.

3 THE INTERVIEWEE

It is fairly safe to address an answer first of all directly to the person who asked the question but then, as you amplify it, turn the head to bring in the other members of the panel. This minimises the possibility that you will have to make a 90° turn to face the next questioner.

A panel often seems rather imposing and formal and it is difficult not to be a little inhibited by it. The suggestions made earlier should be as helpful with this type of interview as with any other.

4 THE QUESTIONS ASKED

Questions are likely to cover the following areas (the emphasis will vary according to your job and background):

(a) work experience
(b) general background
(c) education
(d) type of post wanted, or reasons for applying for the particular post
(e) reasons for taking up secretarial/business career
(f) the qualities required for the job
(g) problems demanding the use of initiative and inventiveness
(h) general interests and hobbies
(i) general knowledge, particularly of contemporary business and economic matters.

PURSUING YOUR ADVANTAGE

The interview having started well, you must ensure that it will continue in the same way.

1 THE INTERVIEWER'S REACTIONS

Just as the interviewer will be judging your reactions to his questions, so you must judge his reactions to your answers. This does not mean that you should deliberately try to create 'the right impression' by giving answers that are untrue or do not represent your opinions. Even if such a procedure were to be successful in obtaining the job for you (which is doubtful, for a pose is difficult to sustain), it would be unlikely to bring you any long-term benefit. Do, however, try to judge how extensive an answer is required and what it will be relevant to include in that answer.

2   SPEECH

Clear speech is not only important during the opening questions but also throughout the remainder of the interview. A regional accent will not normally affect your chances, provided that it is not so pronounced that it clouds the clarity of what you say. Try to remember the following:

(a)   speak with reasonable grammatical correctness (though not to the point of pedantry)

(b)   avoid an over-abundance of slang or colloquial expressions

(c)   speak *to* the interviewer (and look at him) rather than looking down at your hands and muttering

(d)   try to avoid mannerisms of speech, such as, *you know* or *well*. This requires prior practice, of course, and an awareness of your own tricks of speech

(e)   do not allow hesitancy over an answer to express itself in the form of . . . *er*, or . . . *um*.

3   ASSESSING THE FUTURE EMPLOYER

The interview is often the candidate's only opportunity to assess the job and the man for whom she might work. Sometimes applicants are offered posts by letter several days after the interview, while at other times the successful candidate is offered the post at the end of the interview and later receives a letter of confirmation. The applicant may have very little time in which to make a decision.

The interview must therefore be used for the interviewee to obtain information as well as for the interviewer to do so. While not taking the initiative away from the interviewer too much, do not hesitate to ask relevant questions, either during the interview if the opportunity presents itself or at the end. In particular it would be interesting to know the type of work, the degree of responsibility involved, the other people with whom you might be working and the possibilities for the future.

It is not difficult, even in a short interview, to gain quite a strong impression of the interviewer and to know whether he is a person for whom you might like to work. A complete lack of *rapport* will quickly show itself, as also will a friendly, pleasant personality. The questions asked by the interviewer and the detail in the information given will also give some clues.

THE ETHICS OF THE INTERVIEW

If you were the interviewer, you would doubtless be very annoyed if a prospective employee did not *arrive* for the interview. It is surprising how many people do behave in this inconsiderate way. The following guidelines on behaviour should be seriously considered:

1. do not agree to attend an interview and then not turn up without informing the firm

2. do not accept the post at the time of the interview and later turn it down, unless you have a very good reason. (Even worse, do not accept the post and then not arrive for work on the day you are due to start.)

It would be easy to say that, as such behaviour would mean that the applicant would not be concerned further with the firm, it would be of no matter. If inconvenience were caused, there would be very little that the firm could do about it. But such an argument would be evidence of an attitude of mind that is going to be obvious in other ways. It shows a disregard for other people and a casual approach that may well, later on, lose a job that is important or prevent promotion.

Employers should have similar standards, of course. There is a tendency in some firms to ask candidates very searching questions about aspects of their private lives that individuals may feel will not affect their work and should be allowed to remain their private concern. If you object to questions that you regard as 'prying', ask the reason for the questions. If you are still not convinced of their validity, then you may decide not to answer them. The extent of your interest in the job may well determine your attitude.

The question of how far prospective employers have the right to delve into people's private lives is a difficult one and depends largely on individual ethical standards.

It is often helpful to students if mock interviews are conducted before they seek jobs. The students can gain experience by being interviewed and by forming the panel. A series of questions that could be used in such practice is given below:

1 QUESTIONS BASED ON INFORMATION PREVIOUSLY GIVEN BY THE STUDENT

(a) Do your interests take the form of active or passive participation?

(b) How important do you consider taking part in some sport is?

(c) Do you consider it necessary to have a language in addition to secretarial skills?

(d) Which part of your course do you consider has been the most valuable?

(e) How much importance do you put on travel?

(f) What type of music/books/sport are you interested in?

2 QUESTIONS ON AIMS AND AMBITIONS

(a) Why do you wish to become a secretary (or why did you take up secretarial work)?

(b) What sort of job are you looking for?

(c) Why did you take 'A' Levels?

(d) What are your long-term ambitions?

(e) Do you consider that you can gain entry into management?

3 QUESTIONS ON THE ROLE OF THE SECRETARY

(a) What is the difference between a private secretary and an executive secretary?

(b) What are the qualities of an effective secretary?

(c) When could there be a conflict between the secretary's loyalty to her boss and to her firm?

(d) What qualities would you look for in your employer?

4 QUESTIONS ON CURRENT AFFAIRS

(a) Do you call yourself a 'political' person?

(b) What implications are there for Britain/world peace/Europe in the recent events in the Common Market/the United States/South Africa/China, etc.?

(c) What do you think of the present state of the British economy/balance of payments/industrial relations?

5 THE 'SITUATION' TYPE OF QUESTION

(a) Your employer is noted for his bad memory. He left yesterday for a business trip and, despite your efforts, he has left his itinerary behind. How can you ensure that he keeps his appointments?

(b) Your boss is busy at an all-day meeting. A client of his, who has already telephoned twice during the week and has not been able to speak to your boss, arrives in your office and angrily demands to speak to him. What will you do?

(c) You have certain reasons to believe that the office junior for whom you are immediately responsible has been taking money from the petty cash. You talk to her about this and she admits having done so. What will you do?

(d) You find out accidentally that your boss is taking action that you believe will be harmful to the firm. What should you do?

(e) You have been unwillingly forced to listen to a piece of gossip about your employer which could affect his position at work. What will you do about it?

(f) Your boss is attending a conference in a foreign country when a civil war breaks out. You hear nothing from him for several days and he does not return on his scheduled flight. How can you attempt to find out whether he is safe and if and how he can return?

(g) Your boss has just left by car to meet an important client who is arriving at Gatwick Airport. You receive a telephone call saying that the client has just touched down at Heathrow, since his plane was diverted by fog. What will you do?

6 QUESTIONS ABOUT THE JOB AND THE ORGANISATION

(a) What makes you think that you could do this job?

(b) Why do you want this job?

(c) What do you think this job will require of you?
(d) What qualities do you look for in your boss?
(e) Can you work on your own?
(f) How well do you get on with older people?
(g) Will you work overtime at short notice?
(h) What do you know about this company?
(i) What starting salary do you expect?
(j) Will you come on a month's trial?
(k) Will you accept the job now?

Employment interviews have been considered in detail because of their importance to every student. There are other formal interviews which you are likely to encounter at work. They will be concerned with performance, pay, difficulties and grievances. Sometimes, inevitably, you will be reprimanded and there are occasions on which people must be dismissed. Others move from one job to another and are interviewed before they leave their old firms as well as for the new job.

The various kinds of interviews are discussed briefly in the remainder of this section.

APPRAISAL

Employee-performance appraisal is the systematic evaluation of the individual employee related to his performance in his job and his potential for development. Such systems will include provision for appraisal interviews at least once a year and preferably more often.

The manager or supervisor may complete a written appraisal of the employee and then discuss it with the person, or may talk to the individual and, with him, complete the appraisal form during the interview.

The interview will have several aims, including the following:

1. informing the employee of his present position in the working group
2. recognising good and efficient work
3. telling the employee where improvement is needed
4. developing the employee's capability in the existing job and training him for promotion or change
5. acting as a record of assessment.

Such an interview ought to be an exercise with the employee in solving any problems, encouraging the employee to think constructively and to work out the way in which improvement and development can be best achieved. The employee must have standards at which to aim and objectives to achieve. The interviewer must help in setting realistic targets. He must discuss rather than judge, listen rather than lecture, and use questions skilfully to help the employee.

REWARD REVIEW

Sometimes organisations use a rather similar system to the appraisal one but link it directly to rewards, usually bonuses or increments, which the employee may receive.

In this case the manager must judge how well the individual has worked during the review period compared with others with whom the reward must be shared. He must discuss with the individual what is likely to be given by way of reward and the reasons and obtain acceptance of these, without making the employee feels disgruntled and dissatisfied.

COUNSELLING

It is now recognised that people's problems outside work or with their work and work-mates can have a significant adverse effect on efficiency and productivity. There is also a genuine desire to make working life as pleasant as possible and to help people with problems.

In some big organisations there are now professionally trained consellors who spend all or part of their time helping and advising staff. Very often, however, individual managers try to assist their staff and will arrange confidential inverviews with any employee who has a personal problem. The problem may have a direct connection with work, in which case the manager may have enough information to be able to discuss the matter in depth, but there are many other problems on which the manager is not competent to give advice. He should seek to help the employee to find someone better qualified to give constructive advice.

Suppose that you have a problem at home, say with a sick relative, which is adversely affecting your work. Maybe you will approach your manager; maybe he has noticed your diminishing efficiency and calls you into his office to discuss it.

What sort of an interview will it be? It is to be hoped that the manager will be sympathetic, and certainly he should listen to you. You may be conscious, however, that you are preventing him from continuing with other work. Also, while *your* major concern may be the solving of the problem of your sick relative, *his* primary purpose is to obtain efficient work from his staff. These two things may seem to go hand in hand but this is not always true.

The best that can happen is that the manager will help you to obtain practical advice by referring you elsewhere (to the Personnel Department, to the Local Authority, to the Social Services or to other relevant agencies) and will give you time in which to settle the problem and become better and more reliable in your work again.

GRIEVANCES

Most organisations now have well-established procedures for handling grievances. Some of the interviews which may be held will be formal, even with union representatives accompanying the employee. There will be a well-planned routine for the interview and the interviewers will have thought carefully about what is to be discussed.

The informal interview with a manager is likely to be unplanned or little planned. The manager has to remember that there is a problem to be solved and that the aggrieved employee is possibly annoyed, frustrated, resentful or suspicious. The best technique is to listen carefully, show that he understands, and ask questions designed to encourage the employee to think about the problem and suggest possible solutions. Most of all, the manager must try to 'defuse' the situation by discussing it in a quiet, rational way. He must not allow himself to argue, criticise or be sidetracked by irrelevancies.

REPRIMAND

As far as is humanly possible reprimands should never be an instinctive response to carelessness, stupidity or dangerous actions. Reprimand (or disciplinary) interviews have a purpose: to improve performance, prevent repetition of errors and to protect the member of staff and others against hazards.

The manager should make sure of the facts, taking whatever time is necessary to investigate, plan the reprimand so that it will be effective (thinking about the member of staff who will respond in an individual way), give the reprimand in private, refuse to argue and be exact about the error committed. The employee must be given the opportunity to explain and discussion should take place on improvements possible.

The manager must not show antagonism towards the individual either in the interview or afterwards.

DISMISSAL

Following the Employment Protection Act of 1975, formal dismissal procedures have been instituted, including warning letters. Cases of unfair dismissal brought before the Industrial Tribunals have brought consideration of what constitutes fair warning to employees. The provision of formal interviews already exists for reprimand or disciplinary matters and it seems logical that this should be extended to dismissal as an additional means of warning employees.

TERMINATION

This section started with the interview for a job. Now we have moved to the other end of the time-span of a job — when the employee is leaving the company, to retire, start a new job, have a family.

It is important to know what makes people leave a place of employment or a particular job. Sometimes it can give helpful insight into changes that should be made in organisation, management, working relationships, work content and conditions. Firms cannot afford to change staff too often. It makes for discontinuity and is costly and inefficient. Moreover, if labour turnover is high, the rumours start flying and future recruitment can be adversely affected.

When people leave jobs because they are dissatisfied, bored, or unhappy in their working relationships, they may be reluctant to discuss this with an immediate superior or even a departmental manager. There is the fear that their references from the firm might be adversely affected if they really said what they thought about the people and the job.

The termination interview is therefore difficult to conduct if a positive result is to be achieved. It may be somewhat more useful if conducted by a person outside the job-leaver's own department (usually a member of the Personnel Department) but even here it is often the judgement of what has been left unsaid that is important.

THE EFFECTIVENESS OF INTERVIEWS

Interviews take place between people: people are fallible. However well-trained the interviewer, and however carefully planned the interview is, the judgements made by the interviewer and interviewee will be subjective. Instinctive and emotional reactions will sometimes cloud rational thought, while lack of knowledge will lead to faulty conclusions or wrong advice. Time is rarely freely available for full discussion. Also, records of interview are often incomplete or non-existent so that interviewer and interviewee, at a later date, may mistakenly rely on inaccurate memories.

It must be added that many people who have to conduct interviews still may not have been trained in the skills at all, may have given little or no thought to the interview beforehand, may lack innate sympathy with the people they are interviewing or with the difficulties of the situation, or may have far from sufficient knowledge to make a successful interview possible. Bearing this in mind it is surprising that the results of interviews are not more disastrous than seems to be the case (although it has been suggested that faulty interviewing is the major reason for up to 30 per cent of the working population being in jobs where they are not as happy, useful or well re-warded as they might be).

There are suggestions that computers may take over the interviewing process, at least for more routine and less important job interviews. Science fiction becomes science fact very fast but there are those of us who believe that relationships between people cannot be replaced by machines, however complex and clever, without losing something which is important. The various interviews at work are of consequence to management and to staff and form part of the basic patterns of social relationships and communication.

EXERCISES

These require reference to other sections as indicated.

1.   You are shortly to be interviewed for a post as a private secretary. What preparations can you make beforehand and what action can you take

during and after the interview to ensure as far as possible a favourable impression?

(*LCC Private Secretary's Certificate*)

2.   As the senior private secretary you have been asked to interview three candidates for a position of shorthand-typist. They are:

>   Miss *X*, aged twenty
>   Mrs *Y*, aged thirty-five (one child, ten years old)
>   Miss *Z*, aged forty-four.

As all have an acceptable educational standard and the necessary paper qualifications in shorthand and typewriting, what other factors will you wish to investigate regarding each candidate? If all prove to be equally suitable, state with reasons who would be your personal choice. In answering, make any assumptions you wish, provided that these are clearly stated.

(*RSA Personal Secretarial Practice Stage III*)

3.   You have been asked to interview a junior secretary who will succeed you as secretary to two executives, one young and one near to retirement. What questions will you ask her and what information will you give her about your job?

(*LCC Private Secretary's Certificate*)

4.   You are secretary to the Chief Accountant of a large organisation. Your assistant is leaving to get married. Draw up the following:
  (a)   a classified advertisement for the post
  (b)   a job description
  (c)   a report on an unsatisfacory candidate that you have interviewed
  (d)   a report on the most suitable candidate that you have interviewed.
(See Sections 5 and 8.)

(*RSA Diploma for Personal Assistants*)

5.   What are the advantages and disadvantages of using a standard 'Application for Employment' form. List the information you would require from persons seeking clerical and secretarial employment in a firm with a number of branches in different parts of the country as well as several offices in various European countries. (See Section 8.)

(*RSA Stage II The Office*)

6.   (a)   Draw up for insertion in a local newspaper a display advertisement inviting applications for **one** of the following vacancies:
    (i) Secretary to the Sales Manager
    (ii) Accounts Clerk
    (iii) Telephonist/Receptionist.

(b)   Write the letter to be sent to the applicants selected for interview.
(c)   Write the letters to be sent to unsuccessful interviewees.
(See Sections 4 and 8.)

(RSA Communication in the Office)

7.   Discuss the view that unsatisfactory interviewing techniques may lead to staff unrest.

8.   To what extent do you consider that managers should give advice on personal problems? Illustrate your answer with some examples.

9.   Interviews cannot ever be completely objective. Comment on this statement.

10.   Developments in legislation and thinking on industrial relations and effective management have in recent years led to the introduction of more formal interviews. To what extent do you consider that the various procedures are an improvement on less formalised methods of discussing performance, salary, grievances and possible dismissal?

13

VISUAL COMMUNICATION

So far this book has been concerned with written and oral forms of communication. This section considers some aspects of the non-verbal medium.

It is said that people remember about twice as much of what they see as they remember of what they hear. Because it is so effective a medium, communication without words takes many forms. The facial expressions and gestures used in conjunction with speech will often convey more meaning than the actual words used. At the very least they will reinforce the verbal message.

We have already recognised that in written verbal communication the visual presentation, that is, the layout of the words, headings and paragraphs on the page, can be a help, or a hindrance, to the reader's comprehension. The presentation of information in the form of a picture can both simplify and give more impact to the information to be conveyed.

This section is concerned with some of the forms of visual communication which are commonly used in business to convey various kinds of information, not necessarily only numerical. In other words, we shall consider the types of charts, graphs, statistical and other diagrams with which a business student should be familiar.

Familiarity here means the ability to:

recognise the different types of diagram
interpret the information they contain
choose the most effective type of diagram with which to present a given
   piece of information.

Diagrams used appropriately will have several advantages over verbal communication. They will convey information vividly, simply and concisely and they will make comparisons and trends more easily and quickly recognisable.

In business, people have to contend with a vast range of data which it is necessary for them to comprehend swiftly. Imagine having to read many pages such as this:

PRODUCTION, PRICES AND WAGES IN THE EEC

During the four years 1965-9, industrial production in Belgium/Luxembourg rose from 112 to 139 (taking 1963 as 100). The comparable figures for France were 109 to 142; for the Federal Republic of Germany 114 to 143; for Italy 106 to 142 and for the Netherlands 116 to 161. The rise for the United Kingdom, however, was only from 112 to 123.

TABLES

The information contained in the above paragraph can be much more readily understood if the figures are tabulated, as in Figure 42. Statistical information is, of course, commonly presented in tabular form, which may be simple, or much more complex (see Figure 43).

INDUSTRIAL PRODUCTION
(1963 = 100)

	1965	1969
Belgium/Luxembourg	112	139
France	109	142
Federal Republic of Germany	114	143
Italy	110	142
Netherlands	116	161
United Kingdom	112	123

Figure 42   Table — industrial production

LINE GRAPHS

The information contained in the table (Figure 42) could be presented in diagrammatic form as the simple line graph shown in Figure 44. Line graphs commonly plot a series of quantities (measured on the vertical scale or scales) against a period of time (measured on the horizontal scale). They thus make quantitative comparisons, but the nature of the diagram tends to emphasise rise and fall rather than quantity. If one wished to emphasise **quantity**, rather than **change**, then a bar chart is likely to be a more suitable choice of presentation.

The simplest form of line graph will plot one set of values over a period of time, as illustrated in Figure 45.

Figure 46 shows a complex set of line graphs entered on the same diagram. Note that the vertical scale of this diagram is a log scale based on the figures for 1970. A log scale does not show actual amounts but the percentage changes which have taken place since the base figure, in this case the average for 1970 = 100 per cent was calculated.

It is also possible to represent two sets of information on the same diagram by the simple expedient of using a common horizontal scale and two different vertical scales, one on the right and one on the left. The graph in Figure 47 illustrates this. Many people find this type of presentation confusing and make the mistake of comparing the two lines without regard to the scales.

RADIOS AND RADIOGRAMS

| | Radios and radiograms[1] | | | | |
| | Pro-duction | Radio sets [2] | | Radiograms | |
	Thou-sands	Thou-sands	£ thousand	Thou-sands	£ thousand
1968	1736	1413	13293	225	7813
1969	1420	1078	10110	198	7301
1970	1312	1219	12415	193	1592
1971	1587	1173	12326	198	7932
1969 1st quarter	403	247	2410	44	1731
2nd quarter	394	289	2643	34	1193
3rd quarter	303	271	2484	49	1700
4th quarter	319	272	2537	72	2677
1970 1st quarter	302	247	2455	42	1634
2nd quarter	335	305	3105	37	1470
3rd quarter	301	247	2592	51	1966
4th quarter	374	324	3270	63	2522
1971 1st quarter	405	280	2976	49	1947
2nd quarter	410	278	2968	31	1280
3rd quarter	347	295	2967	52	2139
4th quarter	426	319	3415	65	2566
1972 1st quarter	356	290	3197	51	2112
2nd quarter	380	324	3510	53	2218
1972 January	114	88	984	18	729
February	114	90	966	16	653
March	128	112	1247	18	730
April	130	104	1120	14	588
May	130	100	1115	17	736
June	120	120	1275	21	895

[1] Including chassis [2] Including car radios

Source: Department of Trade and Industry. Reproduced from *Monthly Digest of Statistics*, No. 331 (July 1973).

Figure 43 Complex table

It would be very easy in Figure 47, for instance, to read off the consumer price for 1920 as being 150, by relating it to the left-hand scale rather than reading it off correctly as just over 45.

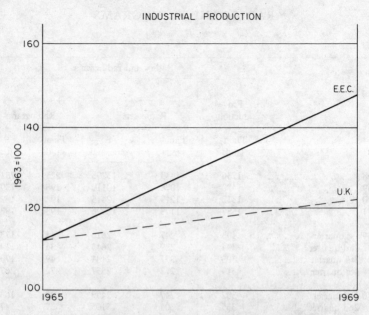

Figure 44 Graph— industrial production

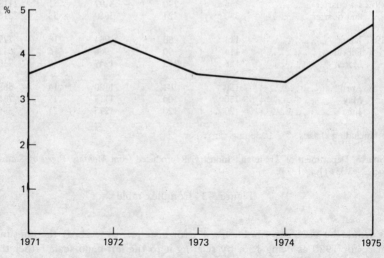

Figure 45 Simple line graph

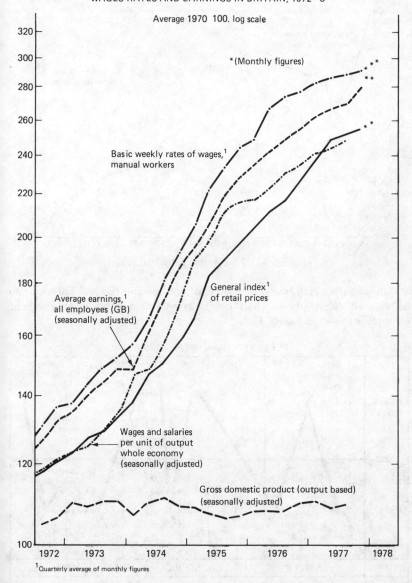

Figure 46   Complex line graph

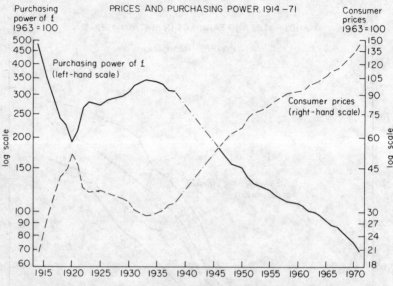

Figure 47   Line graph with dual scale

The quality which line graphs have, of emphasising rise and fall, can also be adapted effectively to chart events as well as quantities. An excellent example is shown in Figure 48.

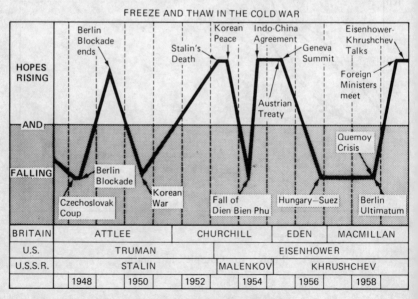

Figure 48   Graph — the Cold War

Z CHARTS

These charts are so called because their shape does indeed resemble a 'Z', as you will see in Figure 49. They are a variation of line graphs and are most frequently used for sales figures. They have the advantage of being able to show effectively three different, but related, sets of information:

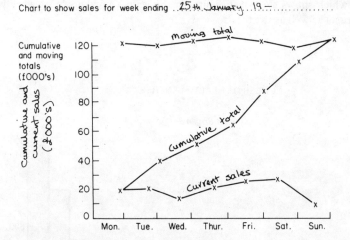

Chart to show sales for week ending ..25th January 19.—.............

Source: *Business Statistics Simplified* (Bell & Mather, 1968)

Figure 49 'Z' chart

(a)   individual figures (current sales in Figure 49)
(b)   the cumulative figures for the whole period (in Figure 49 the whole period is one week)
(c)   a moving total.

In Figure 49, (c) is a moving weekly total. It can be found by adding the totals of the preceding seven days, for example:

	Daily total	Moving total	
Monday	2		
Tuesday	3		
Wednesday	6		
Thursday	5		
Friday	4		
Saturday	8		
Sunday	7	35	
Monday	6	39	*(omit last Monday and add this Monday)*
Tuesday	2	38	*(omit last Tuesday and add this Tuesday)*

BAR OR BLOCK CHARTS

The chief visual advantage of these charts is that they emphasise **quantities** (see Figure 50, a simple vertical bar chart). More than one set of information can be included on a block chart, just as it can on a line graph, and the bars can be presented horizontally where the lettering makes for easier reading. Figure 51 demonstrates this advantage and is also an example of a divided bar chart which shows the constituents (in this case a breakdown of weekly expenditure) as well as the totals.

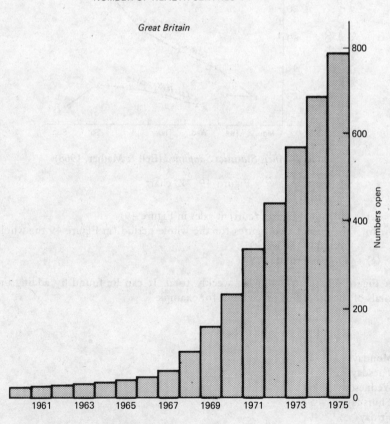

NUMBER OF HEALTH CENTRES[1]

Great Britain

1 Number of health centres open at the end of each year.
Sources: Department of Health and Social Security;
Welsh Office; Scottish Health Service, Common Services Agency

Figure 50 Bar chart

EXPENDITURE PATTERNS: BY TYPE OF HOUSEHOLD

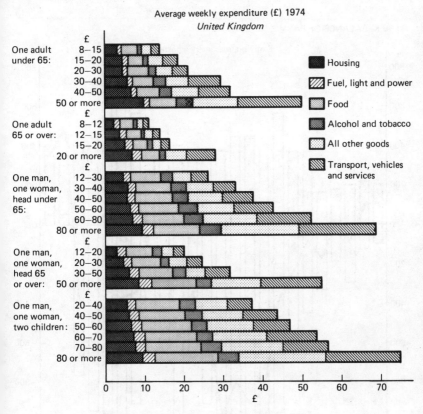

Figure 51 Horizontal compound bar chart

Yet another variation is the floating bar chart, where the bar 'floats' above and below a zero line (see Figure 52).

Population pyramids are complex bar charts which are used to show the population structure of a country. Figure 53 shows the structure of Great Britain's population in 1974 and the divisions of the bars classify the population according to marital status.

GANTT CHARTS

Gantt charts are used to compare actual performance against planned, anticipated or target performance. A Gantt chart could, for example, be used to show the extent to which a shorthand student was succeeding, or failing, to increase her speed in comparison with the performance that her teacher could

U.K. BALANCE OF PAYMENTS, 1972–77

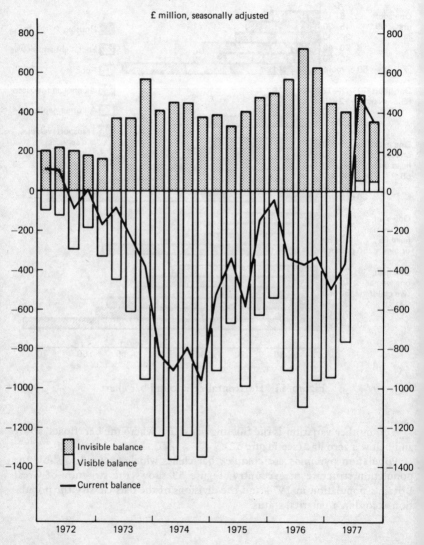

Figure 52   Floating compound bar chart

POPULATION STRUCTURE: BY AGE, SEX, AND MARITAL STATUS, 1974

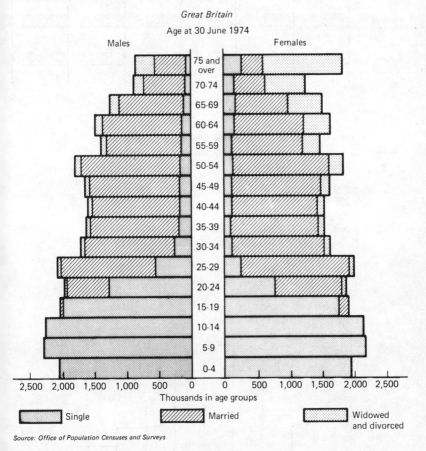

Great Britain

Age at 30 June 1974

Males   Females

Thousands in age groups

Single   Married   Widowed and divorced

Source: Office of Population Censuses and Surveys

Figure 53   Population pyramid

reasonably expect. Our example in Figure 54 shows actual sales of a commodity set against planned sales over a period of six weeks.

HISTOGRAMS

A histogram shows the frequency of occurrence of the subject being studied within defined limits (called 'class limits'). For example, the mileage recorded by 100 salesmen for a certain company during the course of one week is shown in Figure 55, first as a table and then as a histogram. Note that the area of each rectangle is directly proportional to the number of observations made in each class of the table.

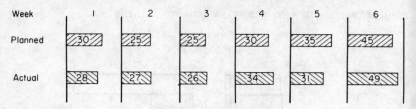

Figure 54   Gantt chart

Mileage recorded by 100 salesmen for a certain
company during the course of one week

Miles			Salesmen
200	– under	220	4
220	″	240	6
240	″	260	10
260	″	280	14
280	″	300	18
300	″	320	15
320	″	340	12
340	″	360	9
360	″	380	7
380	″	400	5

Figure 55   Histogram

FREQUENCY POLYGONS

If we use the information given in Figure 55, plotting it as a series of dots
rather than as bars, we can join up the dots to produce a continuous line, as
shown in Figure 56. This is called a 'frequency polygon'.

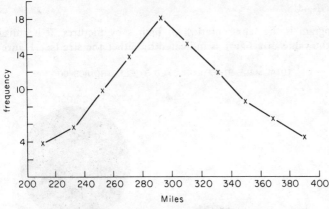

Figure 56   Frequency polygon

PIE CHARTS

The pie chart, like the pictogram (see below), has considerable visual impact and also simplifies information effectively. Both are therefore used to convey information to the layman. They will be frequently used in a newspaper or poster presentation of statistical material. Pie charts can only be used effectively when there are not more than seven or eight segments and when it is wished to show the relative proportions of figures that make up a single overall total. Figure 57 shows two pie charts in which the segments add up to the respective total weekly household incomes. Why do the two pies vary in size?

SOURCE OF HOUSEHOLD INCOME, 1974

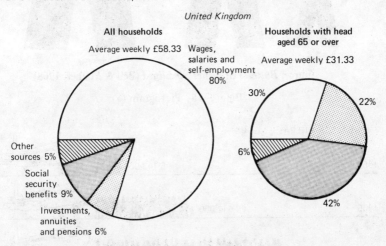

Source: *Family Expenditure Survey, Department of Employment*

Figure 57   Pie charts

PICTOGRAMS

A pictogram is the representation of figures by pictures. It is a diagram in which the value of a figure is indicated by either the size (see Figure 58) or

TOTAL MALE STAFF EMPLOYED BY ELECTRONICS CO.

107,000

75,000

40,000

1945   1955   1965

Source: *Business Statistics Simplified* (Bell & Mather, 1968)

Figure 58   Pictogram (a)

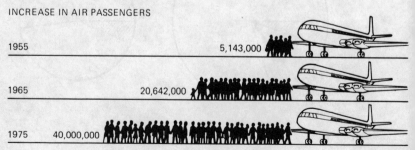

INCREASE IN AIR PASSENGERS

1955   5,143,000

1965   20,642,000

1975   40,000,000

Figure 59   Pictogram (b)

the number (see Figure 59) of figures that are shown. Pictograms have more visual appeal than, for example, bar charts, and they are easily understood irrespective of language or numeracy problems. Generally the second technique, that shown in Figure 59, is more satisfactory.

STATISTICAL MAPS

These are simply maps which are shaded or marked in such a way as to convey statistical information (see, for example, Figure 60). In this figure shading is used to denote the sharing of industrial employment between areas. The large figures express the percentage of the national total of additional employment. Smaller figures show the relationship between this percentage and existing industrial employment. Note that the size of the percentage is indicated by the scale of the figure as well as by the number. The variety of information that may be shown on one statistical map is well illustrated by this example.

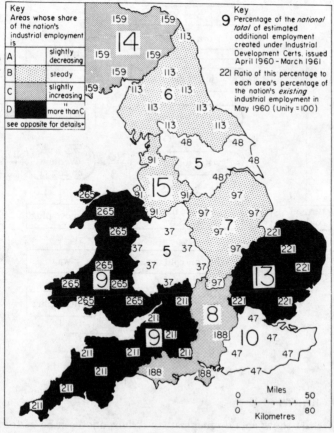

Figure 60   Statistical map

If a computer were to be programmed to perform the simple task of running a bath, the first step would be to produce a flow chart like this, then to use it as a basis for the program. Actions are shown in rectangular boxes and decisions in boxes with curved ends.

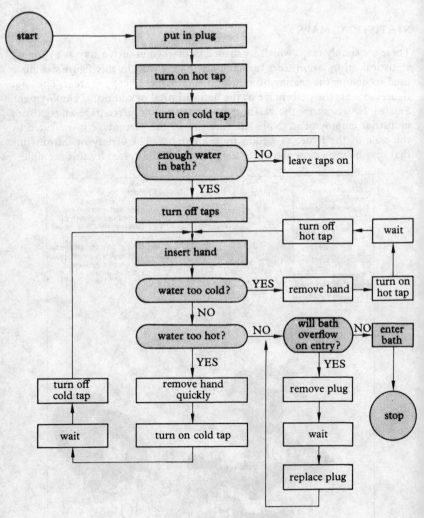

Figure 61   Flow sheet

FLOW CHARTS

A flow chart shows in a diagrammatic way how a job can be performed by charting in some detail the logical sequence of action or thought involved.

It is a technique used by systems analysts. A flow chart must have a single start-point and a single end-point. Between these two there can be any number of branches or limbs. If a computer were to be programmed to perform the simple task of running a bath, the first step would be to produce a flow chart like the one shown in Figure 61 and then to use it as a basis for the programme. Actions are shown in rectangular boxes and questions in boxes with curved ends.

ALGORITHMS

These are a type of flow chart, and the one shown in Figure 62 is designed to facilitate decision-taking. In other words, it directs the reader, by a set of simple yes/no responses, to the answers to the complex question: 'What shares should I buy?' Such diagrams can also simplify the complex instructions needed to direct someone, for example, to find the fault in an electrical type-writer.

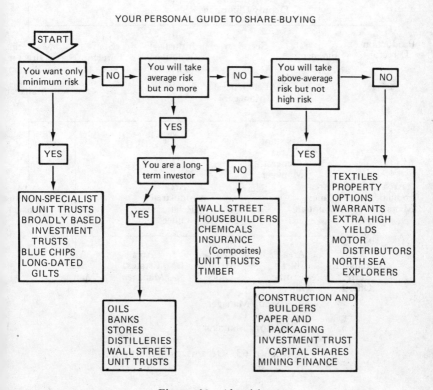

Figure 62   Algorithm

ORGANISATION CHARTS

An organisation chart is rather like a family tree of an organisation. It indicates the interrelationship, the responsibilites and the authority of various units. The diagram can be one which either shows the whole organisation or shows only a section or department. Figure 63 shows the organisation of an imaginary body, the Plastic Novelties Board.

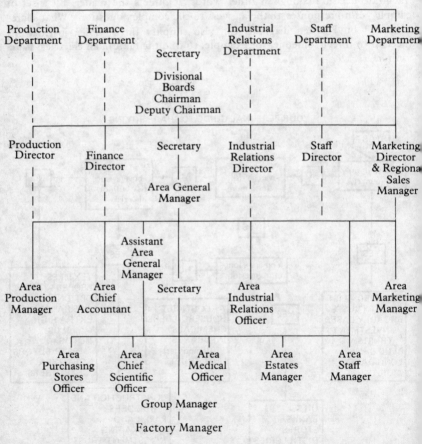

Figure 63   Organisation chart

VISUAL CONTROL BOARDS

Some organisations maintain their charts and graphs in the form of wall displays, using elaborate, pre-manufactured visual control boards. There are a number of these on the market and it is not possible to detail all of them. It is important, however, that the system selected should be suitable for its purpose and that it can be kept up to date. This does not necessarily mean that it will be an expensive or complicated system.

THE USE OF CHARTS AND GRAPHS

Some of the particular uses of certain visual presentations have already been mentioned. The following general points should also be noted:

(a)   statistical information is much more clearly grasped when it is presented on a graph or chart than when it is written
(b)   visual systems enable greater control to be exercised
(c)   planning is made easier
(d)   comparison is facilitated
(e)   charts can be built into a comprehensive range.

These comments made the basic assumption that suitable charts for the purpose will be used, that they will be prepared carefully and that they will not be allowed to become out of date. Given that these conditions are observed, then the visual presentation of information can be time-saving and valuable.

EXERCISES

1.   Present the following information in the form of a table. What further data would be required to make the table more informative?

In 1966 the total number of accidents to the ABC Company male employees was 364 and to female employees 204. In 1967 the total number of male accidents was 418 — a rise of 54 — and the total number of female accidents was 235 — a rise of 31. In 1968 the total number of accidents remained roughly constant, the corresponding figures being 410 and 231 and it is felt that this small reduction in accidents was due to many of our employees being laid off during the recession in the motor industry. In 1969 there was a rise in male accidents of no less than 194 to a total of 604. Part of this rise is accounted for by the exceptionally icy condition of the roads in November and December 1969.

(SCCAPE Advanced Secretarial Certificate)

2.   Suggest one method of presenting each of the following items of

information in a visual form, giving reasons for your choice and indicating what 'audience' you have in mind for each:

    (a)   the sizes of shoes sold by one shop in one day

    (b)   the number of cars produced by British car manufacturers over
a five-year period (in 10,000s)

    (c)   the percentage of income spent on rent/mortgage repayments,
food, consumer durables, clothes, other items.

3.   (a)   What are the advantages of recording statistical data in graphic
form?

    (b)   Explain the difference between a line chart and a bar chart and
give an example to show when each might be used.

(LCC Private Secretary's Certificate)

4.   Using reference books in your library, find out where there is the
following information:

    (a)   index of industrial production

    (b)   index of retail prices

    (c)   sales of vehicles

    (d)   census details on types of dwellings

    (e)   local government finance

    (f)   industrial absenteeism.

5.   What is the value of using visual communication in addition to, or
instead of, written communication?

6.   Describe and illustrate three different types of charts and give two
examples in each case to show how such charts might be used in the
office.

(LCC Private Secretary's Certificate)

7.   The term ' — chart' is used for a variety of ways of presenting statistical
information. Give five terms which could be used for filling in the blank
space and describe in each case how such a chart would be used.

(LCC Private Secretary's Certificate)

8.   Present the statistics contained in the following passage in an appropriate
visual form other than a table. Give your chart a suitable title.

The fantastic expansion of local authority social services is of course
the obvious boom story: up by 50 per cent from 1969 to 1971, from
£267 million to £401 million. The number of social workers rose over
the same year from 7,000 to nearly 11,000, outstripped nevertheless by
the increase in 'other social service staff' — presumably administrative —

from 6,000 to 12,000. The largest increase in the work of the departments was a staggering rise in the numbers of children in care — from 71,000 in 1970 to 87,000 in 1971, most of this due to children in remand homes and approved schools coming under local authorities since the Children and Young Persons Act 1969. There was a gradual but alarming increase in the numbers taken into care because of bad home conditions (up 300 per cent since 1959) and those abandoned or lost (up 400 per cent since 1959). The numbers of old people in residential homes continued its upward march, from 82,000 in 1959 to 117,000 in 1970, reflecting as much a decrease in community concern as an increase in statutory provision. The overall picture given by the statistics is not an encouraging one: burgeoning social services only beginning to discover the extent of need and an almost stagnant health service.

(New Society, 1 February 1973)

9. Use the information contained in Figure 53 (p. 239) to write not more than 300 words in prose under the heading 'The Population Structure of Great Britain'.

10. Use the information in Exercise 2 of Section 6 (pp. 99—100) to devise a flow chart entitled 'How to obtain Exceptional Needs Payments'.

14

THE PLACE OF COMMUNICATION

An organisation cannot succeed without good human relations. A body which pays insufficient attention to good human relations can be recognised by its high labour turnover and the inefficient, disinterested work of its employees. An employee needs satisfaction from the work itself and happiness in his/her relations with fellow employees. She needs to know what is expected of her, what her responsibilities and authority are, and what constitutes a job well done. She needs to feel that her efforts are appreciated and that what she is doing is of value to the organisation.

The secretary's most immediate concern in this area is her relations with her boss. Working for someone one admires makes it easy to try hard to earn his/her respect in return. But we all have human failings, and we need to extend to others the same tolerance which we allow to ourselves. We readily excuse some failure of our own, a mistyped letter or a lapse of temper, on the grounds of a headache or some personal worry. We should recognise that others have similar problems from time to time.

If your employer is friendly and informal, do not allow yourself to become too familiar. Always respect any confidences made to you. The temptation to gain prestige by passing on information is a real one, but your boss is unlikely to trust you again if you fail in this way. Be helpful with suggestions and give your opinions if they are sought. You may tactfully query a decision if you think some important factor has been overlooked, but never forget who is in charge. If you are right and he is wrong, your responsibility ends when you have stated your views and you must accept this.

In *The Business Executive* (Pitman, 1969) H. E. Light states:
'Good human relations are based on effective communications, teamwork and the contribution of all who are working together for a common end.'

There can be no doubt that a simple definition of the process of communication is often inaccurate unless, along with stating that it is the conveying of meaning from one mind to another, we also indicate that we are talking about relationships and the establishment and maintenance of co-operation. If we do not thus expand our definition, then the statement that poor communication is a major problem can be misleading and dangerous. It may lead to the conception that if we solve any difficulties in conveying meaning, then we shall at the same time solve the underlying causes of unrest and dissatisfaction at work. Unfortunately this is far from being the truth. Effective communication must involve three things: language, structure and attitudes.

LANGUAGE

Language is our basic tool. As far as this book is concerned the language is English. We have seen in previous sections many examples where the ineffectual use of English hinders or even prevents communication. We have seen, too, that the rules of English will assist in the conveying of information. Some people might argue that the strict rules of our language are a deterrent to good communication in that they might stifle individual expression. This is not a valid argument. In order to express ourselves to other people, it must be systematically organised. As was said in the section on Oral Communication, words on their own have very different meanings for different people. The meaning that one wishes to convey can be imparted only by using words in relationships with other words and in forms that will be acceptable to the listener or reader.

Everyone will agree that the system of language that gives us a relationship between sound and object is artificial. Even onomatopoeic words vary from country to country. The 'buzz' of a bee to an English child will be 'bourdon' to the French, 'Summen' to the German, 'ronzio' to the Italian and 'zumbido' to the Spaniard. However, in each language there will be a grammatical system, a set of conventions or a system of distinctions or relationships that are necessary for thought and communication to be organised and for understanding to be facilitated.

In *Linguistics and Your Language** Professor R. A. Hall stated:

'There is no such thing as good and bad (correct and incorrect, grammatical and ungrammatical, right and wrong) in language.

Correct can only mean "socially acceptable", and apart from this has no meaning as applied to language.'

This may be true, but the use of a language does also mean having some tradition and some rules. To be able to speak a language implies an ability to be able to speak it sufficiently correctly to enter into communication with other people. There is nothing to stop a speaker of English from ceasing to use that language and switching to a version based on personal preference, but this course may lead to total isolation.

The rules of language have the force that they have because most people using the language impose them among themselves. They cease to have force when nobody minds any longer whether or not they are observed. For instance, many people today do not object to ending a sentence with a preposition. Because English is a living language, changes in its rules, as in the meaning of individual words, will always take place. It will be a sad day for the language when they cease to do so. However, if one moves too far away from what is

* R. A. Hall, *Linguistics and Your Language*, Doubleday & Co., 1960.

usually considered correct usage then the risk of misunderstanding exists. Incorrect or careless speakers or writers can reduce their remarks to gobbledygook.

To sum up: the importance of using language that conforms with the existing rules lies not in the merit of being an academic purist or pedant, but in the merit of communicating well. Minor infringements of the rules do not matter *per se,* but they may be socially unacceptable to the recipient or eventually lead to much greater infringements that can distort meaning.

Distortions, as we have seen, can take place in speech or in writing. They can be distortions of the rules of spelling, punctuation, grammar or syntax, for example,

> The housewife put the casserole of jugged hair in the oven.
> The only student I have ever met who ever believed his ears was blind.*
> Running down the road, the car hit her.

They may alternatively be the distortions that come through the development of specialist descriptions and specialist 'languages'. The following words and phrases serve as examples:

> *interlocking directorships* — the means and arrangement under which individual directors have seats on the boards of various companies within the same group.
> *multifunctional utilisation* is a distortion caused by using long words. 'Translated', it means 'many-purpose uses'!
> *stochastic* is an overused term in management studies. It is often meaningless because few people are familiar with it. The dictionary definition says 'pertaining to conjecture (to guess, to aim at a mark)'. When last seen by your authors in use in a book, the word was defined as 'chance', a simple explicit term that could have been used in the first place.

Frequently distortion of this type seems to occur when the specialists developing new techniques are also people who have not specialised in the use of the English language and they therefore alter the meaning of words from that of common usage. New words may also be coined. These are called 'neologisms', and some of the more recent ones include:

> *radar* — radio detection and ranging — a system developed during the Second World War
> *cosmonaut* — the title given to Russians who make space flights (as opposed to *astronaut,* the term used by the Americans)
> *quasar* — quasi-stellar objects. These are strange objects in the universe which appear to be extremely remote and superluminous. In addition to sending out light, they are strong radio sources and it was through this that they were first identified in 1963
> *bikini* — there is no very clear definition of the origin of this word as

---

* Eric Partridge, *Usage and Abusage,* Penguin, 1965.

applied to a minute two-piece bathing-suit, but it is suggested that there is a connection with the Bikini Atoll in the Pacific, where one of the early atomic tests was carried out. The sight of a shapely female form so scantily clad is perhaps assumed to excite an atomic reaction from the watching male.

If the growth of these secondary languages is not checked, then communication is likely to deteriorate, not improve. Laymen have to become aware not just of the existence of these languages, but also of their meaning. The specialists need to learn to use words more carefully.

The following may be ways in which better use of language can be achieved:

1. the effort now being made to encourage scientists, technicians and administrators to improve their ability to communicate with laymen must be sustained and strengthened
2. children at school must be taught not only to seek freedom of expression but also to seek the three cardinal virtues of Accuracy, Brevity and Clarity when they write
3. those people who move into industry, commerce and government with a good command of the language should be prepared to find colleagues of whom this is not true and should be made aware of how important it is that their own individual standards should not be lowered
4. the standard of speech and writing in the media; press, television and radio, particularly where advertising matter is concerned, should be improved.

The budding secretary may feel that this is mere academic theorising of very little practical value to her in her prospective career. Not so. There are many ways in which even the most junior member of an organisation can both protect her own standards and seek to improve those of the people with whom she comes into contact, providing that she realises that all changes take time and tact. However, although the time taken in achieving effective communication may be longer initially, it will be time saved in the long run.

Here are some suggestions about ways in which the secretary can concern herself with the effective use of language.

1. Examine, as objectively as possible, your own deficiencies in the use of appropriate language and remember that everyone has deficiencies and that you will be no exception.
2. Apppreciate how different presentation or the use of a different medium of communication can assist effectiveness.
3. Learn to appreciate clear, simple communication by others.
4. Keep jargon to a minimum.
5. Get into the habit of planning all communication carefully, whether oral or written.
6. Extend your knowledge of language, including specialised terminology, by reading.
7. By example try to make your superiors aware of improvements that can be made.

8. Question any lack of clarity where and when possible.
9. Always try to use clear and simple forms of expression even when these conflict with the superior's ways, provided that there is effective communication.
10. With colleagues and subordinates, gently draw their attention to failures to use communication effectively.
11. Progress gradually to a position where unsatisfactory communication, written, typed or otherwise prepared for your use, is unacceptable.
12. Be aware of the need of training your subordinates and take every opportunity to provide pertinent help, both individually and through formal training, not just destructive criticism.
13. Be aware yourself and encourage an awareness in others of the cost-effectiveness of the efficient use of language.

STRUCTURE

A systematic approach is needed for language. Similarly a structured framework for the flow of information within a firm is required. This framework must include the practical arrangements for the interchange of information, such as telephones, telex, mail systems and meetings. It must also establish the disciplines which ensure that people talk or write about the necesssary facts to those people who should know about them.

The secretary is not normally in a position where she can impose such a structure, for she is seldom considered part of the management team. She has to learn to work within the existing system, to use it to the greatest advantage and to avoid its pitfalls. Any planned structure will generally be imposed on the organisation by top management and any major changes in it will have to be made by these people rather than by anyone lower down in the hierarchy.

In the modern efficient company the communication system will have been conceived and designed together with the organisational structure. The complexity of the system, and its formality, will often be governed by the size of the organisation. A small office will not require the disciplined methods and degree of standardisation and regulation that might be necessary in a large company. For instance, a standard letter format need not be devised for the firm that employs only one typist, but it might be highly desirable in the company employing a total of forty secretaries, shorthand, audio and copy typists. Structures are therefore designed to enable co-ordination, co-operation and rationalisation to be achieved and should be chosen to suit the individual needs of each organisation. They need to be well planned, with a degree of order and discipline, but not so rigidly as to stifle individual freedom of expression entirely and they must take into account existing informal groupings.

Where problems arise, it is often because no systematic formulation of the means of communication has been devised. Existing systems may well have grown up piecemeal as the organisation has expanded, with each section establishing its own systems with a blatant disregard for the need for co-ordination and co-operation with other departments. So, a form might be designed by one section, to be filled in or used by another group which has not been consulted.

A similar fragmentation has existed in the past with, for example, accounting procedures. These, in most companies, have now been studied and controlled. Such study is now being extended to other fields. The introduction of computers, the establishment of procedures such as Clerical Work Measurement and the availability of sophisticated means of communication, like the Post Office 'Confravision' service, are all tending to encourage and even require the study of communication structures.

They also point to the significance of communication in any enterprise and the clear advisability of establishing, even informally in small organisations, a logical skeleton for giving information or instructions and discussing matters of business. This skeleton needs careful construction. All the bones and joints must be connected and each must have either the freedom of movement or the rigidity desired for it to preserve its function in the whole. Injury or dislocation of any part can cause a limitation of the over-all facility of the structure. For instance, bad telephone techniques can affect the profitability of a firm if customers trade elsewhere because they can get no satisfaction when they telephone the Sales Department. Production of the wrong parts can follow from a carelessly worded memo or an inaccurate drawing. Strikes may ultimately result because the grapevine, with all its concomitant evils, is swifter than the formal lines of communication.

These examples show the compulsion upon management to establish suitable systems of communication. Furthermore, they stress that all members of an organisation must somehow be persuaded to follow the systems. This requires much training and is a long and uphill process with existing members of an organisation because, as will be shown later, they are often resistant to change. The task may be easier with new members of staff provided that good induction training is undertaken.

The secretary can play a positive part here. Even when formal induction training is provided by a firm, the secretary can reinforce it in her own department. She may in some companies be formally responsible for any such training of staff under her.

The secretary also bears a responsibility for maintaining the structure of communication with her boss and, on his behalf, with other departments or outside contacts. She can have some influence on improving structure also. Here are some of the ways in which she may be effective. She can:

1. make sure that she knows what the structure should be
2. consistently channel all her own communication correctly and in the appropriate form
3. be aware of the deficiencies in the structure and try to avoid failures of communication because of these inadequacies
4. make subordinates aware of the structure and train them to follow the correct systems
5. show her superior an awareness of the need for effective structures

6. ask for information that she needs but does not get (or alternatively say when she is being inundated with information that she does not need)
7. effect minor modifications after consulting others concerned and sometimes suggest major modifications.

ATTITUDES

All communication is between people even when the computer is an intermediary. Thus the study of communication is always linked with a study of relationships and attitudes. We have already referred in previous sections, particularly Section 11, to ways in which attitudes can raise barriers to effective communication.

One of the most rigid attitudes that has to be overcome is that which governs people's reactions to the suggestion of any need for training in communication skills. First, tradition dies hard and people frequently tend to feel that existing routines must of necessity be better than proposed and untried methods. Second, there is a natural aversion to admitting that one may not be totally proficient at a skill that one has been exercising since birth, namely, communicating with other people.

Both these feelings must be overcome before the use of language or the development of structures can be facilitated. Each of the attitudes is a symptom of insecurity, one of the commonest barriers of all. If confidence in one's own prowess is shaken, then one's inability to communicate is intensified. So the process of persuading people to accept their inadequacies must be a slow and tactfully conceived one. It must build on existing strengths rather than concentrate on weakness.

Insecurity sometimes also results from the 'Them and Us' syndrome. As long as the work-force regards the management as inherently 'out to do us down' and the management regards the work-force as only interested in its pay packet, then mutual trust is hard to establish. This is one reason why the grapevine story often seems more plausible than management's own tale. There is a tendency to believe unofficial sources on the assumption that they may reveal truths that management is trying to hide. Much of this distrust stems from the different frames of reference known by management people who have never been shop-floor workers and by men who not only work on the shop floor but who also may have received a part of their education through trade-union courses.

Our upbringing and environment very often govern our attitude to work in general. It cannot be denied that some people are work shy. Many more lack interest in their work, and this attitude merits great consideration. It may be that the work itself is not very interesting or that the worker is not given sufficient incentive by the employer to take a full part in the organisation. The cause of this is often lack of communication.

Attitudes can also change from day to day. They may depend on one's state of health, the weather or having had a quarrel with one's boy friend.

They may even be affected by the time of day. There are, it is said, two distinct groups of people, the larks and the owls. The latter group are likely to be well suited to night work, but grumpy at nine in the morning, while the former will head for bed at ten p.m., but have no difficulty in getting to work on time in the morning. Each group may find the other's behaviour irritating.

All these attitudes and changes of attitude can and do affect the ways in which we communicate and our success in doing so. It is necessary to consider our relationships with other people and develop the ability to recognise moods in ourselves and in others.

The effect on written communication may be somewhat different from the effect on oral communication, where it is possible to make instantaneous changes of approach according to the reaction of the listener. When we write letters we cannot judge exactly what mood our recipients will be in when they read them. However, it is possible to make certain valid generalisations.

1. If the tone of a communication is always courteous, then offence through bad manners will not occur.
2. The likely standard of education of your readers will determine the vocabulary used.
3. A simple clear style will always be more easily understood.
4. Accuracy will always be appreciated, even if the recipient does not agree with your views.
5. One may have some knowledge of the particular outlook of a prospective reader. For instance, is he in general favourable to certain kinds of project?
6. Communications intended for a wide audience should not include specialist language that may confuse and annoy the readers.
7. Communications should be kept as short as possible to avoid wasting the recipient's time.

The secretary has a particular interest in becoming aware of the attitudes of her own employer because she works in close contact with him. She should also consider her own approach to, and her relationship with, other people with whom she has contact in the course of her work. She may find it helpful to:

1. develop an instinct for self-awareness and self-criticism
2. guard against any prejudice or pre-conditioning which might impair her judgement
3. show a willingness to change her attitudes
4. think more about other people and how she appears to them
5. consider other people's problems and learn to respect and understand their points of view
6. appreciate that various approaches may be needed.

A QUESTION OF CHOICE

The structure of communication and the attitudes of people still leave some choice of presentation. In addition to the choice of specific words and phrases the following should be considered:

> Medium
> Tone
> Time and Place
> Amount.

1   MEDIUM

The primary choice here will be between oral or written or visual presentation, but within these broad categories further decisions must be made. Some of the possibilities are now given.

Oral communication

(a) face to face
      (i) to an individual
      (ii) to a group, that is, in a meeting
(b) by means of the telephone

Written communication

(a) telex/telegram
(b) letter/memorandum
(c) report
(d) instructions
(e) publicity material
(f) constitutions and rules

Visual communication

(a) tabular presentation
(b) pictorial presentation
(c) chart
(d) graph

Combined presentation

(a) oral communication reinforced by written communication
(b) written and visual communication

2   TONE

Again, there is a primary choice between a formal and an informal approach. In addition the particular tone of the communication will vary according to the content, situation and people concerned. The tone might, for instance, be authoritative, genial, sympathetic, harsh, light-hearted, non-commital or persuasive.

3   TIME AND PLACE

The time and place of communication should be chosen according to the situation, the people involved and the degree of urgency to convey the information. For instance, it would be inappropriate for the secretary to interrupt her boss when he is at an important meeting in order to tell him that his wife has telephoned to thank him for some flowers just delivered for her birthday. On the other hand, the employer might well interrupt the secretary when she is transcribing some letters to instruct her to make some travel arrangements for him as he has received an urgent message which will necessitate his flying to Brussels on the first available flight.

4   THE AMOUNT

The amount to be communicated may involve the following choices:

(a)   how much can be communicated at any one time to the particular people;

(b)   how much time needs to be spent in planning the communication;

(c)   what medium is most suitable — for instance, a complex job instruction may demand the use of writing and illustration so that a permanent manual is produced, whereas a simple directive to 'go and collect two reams of A4 headed paper from the stores' can easily be conveyed orally.

FEEDBACK

When the communication has been planned and delivered, the final step is to ascertain that it has been understood. This means obtaining a feedback from the recipient. This may be a written reply to a letter or memo, but there are many occasions with both oral and written communication where no specific reply is demanded.

Feedback may be acquired by waiting until the task has been performed or the instructions followed. However, this is hardly a satisfactory method because it does not allow for early correction of misunderstanding or mistakes. With talk it is possible to get early feedback by watching people's expressions, though this is by no means a foolproof method. Much more satisfactory is the posing of questions. These must be framed in such a way that they prevent the monosyllabic answer. 'Do you understand?', for instance, might produce the answer 'Yes' but this will not tell you if the understanding reached by the recipient is comparable with your original meaning. It is far better to pose questions such as:

What steps do you think we should take?
Where can you get this information?
Who else should be consulted, and why?
In what order will you tackle these jobs?
How are you going to approach the task?

If the feedback indicates that understanding has not been reached, it is useless to blame the recipient. Maybe he was not concentrating on what you said. Ask yourself why. Perhaps you expressed yourself in such a confused way that he could not take in your communication. Perhaps you chose a moment when he was busy on another task. Did you include so much irrelevant detail that the primary message was obscured? Was your attitude to him one of impatience? Maybe you failed to get his attention right at the start.

There may be hundreds of reasons why any particular communication fails. The significant factor in improving communication will be your willingness to consider how *YOU* have failed rather than how your recipient has failed. If you get your own side of the communication process right, then you can look at the other people.

A similar truth holds when you are the recipient of a communication. If you have to read a letter several times, is it because the letter was badly written or because you are not giving it your proper attention? Communication demands concentration on the part of the giver and the receiver, whatever form it takes. It also demands perpetual consideration for the other person or people involved in the process.

EXERCISES

Up to now the exercises have been fairly limited in scope to allow you to concentrate on each section in turn. Some general questions follow and Section 15 includes exercises which will give you the opportunity to combine various skills, as one has to do in the practical office situation.

1.   A manager is proposing to move a department of a business to another location. What forms of communication should he use to consult (and persuade) the employees about the plan and to put the plan into operation?

(LCC Private Secretary's Certificate)

2.   Your company has decided to institute a suggestions scheme. The procedure to be followed has been drawn up and must now be communicated to the employees concerned: some 350 persons accommodated on two floors of an office block and a factory building a short distance away. Suggest an efficient method of ensuring that all employees are made aware of this scheme.

(LCC Private Secretary's Certificate)

4.   What role should the secretary play in the maintenance of good communication?

5.   Why is the meaningful use of language so important in achieving good communication?

6.   We have heard more and more today about 'communication in industry'. Describe how to secure an effective communication system, discuss the objectives and consider the possible channels of communication, giving your views on the effectiveness of each.

7   'The advantages of a written communication tend to outweigh its disadvantages.' Discuss.

(Scottish HND in Secretarial Studies)

8.   An office manager has decided to introduce flexitime working for his office staff of thirty. The new system has been explained to them at a briefing meeting. What method(s) should he use to obtain his employees' views?

9.   A sales clerk working in a large department has thought of a change in office procedure which she believes will lead to a saving in costs. Comment on the suitability of each of the following methods of bringing her idea to her superiors' notice:

> the monthly departmental meeting
> a memo to the Sales Manager
> talking to her immediate supervisor
> the firm's suggestion scheme
> a telephone call to the Sales Manager, seeking an interview.

10.   A merger between a small firm and a much larger group of companies has been decided. The news will shortly be published in the press. How and when should the directors of the company inform their employees of the change?

11.   An office manager discovers that two of his staff have been frequently using the office telephone to make private calls. He can *either*

> (a)   issue a circular memo addressed to his staff, reminding them that this practice is against company rules, *or*
> (b)   call them privately either (i) singly, or (ii) together into his office and reprimand them.

Which choice do you think he should make?

15

LONGER EXERCISES

This section offers eight complex exercises which use a variety of means of communication. They give students an opportunity to produce several related pieces of work on a single topic and to apply their knowledge of other subjects in the cross-discipline approach which has been introduced in Business Education Courses. The class discussion which may precede written work in many of the exercises should enable students to 'pool' any practical experience or special knowledge they may already have to a consideration of the communication and organisational problems inherent in particular situations. The exercises are graded in order of length and difficulty, the shorter or simpler ones appearing first.

1 OPENING AN EXTENSION TO THE COLLEGE
(Adapted from *SCCAPE Secretarial Certificate*)

This exercise involves:

(a) class discussion
(b) writing of letters, memos, notices
(c) typing a draft programme.

INSTRUCTIONS

The college in which you are a secretary is to open an extension. The deputy principal says, 'Rough out notes for the official programme; order of events on the left of the page; letters, action and arrangements on the right; add some general reminders; 600 people enough for the hall; guests, staff and limit of 500 students, warn our Mrs Beveridge she's doing buffet teas; opening and closing by Rev. J. MacIntosh and Father Bryan; see Dr Murray about singing; if orchestra, then stands and lights; hymn sheets or print in programme; two of Town Council, one to speak; reply by county architect; county education convenor and three others; he'll speak; bouquet to wife; MP to unveil plaque, bachelor; reply by contractors' representative; gift of books to college; principal to reply; bouquet to wife; I can wind up; staff in academic dress; police parking; flower arrangements, Miss McLeod up to £15; senior students as guides and two on platform; staff to classrooms after; platform party use dressing rooms behind stage; see head janitor soon; college badge in colour; get outside printers' quotes and time.'

Draft the letters and memoranda mentioned and send copies to the deputy principal for his approval, with a covering memo which includes a list of the last-minute arrangements which will have to be made or checked during the last few days before the opening.

Finally, write an account of the occasion for publication in the local paper.

SOME POINTS TO CONSIDER

How long should the ceremony be?
What is a suitable order of events?
Who should present the bouquets?
How many guests?
Who will they be?
How is the platform party to be selected?
How are the students to be selected?
Can you suggest any suitable displays or exhibitions to illustrate the work of
  the college which guests might also enjoy on this occasion?
How can the necessary information best be conveyed to members of staff, by
  memos, meetings, notices?

2 ORGANISING A CONFERENCE
   (Adapted from *LCC Private Secretary's Certificate*)

This exercise involves:

  (a) class discussion
  (b) writing of letters and memos
  (c) some reference-book research

INSTRUCTIONS

Your employer is at present abroad on the company's behalf and will be away for six weeks. He is, however, the Honorary Secretary of a professional association which is holding a one-day conference in your town one week after he returns. Your employer has therefore been obliged to leave you to make the necessary administrative arrangements for the fifty people coming from all over the country who are attending the conference. The four speakers for the conference have already accepted invitations. They will require accommodation and two of them are bringing their wives. It has also been decided that the association's annual dinner, to which wives and guests are also invited, will be held on the evening of the same day as the conference.

Write a report to your employer detailing the arrangements you have made and enclosing copies of all correspondence. Add a list of any outstanding arrangements which will have to be made after his return.

Write a check-list for yourself of all last-minute arrangements, the matters with which you will have to cope on the day, the information, handouts, lapel badges and equipment which you will need.

EXERCISES

(a)   Plan the day's programme.

(b)   Arrange the conference venue. What facilities, for example conference room, catering arrangments, will be needed?

(c)   Write to delegates, enclosing copy of the programme, appropriate maps, travel details and offering to arrange overnight accommodation and other help.

(d)   Write to speakers giving similar information. Ask what visual aids or preparation of handouts they would like. Offer assistance with transport and details of overnight accommodation and information about local places of interest for their wives.

(e)   Make arrangements for the dinner menu, price, seating arrangements, entertainments if appropriate.

(f)   Obtain information on: map for delegates, train times, places of local interest, local entertainment, telephone numbers of taxi firms, etc.

3   SECRETARIAL INSTRUCTIONS

This exercise assumes that the secretary has taken notes from her boss on a Thursday morning. She has in her possession all the relevant correspondence, names, addresses, etc.

The exercise involves:

(a)   planning
(b)   a draft letter
(c)   a memo
(d)   an itinerary.

INSTRUCTIONS

The following is information dictated to the secretary:

> Write to my Bank Manager — personal, of course — heading Account No. 883980. Thank him for his letter et cetera. You've got it. Agree with his comments — propose to increase amount in special accounts each month to £120 — that's the account number 883980. Ask him to let me have the necessary form. I think I need to do this because of the recent increase in rates/mortgages — rates have gone up 15p in the pound — and probable increase in petrol and car insurance. Usual regards et cetera.

> Do an internal memo about this Staff Association invitation to Mr James. Say that I shall be pleased to speak to them — will give some sort of general survey of our activities. Get a suitable date from my diary. Sign it yourself.

> I'm going to Scotland for this meeting next Wednesday. Don't want to stay at Loch Lomond more than one night. Book me flights. Heathrow/

Glasgow. Hired car at airport for use during stay — ask for Mercedes or Daimler with chauffeur. Book hotel — evening meal. Do me an itinerary. Get cash.

EXERCISES

Now carry out the instructions by:

(a)   listing all the work necessary in the order in which you consider that it should be done
(b)   writing the necessary items.

4   THE FIRM'S NEWSLETTER

You work in the Public Relations Department of your firm. The manager has decided to produce a monthly newsletter for circulation among the firm's 1000 employees.

You have been asked to consider this project and write a report for the departmental manager. Your report should recommend the most suitable reprographic method for production of the newsletter, include suggestions for the most suitable methods of collecting news (for example, posters, memos, meetings) and enclose sample articles based on the following items of information which you have just received.

(a)   One of the electrical apprentices has received an 'Apprentice of the Year' award from the local technical college which he attends on one day a week.
(b)   The secretary of the firm's staff association has asked you to prepare a display advertisement for the annual dinner/dance which is to take place in a month's time.
(c)   The cricket club secretary has told you of the firm's team's successes in the local league and asked you to write an article for him. He has also asked for your help in obtaining volunteers to assist in preparing the cricket club teas on Saturday afternoons for the rest of the season.
(d)   You have recently attended the presentation to the Sales Director of the firm on his retirement after forty years' service. There will be a photograph for inclusion. Write the caption.

Invent any necessary details to prepare your articles.

5   THE SECRETARIAL POST

The exercise could involve:

(a)   a letter of application and *curriculum vitae*
(b)   drafting an application form
(c)   completing a job specification
(d)   write a letter of application and *curriculum vitae* for the following post:

Personal Assistant/Executive Secretary
for Group Managing Director

The Managing Director of the Tilley Group requires a Personal Assistant/Executive Secretary. Experience of operating at senior level essential. Must have first-class shorthand and typing, be capable of working on own initiative and have the ability to keep office running smoothly during his frequent absences abroad.

An excellent salary is offered with attractive benefits. This is a demanding but interesting job with frequent high-level executive and international contacts that requires a high level of confidentiality.

(e)   shortlist the letters of application written for exercise (d)

(f)   carry out interviews of shortlisted candidates and make a final choice

(g)   write letters to be sent to the unsuccessful candidates and to the successful applicant.

EXERCISES

(a)   Read the following information and add whatever other detail you consider necessary.

JOB SPECIFICATION

A.   LEVEL   Senior Secretarial with responsibility for supervision

B.   DUTIES

    1. Preparation and transcription of correspondence, reports and financial statements, including much confidential material

    2. Organisation of employer's travel arrangements

    3. Organisation of the work flow in the office for the following staff:

        (a) shorthand typist (deputy to Personal Assistant)

        (b) audio typist

        (c) clerk typist.

C.   RESPONSIBILITIES

    1. Assisting the Group Managing Director in a variety of work

    2. Supervision of the staff mentioned in B3 above

    3. Responsibility for the confidential files

D.   TRAINING AND EDUCATION REQUIRED

    1. Good background education, preferably to at least 'A' level in two subjects including English

    2. Shorthand 120 w.p.m., typing 60 w.p.m.

    3. Experience in senior post for at least two years

E.   ECONOMIC AND WORKING CONDITIONS

    1. Salary £1600—£2000 depending on age and experience

    2. Holidays — eighteen working days

    3. Hours of work must be flexible but normally will be a five-day week, 9.15 to 5.30

4. Non-contributory pension scheme
5. Canteen facilities
6. Own modern office with IBM electric typewriter (latest model).

(b)   Draw up an application form that could be used for applicants for this post.

(c)   Make out a list of questions that you would want to ask at the interview.

(d)   Shortlist the letters of application written in reply to the exercise in Section 4.

(e)   Carry out interviews of shortlisted candidates and make a final choice.

(f)   Write letters to be sent to the unsuccessful candidates and to the successful applicant.

6   THE MEETING

There follows a series of instructions for an exercise with a meeting as a central feature. The exercise involves:

(a)   drafting an agenda
(b)   holding a meeting (the use of a tape recorder is helpful)
(c)   writing the minutes
(d)   preparing a report
(e)   drafting an advertisement
(f)   preparing a press release
(g)   a series of letters.

It is suggested that a class could be divided into several groups, each carrying out different tasks, for example,

GROUP 1   draft agenda
hold meeting
prepare press release

GROUP 2   write minutes
draft advertisement

GROUP 3   prepare report
write letters

Groups 2 and 3 would attend the meeting to take notes so that they could respectively write the minutes and prepare a report afterwards. They would not participate in the meeting.

INSTRUCTIONS

You are a group of people who have met regularly to discuss the feasibility of forming an area environmental body to act as a watchdog in your locality. The area chosen should include rural and urban sections if possible.

(a)   Prepare for your meeting. Draft the agenda. Elect a Chairman. Your meeting will need to discuss some or all of the following items, but you may wish to include others:

(i)   THE BROAD AIMS OF THE GROUP You must consider what other groups already exist so that your aims do not conflict with theirs.

(ii)   THE FEASIBILITY OF SUCH A SOCIETY Some of you may feel that it is either not feasible or not necessary. However, for the purpose of the exercise it must be assumed that there is sufficient public concern in the area for you to be reasonably certain of adequate support for a public meeting.

(iii)   THE PARTICULAR NEEDS OF THE AREA For instance, is there a problem with road traffic, housing development, office development, industrial pollution, aircraft noise?

(iv)   PUBLIC MEETING You must decide when and where this should be held, who is to be asked to chair it and to which people you are going to send special invitations. You must also decide how you will publicise it.

(v)   PRESS RELEASE You must decide what form your press release will take.

(b)   THE MEETING   When you have discussed and agreed your agenda, you can hold the meeting. This should take no more than three-quarters of an hour. Your Chairman must see that everyone has an opportunity to present her views and that notes are taken for minutes.

(c)   MINUTES   When the meeting is over, the minutes must be drafted.

EXERCISES

The following are the tasks which the Secretary to the meeting would then have to perform:

(a)   write a report for the public meeting, making it about 350 words long and summarising the discusssion at the meeting

(b)   draft an advertisement for the public meeting for insertion in the local newspaper

(c)   write a press release of not more than 200 words

(e)   write letters to at least two of the people whom the meeting has decided should be invited to the public meeting, choosing people to whom you will send very different letters

(e)   write a letter to the person whom you hope will chair the public meeting, explaining your purpose and asking him or her to accept the job.

7   HAS COMMUNICATION FAILED? A SITUATION EXERCISE

This case study brings together in one exercise a number of problems that might be encountered by secretaries in supervisory roles. The exercise involves:

(a)   discussion

(b)   report-writing

(c)   redesigning an organisation chart
(d)   redrafting a memo.

INSTRUCTIONS

Read the following information:

The exercise is concerned with a general administrative office in a small manufacturing company as outlined on the chart in Figure 64. The staff in the
office and their immediate superiors are described below:

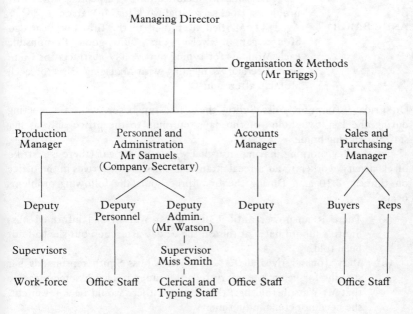

Figure 64   Exercise 7 – organisation chart

STAFF

MR SAMUELS	Company Secretary with Accountancy qualifications. Aged 38. Two years with the company. Approachable but will not tolerate inefficiency in his subordinates. Doesn't like to be 'caught out'.
MR WATSON	Unqualified. Aged 49. 24 years with the company. Resents younger people who might threaten his position. Miss Smith's immediate superior.
MISS SMITH	Aged 35. Unmarried. Combines her supervisory responsibilities with the job of Secretary to Mr Samuels. She is responsible for the work-flow in the office and Mr Samuels has given instructions that all work should pass through her.

CLERKS

MARGARET GREEN	Three 'O' levels. Aged 16+. Responsible for filing. Has been with the firm for three months. Predecessor 'showed her the ropes' for two weeks.
SUSAN YOUNG	Six 'O' levels. Aged 26. Married. Deputises for Miss Smith. Been with the firm for four years.

SHORTHAND TYPISTS

MARY JONES	Aged 17. Came from secretarial college two months ago. Reasonable qualifications. Suspected 'love life' problems. Does secretarial work for Mr Watson.
ANNE BRIGHT	Aged 42. Married. Returned to the firm one year ago after a gap of twelve years. Quite good. Responsible each Monday for typing out weekly abstracts for Company Secretary's meeting with Managing Director each Monday afternoon.

On Friday afternoon, Miss Smith, the office supervisor, was at a meeting during the last two hours of the day, returning to the office only as her staff were going home.

On Monday morning, having struggled with a power cut (there is a strike of electricity workers) and a recalcitrant car, Miss Smith arrives in the office on time at 8.30 a.m. During the first three hours the following problems occur.

(a)   There is no power until 9.30 a.m. Mr Watson had informed Miss Smith's subordinates of this on the Friday afternoon but she had not been told.

(b)   Mary Jones arrives at 9.35 a.m. When Miss Smith reprimands her sharply for being late, Mary tells the supervisor with some pleasure that Mr Watson told her, that, because there would be a power cut, she need not come in on time.

   'After all, I shouldn't have been able to use my electric typewriter, should I?'

   She threatens to complain to Mr Watson about Miss Smith's tone.

(c)   At 9.45 Mr Briggs comes in and starts talking to the staff and giving out some sheets of paper. When Miss Smith enquires, he is surprised that she does not know that he is going to be in the section for the next three weeks doing an O & M survey.

   Further checking reveals that Mr Samuels had a memo about it (Figure 65).

(d)   At 10.00 Miss Smith goes to the filing cabinet to obtain information on staff holidays for Mr Watson. The file is missing. Later she discovers it on Mr Samuels's desk.

(e)   Mr Samuels has given Anne Bright a long report which he has said must be typed in triplicate by 12.15 p.m. Miss Smith discovers this only when Anne fails to give her the weekly returns for checking at 11.30.

MEMORANDUM

From: O & M Officer   To: Company Secretary

Date: 3rd December 19--   Subject: Administration

The Managing Director has agreed that an O & M
survey of your Administration is long overdue.   I
propose to commence this survey on Monday 21st
February 19-- and shall be visiting the office.

R. Briggs

Figure 65   Exercise 7 — memorandum

EXERCISES

(a)   Resolve the problems. You may need, among other things, to consider
the following, although not necessarily in the order in which they are
given, or even as separate points.

  (i)   What failures of communication exist?
  (ii) How should Miss Smith have reacted to the situation?
  (iii) What action should have been taken to prevent these problems
        from occurring, and by whom?
  (iv) How would you deal with the situation (a) in the short term,
        (b) in the long term?

(When dealing with (iii) and (iv) the group may wish to consider each
person in the exercise in turn or concentrate on the supervisor and Mr
Samuels.)

(b)   Rewrite Mr Briggs's memo.

(c)   Assume that you are Mr Briggs and that you have come into the department following the rewritten memo and have been able to carry out a
comprehensive survey. Write your report to the Managing Director,
copy to Mr Samuels, giving your analysis of the situation and your
recommendations. Do not change any of the details in the exercise
(except those referring to Mr Briggs), but invent any other information
that you consider necessary.

(d)   As Mr Briggs, amend the organisation chart in accordance with your
report.

8   THE MOVE

This exercise is based on an article published in *Personnel Management* relating
to a move made by one firm. When the exercise is completed students may be
interested to read the article, which is reprinted in Section 16, Appendix 5.

The exercise involves:

(a)   class discussion
(b)   a circular letter
(c)   an agenda
(d)   a meeting (the use of a tape recorder is helpful)
(e)   oral reports
(f)   minutes

INSTRUCTIONS

Read the following information:

A company manufacturing a consumer product with highly technical equipment decided that their existing premises were too old and cramped to cope with further expansion and that they should move to a new £4 million, 16-acre site, two and a half miles away.

The following facts may be relevant.

1.   The company employed nearly 2000 employees on production and distribution.
2.   Enormous stocks were held — about £5 million.
3.   They have 30 per cent of the existing market for similar products.
4.   Their products go to some 4500 dealers.
5.   The company had a high proportion of long-service employees whose expertise it valued.
6.   Choice of site was made in the summer of 1970.
7.   Rumours of the move were already current at this time.
8.   The move was proposed for June 1972 (usually a slack period).
9.   Production was to be gradually transferred over a four to eight-week period.
10. To avoid distribution problems, it was decided to transfer the bulk of stock in advance with immediate stocks being transferred over a long weekend.
11. There would be no redundancies.
12. Industrial relations had been good over the past few years with some very satisfactory negotiations over both payment systems and working arrangements.

EXERCISES

(a)   Answer the following questions:
      (i)   What information should have been given and to whom?
      (ii)   What opportunities for discussion should there have been?
      (iii) Timing: what should the time-table of communication have been.
      (iv)   What media of communication should have been used at various stages?

(v) What are the main problems that could have arisen from communication failures and what might the consequences have been?

(b) Draft a letter to all employees informing them of the impending move and proposed arrangements.

(c) As an alternative to class discussion, draft an agenda and hold a meeting of the company's Board of Directors to discuss arrangements. For this exercise it is suggested that half the students be given time in which to prepare roles and plan short reports, to be given orally, on, for instance, finance, movement of plant, security, co-ordination with unions, discussions with employees.

The remainder of the class should take notes at the meeting and prepare minutes afterwards.

(d) Class discussion on the efficacy of the measures proposed at the meeting could follow.

Appendix 1

SKIP TEST ANSWERS
AND SUMMARY OF CORRESPONDENCE

GRAMMAR

Dear Sir,

Owing to the bad weather last week, we were unable to complete the laying of your lawn. I should be very pleased if you could let me know when it will be convenient for us to return to finish the work.

With reference to your query about the price of shrubs, you will have our estimate for this by the end of the week.

Mr Brown, our consultant, whom you met some time ago, will be able to meet you and me next week at a time to suit you to consider what herbaceous plants will suit your soil.

We apologise for his not contacting you earlier, but he has unfortunately been ill. He would be glad if you could give him some idea of your preference as to colours in this border. Do you wish them to be different from one another or of similar hues? If you want two colours only, would you like fewer of one plant or an equal number of each type?

All of the plants we sell have, of course, our usual guarantee.

Yours faithfully,

PUNCTUATION

At the Annual General Meeting of Traders Limited held on 16 April 19 — —, the Chairman said,

'It is with pleasure that I am able to announce the results for the past financial year. Profits have risen by 20 per cent after tax and happily, your Board's concern with the rising cost of materials, which I expressed last year, has not been entirely justified. It is true that costs have risen. When do they not do so?

'Our increased sales, particularly on the export side, have, however, enabled us to show increased profits. In addition the continued streamlining of the process, rationalisation of staff, together with reorganisation of departments, improved advertising methods and the success of the new name, "Tradex", have contributed to progress. I anticipate that in two years' time our change-over to the new machine will be complete and that we shall then see even greater returns than are apparent now.

'The dividend of 10 per cent that we are able to declare is largely the result of intensive work by the staff and they deserve our thanks. Good staff are hard to come by and we appreciate their many qualities: integrity, intelligence, adaptability, patience and, above all, the will to work hard.'

SPELLING

The old-fashioned *practice* of writing out correctly one's *errors* in spelling may still *definitely benefit* those students who *occasionally* find *difficulties* in this area. An *efficient* secretary must be able to spell *accurately*; even the most *capable* should keep a *dictionary* in her desk. Some of the following words are commonly misspelled:

advertisement	management
academic	psychological
conscientious	recommendations
explanations	statistical
interpret	exhibit
instalments	signature
disappear	objectionable

SUMMARY OF CORRESPONDENCE

Summary of correspondence between J. Maggs, 5 Maple Grove, Bingley, Wilts., WB4 6LM and the Reliable Insurance Company, Broadgate, Bradford, BD1 5CX, about a comprehensive motor insurance policy, between 14 and 28 March 19 — —:

Mr Maggs queried the quotation of £65, asking for a no-claim bonus and a reduction for his agreement to pay the first £25 of damage.

The Reliable Insurance Co. agreed to a no-claim bonus allowance of £18.50 on receipt of proof of the bonus from Mr Maggs's previous insurers, plus an allowance of £10 for his acceptance of responsibility for the first £25 of any damage.

Mr Maggs accepted the revised quotation of £36.50 and enclosed proof of his previous no-claim bonus.

The Reliable Insurance Co. confirmed the revised premium and sent proposal forms for Mr Maggs's signature.

Mr Maggs returned the signed forms, and enclosed his cheque for £36.50. He requested that cover should be arranged as soon as possible. (120 words)

Appendix 2

EXTRACTS FROM THE MEMORANDUM AND ARTICLES OF ASSOCIATION OF A LIMITED LIABILITY COMPANY

FIRST SCHEDULE TO THE COMPANIES ACT 1948, TABLE A, PART 1

GENERAL MEETINGS

47.   The company shall in each year hold a general meeting as its annual general meeting in addition to any other meeting in that year, and shall specify the meeting as such in notices calling it; and not more than fifteen months shall elapse between the date of one annual general meeting of the company and that of the next.

48.   All general meetings other than annual general meetings shall be called extraordinary general meetings.

NOTICE OF GENERAL MEETING

50.   An annual general meeting and a meeting called for the passing of a special resolution shall be called by twenty-one days' notice in writing at the least, and a meeting of the company other than an annual general meeting or a meeting for the passing of a special resolution shall be called by fourteen days' notice in writing at the least. The notice shall be exclusive of the day on which it is served or deemed to be served and of the day for which it is given, and shall specify the place, the day and the hour of meeting and, in the case of special business, the general nature of that business, and shall be given, in manner hereinafter mentioned or in such other manner, if any, as may be prescribed by the company in general meeting, to such persons as are, under the regulations of the company, entitled to receive such notices from the company:

Provided that a meeting of the company shall, notwithstanding that it is called by shorter notice than that specified in this regulation, be deemed to have been duly called if it is so agreed —

(a)   in the case of a meeting called as the annual general meeting, by all the members entitled to attend and vote thereat; and

(b)   in the case of any other meeting, by a majority in number of the members having a right to attend and vote at the meeting, being a majority together holding not less than 95 per cent in nominal value of the shares giving that right.

51. The accidental omission to give notice of a meeting to, or the non-receipt of notice of a meeting by, any person entitled to receive notice shall not invalidate the proceedings at that meeting.

PROCEEDINGS AT GENERAL MEETINGS

52. All business shall be deemed special that is transacted at an extraordinary general meeting, and also all that is transacted at an annual general meeting, with the exception of declaring a dividend, the consideration of the accounts, balance sheets, and the reports of the directors and auditors, the election of directors in the place of those retiring and the appointment of, and fixing the remuneration of, the auditors.

53. No business shall be transacted at any general meeting unless a quorum of members is present at the time when the meeting proceeds to business; save as herein otherwise provided, three members present in person shall be a quorum.

55. The chairman, if any, of the board of directors shall preside as chairman at every general meeting of the company, or if there is no such chairman, or if he shall not be present within fifteen minutes after the time appointed for the holding of the meeting or is unwilling to act the directors present shall elect one of their number to be chairman of the meeting.

58. At any general meeting a resolution put to the vote of the meeting shall be decided on a show of hands unless a poll is (before or on the declaration of the result of the show of hands) demanded —

Unless a poll be so demanded a declaration by the chairman that a resolution has on show of hands been carried or carried unanimously, or by a particular majority, or lost and an entry to that effect in the book containing the minutes of the proceedings of the company shall be conclusive evidence of the fact without proof of the number or proportion of the votes recorded in favour of or against such resolution.

60. In the case of an equality of votes, whether on a show of hands or on a poll, the chairman of the meeting at which the show of hands takes place or at which the poll is demanded, shall be entitled to a second or casting vote.

POWERS AND DUTIES OF DIRECTORS

86. The directors shall cause minutes to be made in books provided for the purpose —

  (a)   of all appointments of officers made by the directors
  (b)   of the names of the directors present at each meeting of the directors and of any committee of the directors
  (c)   of all resolutions and proceedings at all meetings of the Company, and of the directors, and of committees of directors

and every director present at any meeting of directors or committees of directors shall sign his name in a book to be kept for that purpose.

PROCEEDINGS OF DIRECTORS

98.   The directors may meet together for the despatch of business, adjourn, and otherwise regulate their meetings, as they think fit. Questions arising at any meeting shall be decided by a majority of votes. In case of an equality of votes, the chairman shall have a second, or casting, vote. A director may, and the secretary on the requisition of a director shall, at any time summon to a meeting of directors any director for the time being absent from the United Kingdom.

99.   The quorum necessary for the transaction of business of the directors may be fixed by the directors and unless so fixed shall be two.

PART II

REGULATIONS FOR THE MANAGEMENT OF A PRIVATE COMPANY LIMITED BY SHARES

4.   No business shall be transacted at any general meeting unless a quorum of members is present at the time when the meeting proceeds to business; save as herein otherwise provided two members present in person or by proxy shall be a quorum.

5.   Subject to the provisions of the Act, a resolution in writing signed by all the members being entitled to receive notice of and to attend and vote at general meetings shall be as valid and effective as if the same had been passed at a general meeting of the company duly convened and held.

Appendix 3

GLOSSARY OF TERMS RELATING TO MEETINGS

Ad hoc   Literally 'to this' or 'for this'; that is, 'for this purpose', for example a committee formed for a special purpose and usually disbanded after that purpose has been achieved.

Addendum   A resolution which adds words to a motion.

Adjournment   The act of extending or continuing a meeting for the purpose of dealing with unfinished business, or of deferring the debate on a motion which is before the meeting.

Agenda   Literally means 'things to be done', but commonly used to describe the agenda paper which lists the items of business to be discussed at a meeting. (The term 'agenda paper' is also used of papers relating to an item or items on the agenda which are provided for members of the committee.)

Amendment   A proposal to alter a motion which has been submitted to a meeting, for example by adding, inserting or deleting words of the original motion.

Ballot   A method of voting employed when secrecy is desired.

Casting vote   A second vote usually allowed to the chairman, except in the case of a company meeting, and used to break a deadlock.

Closure   A motion submitted with the object of ending the discussion on a matter before the meeting.

Committee   A person or body of persons to whom general or specific duties and authority have been delegated by a parent body, for example a committee in lunacy may consist of one person appointed by a court.

Co-opted   Invited to join the deliberations of a meeting or series of meetings, but not entitled to vote. (**Co-optative** members have a vote.)

Debate   Discussion on a motion put before a meeting, prior to putting the motion to a vote.

Ex officio   Literally 'by virtue of office or position' as, for example, when a person attends a meeting not in his capacity as a member but by virtue of his office.

Executive committee   A committee with powers to put decisions into effect.

Form of proxy   A document in writing by which one person authorises another person to attend a meeting and vote on his behalf.

Formal motion   A motion intended to alter the procedure of a meeting, for example to adjourn the meeting.

In camera   Held in private — the public excluded.

Lie on the table   A letter or document on which a meeting decides to take no action is said to do this.

Majority   Unless otherwise indicated, this may be taken to mean a 'simple' majority, that is, a number which is greater than either the number voting against or abstaining. (An 'overall' majority is a vote which is more than half of the total number of votes cast.)

Minutes   A written record of the business transacted at a meeting.

Motion   A proposition or proposal put forward for discussion and decision at a meeting.

Nem con.   *(nemine contradicente)*. Without dissent.

Next business   Motion to move to next business, which is a method of curtailing discussion (and delaying discussion) on any matter before a meeting.

Order of business   The intended order in which items of business, as set out on the agenda, are to be taken. This order may be altered by resolution of the meeting.

Point of order   A question regarding procedure or a query relating to the rules (constitution, standing orders) raised during the course of a meeting and decided on by the chair (for example, lack of quorum).

Poll   The taking of a vote, the number of votes recorded.

Proxy   A person (or document of authority) authorised to attend a meeting and vote on behalf of someone else.

Quorum   The minimum number of persons entitled to be present at a meeting which the regulations require to be present in order that the business of the meeting may be transacted validly.

Resolution   Although the words 'motion' and 'resolution' are often used indiscriminately, a 'motion' is a proposal put to a meeting, whereas a 'resolution' is a proposal which has been accepted by the meeting.

Rider   An additional clause or sentence added to a resolution and proposed, seconded and voted upon in the same manner as the resolution.

Right of reply   Right of mover of a motion to reply once to discussion of it before the vote.

Sine die   'Without an appointed day'; indefinitely. Thus a meeting adjourned *sine die* necessitates fresh notice for the adjourned meeting.

Standing committee   A permanent committee, such as the housing committee of a local authority.

Standing orders   The name given to rules regulating the conduct and procedures of certain deliberative and legislative bodies, such as the permanent standing orders of local authorities.

Status quo   The existing state of affairs.

Sub-committee   A committee appointed by a parent body for a certain specific purpose or to relieve the larger committee of some of its routine work. It usually consists of some of the members of the appointing committee, but specialist non-members are often co-opted.

Substantive motion   A motion which has been amended.

Ultra vires   Beyond the legal powers possessed by the organisation.

Appendix 4

TELEPHONE SCRIPT ERRORS

The secretary made the following errors:

(a) She did not greet the caller properly, for example,
'Good afternoon. Sales Manager's office. This is his secretary, Miss Jones, speaking.'
(b) She was not helpful
(c) Her tone was brusque
(d) She used unsuitable language such as,
'Just a sec.'; 'O.K.'; 'Hang on'
(e) She had no pencil or paper handy
(f) There was no proper telephone message pad
(g) She was not careful enough when taking the message
(h) The message was not rewritten correctly with full information
(i) She did not obtain the name, firm and telephone number of the caller
(j) She carried on a conversation with someone else.

Appendix 5

THE STORY BEHIND THE MOVE

PERSONNEL AND TRAINING IN PRACTICE — THE STORY BEHIND EMI RECORDS' MOVE INVOLVING 2000 EMPLOYEES AND £5 MILLION WORTH OF STOCK

RECORD OF THE MOVE

Just two years after deciding that their premises at Blyth Road, Hayes, were too old and cramped to cope with further expansion, EMI Records were happily installed at a new £4 million 16-acre site, on the Uxbridge Road, two and a half miles away.

Not much of a move in terms of distance, perhaps, but with nearly 2000 employees covering both production and distribution of records and tapes, enormous stocks of the records themselves and a big investment in highly technical equipment, EMI were faced with a number of taxing problems — both in production and human terms.

EMI Records have the lion's share of the record business in this country, about 30 per cent of the total market. Their records go to some 4500 dealers, who rely on delivery of new stock within 24 hours of placing their orders. The records which have to be held in stock for this operation at the new distribution centre are worth about £5 million and a day's production from the presses next door, 112 of them, amounts to some 300,000 records.

When it came to choosing a new site the company had to consider their distribution system. Prior to 1966, EMI had used a chain of distribution centres spread throughout the country, but these were then abandoned in favour of a single, central warehouse at Blyth Road. Distribution these days relies heavily on British Rail and so any new warehouse would need to be near the major London railway stations. In addition the company had a high proportion of long-service employees whose expertise they valued and so there was some pressure to remain in the Greater Hayes area.

PREPARING TO GO

The choice of site was finally made in the summer of 1970 and preparations began almost at once. Rumours of a move (to the North-east of England or even further afield) were already current, and the company's first move was to make sure that all employees were kept fully informed and involved. A company notice in August 1970 announced the move on the same day that the managing director and personnel manager met senior union representatives from ASTMS, APEX, DATA, AUEW, and TGWU and told them of the proposed move. All employees, both manufacturing and distribution, attended a mass meeting the same afternoon and were told of the company's plans for moving by the personnel manager and the two divisional heads directly involved in the project.

These were, broadly, that the move should take place in June 1972 (usually a slack period in the record business) and that the production should be gradually transferred to the new site over a period of four to eight weeks. The distribution side presented more problems and in order to make any break in supply to dealers as short as possible, it was decided to transfer the bulk of the stock in advance of the move, with immediate stocks being transferred over a long weekend.

One of the company's first tasks, through the personnel department, was to assure the unions that no redundancies would be caused by the move and a statement was issued to that effect. In fact, all but four of EMI Record's employees are still with them on the new site and those four are currently still employed elsewhere in the EMI Group.

Nine months before the move date, two liaison committees were set up with the intention of providing an opportunity for consultation and negotiation with employees. These committees, chaired by the personnel manager, Mr Edwin White, were for salaried and hourly paid staff, respectively, and included senior shop stewards from the five unions recognised by the company. These committees could meet as often as their members required and were able to discuss and negotiate upon matters arising from the move.

At the same time, and in addition to the high-level liaison committees, departmental discussion groups were formed in which representatives from each of the main departments could thrash out more specific problems associated with the layout of the new site. In both cases the company's intention was to involve the employees in the move as much as possible. Employees were encouraged to visit the new site, which was by then in the throes of reconstruction, and to comment on the arrangements there.

The fact that involvement in the project did indeed take place was, the company feels, largely due to the efforts made over the past few years in the industrial relations area. A number of major changes in payments systems and working arrangements have meant that the confrontation between management and union has been kept to a minimum. For example, EMI Records negotiated a system of twelve-monthly agreements for most employees which has largely eliminated wage drift as well as removing a considerable source of friction. Bonus schemes were almost completely eliminated by May 1970 in favour of standard time work at all-in rates. Shift working was introduced at the same time and has now spread to a number of production areas.

In the event the move date happened to coincide with a period of freak demand for records — almost at the level of the pre-Christmas rush. The company's plans held good, however, with a pilot production run in the new press room being gradually built up to full production levels. The distribution warehouse closed down at the old site on Wednesday evening and current record stocks were transferred to the new site over the following four days — with stringent security precautions. Business was 'as usual' on Monday morning.

HARDLY A HITCH

Few serious problems have been experienced with the new site, which offers potential for something like 50 per cent expansion for the company. Transport, particularly for the part-time female staff, was recognised as a problem, but a temporary free bus service has taken care of things for the time being. Working conditions at the new site are much improved and the company feels that it has been successful in what, from a personnel point of view, it regards as primarily an industrial relations exercise of some magnitude.

(*Personnel Management*, Journal of the Institute of Personnel Management,
September 1972)

Appendix 6

EXAMINATION PAPERS

THE LONDON CHAMBER OF COMMERCE AND INDUSTRY
PRIVATE SECRETARY'S CERTIFICATE
EXAMINATION

JUNE 1974

INSTRUCTIONS TO CANDIDATES

You are allowed 2½ hours and can obtain a maximum of 100 marks. *Answer ALL THREE questions.* Notice that the marks obtainable are shown below each question or section.

Put a line through any rough work.

1. Super-Temp is a secretarial agency which supplies temporary staff for local firms which are short staffed owing to holidays, illness, overwork or other reasons. Temporary secretaries are employed by and paid by the agency, which engages them on a permanent basis, either full-time or part-time, and sends them to work in the offices of local firms as the need arises.

   When the temporary secretary first arrives a firm explains her exact duties, although she is of course usually fully trained. She will work at a given firm for any period from half a day upwards, but seldom spends more than two or three weeks there. This might be unsettling for some girls, but Super-Temp tries to employ staff who enjoy variety. The girls sometimes need to travel fairly long distances, though fares are refunded by the agency. Full-time staff can earn up to £40 per week and part-timers *pro rata*.

   Super-Temp plans to distribute hundreds of copies of a recruiting leaflet to local houses. The object is to find housewives with secretarial training and/or experience who would like to join the staff of Super-Temp. An open evening will shortly be held on the agency's premises, so that interested persons can learn more about the life and work of a temporary secretary. They will be able to meet some of the staff, listen to a talk by the Manager, and so on. There will be suitable light refreshments.

Attempt ONE of the following exercises, inventing any necessary MINOR details:

Either (a) Prepare the full text of a suitable recruiting leaflet. You need to present all the relevant particulars attractively but crisply. Circular letter format should be used.

Or (b) As a junior reporter for a local newspaper, you have attended the open evening. Draft a brief feature article about Super-Temp and its activities. You must assume that your readers do not know anything about temporary work.

NOTE: You may choose whether the evening was a success or a failure, provided you clearly indicate why. This exercise tests your ability to report and put forward reasoned views.

(30 marks)

2. Your employer will shortly be addressing a business conference on the subject of the benefits resulting from the existence and operations of multinational companies. Prepare a summary in not more than 170 words of any *relevant* material in the following extract which might help your employer when he prepares his talk.

The multinational company has become an ogre to many people. There are few complaints that have not been laid at its doorstep. One school of thought sees multinationals are rapacious marauders, infiltrating the poor developing countries and siphoning off their resources.

Many attitudes towards these international giants are wholly irrational. Suddenly discovered by a rash of authors, the multinational is exposed in all its supposed forms as a phenomenon of our times. But surely the multinational has been with us since the days of the Hudon's Bay Company?

Politicians agonise about the foreign investment the international companies bring — for example, Britain worries about whether American investment in this country is good or bad. Then we are horrified if Henry Ford suggests that he might not build his next factory in Britain.

In fact the international investment that the multinational company brings with it is, as most economic liberals have long believed, a good thing for both investor and host country. Far from exploiting the developing countries the multinational is capable of doing them a power of economic good. A number of important facts must be borne in mind when weighing up the situation.

Firstly, although the investment in underdeveloped countries obviously takes out more than it puts in (since companies must be profitable) this in effect constitutes the premium required from the underdeveloped country in order that it may benefit from the installation of new economic enterprises.

Secondly, even when taken collectively the multinationals have only a small influence on the balance of payments and the national economies of the countries involved — contrary to popular myth.

Thirdly, multinationals are not quite the band of international privateers*; untrammelled by government regulation, that so many people see them as. Indeed, they are bound by a maze of fiscal and exhange regulations.

There are many risks which the multinational company has to take, and part of its profits are needed to safeguard it against them: nationalisation, for example, compulsory local material purchasing, or even the dangers of loss through war or civil commotion. Indeed, the notion of the multinational as an organisation more powerful than the states in which it operates, and able to trample on regulations obeyed by more ordinary businesses, is quite mistaken.

What can sometimes be argued is that multinationals, by switching funds about the world, can endanger national economies, damage balances of payments and threaten weak currencies. But against this there is clear evidence that in recent years there has been a switch —multinationals have begun to look to developed countries rather than developing countries in which to invest — and that this is a source of real concern to the Third World. Here is evidence of the vital role played by these international giants in aiding the growth and prosperity of underdeveloped nations, in bringing employment, in creating stability (political as well as economic) and — we must not forget — in earning a good return on the huge capital sums involved. (492 words.)

(Adapted from an article in the *Sunday Times,* 25 March 1973)

(30 marks)

3. Answer both part (a) and part (b)
   (a) Read the following extract from a booklet entitled *Extending Your House,* published by the Consumers' Association and answer the questions which follow it.

Most gas appliances must be separated from any combustible material in the structure of the building either by a shield of non-combustible material or by an air space.

The flue requirements of gas appliances often depend on the size of the room. Some appliances do not connect directly to a flue: a gas cooker does not, nor a water heater below a certain size — for instance, a sink water heater. You can install a gas water-heating appliance without connecting it to a flue only if the room is large enough and has a specified amount of per-

---

* privateers = pirates

manent ventilation. In a bathroom a gas water heater should be of the room-sealed type with a balanced flue.

(i)   A householder fixes a gas water heater directly on to a brick wall. Is this permitted? Give your reasons.

(ii) A householder proposes to install a gas cooker in a very tiny kitchen which lacks ventilation. Is this permitted? Give your reasons.

(iii) A householder fixes a sink water heater over the hand-basin in his bathroom. There is no flue. Discuss how one should interpret the regulations on this point; is there any ambiguity?

(iv) A householder shows the foregoing regulations to a builder, who says he has not read them before. What evidence do you notice which might indicate that a builder is, or is not, likely to have seen this extract?

(15 marks)

(b)   Read the following extract from an article entitled 'There's none so blind . . . .' from *New Statesman,* 21 July 1972, and answer the questions which follow it:

Last month an unfortunate ophthalmic optician was struck off the Register of Opticians by the General Optical Council for the heinous crime of allowing his firm's name to appear in two Scottish telephone directories in heavy type. In so doing he had contravened the rules on publicity made under Section 25 of the Opticians Act of 1958, and by such contravention had apparently rendered himself unfit to serve the public by grinding lenses or fitting spectacle frames.

Ordinary and ignorant members of the public such as myself could be excused for thinking that a bold-type entry in the telephone directory might be exactly the kind of aid that any citizen needing the services of an optician would welcome, as he peered at the columns of otherwise grey and unreadable print. But this is not the view of wiser and more percipient mortals, such as the members of the General Optical Council, who regard the use of heavy type as a piece of vulgar self-aggrandisement. Some 40 ophthalmic opticians, including last month's victim, had previously been warned against continuing the use of bold letters. The victim had apparently ignored this solemn admonition, with the result that one of his fellow traders, irritated by the unfair competition, informed the Council.

(i)   In a few lines, draft a regulation which roughly sums up the content of Section 25 of the Opticians Act of 1958. Use the passage to give you clues, and word the regulation as it might appear in the Act.

(ii) The writer describes what happened to a person who broke the law. What reasons have you for thinking that the writer sympathises with the person concerned and disapproves of the law?

(iii) Do you regard the passage as flippant, serious, satirical or a mixture of these? Give examples from the passage to support your interpretation.

(iv) Using your own words, explain what you understand by any TWO of the following words or phrases in the passage:

      ophthalmic   *bold-type entry*
      percipient   *solemn admonition*

(25 marks)

JUNE 1975
INSTRUCTIONS TO CANDIDATES

You are allowed 2½ hours and can obtain a maximum of 100 marks. *Answer ALL THREE questions.* Notice that the marks obtainable are shown below each question or section.

Put a line through any rough work.

1. The Westshire District Council runs four municipal swimming pools. Three are indoor pools and are heated. The fourth is an outdoor pool and it is not heated. The Council must decide whether or not to install heating in the outdoor pool, and one of the officers of the Council has been asked to look into the various advantages and disadvantages. He is not an expert, but having studied the various points and spoken to experts he is to submit a brief report to the Council giving his recommendation.

    There are several arguments in favour of heating the outdoor pool: to allow swimmers to use it in winter; to take the chill off the water during cool summers; to ensure that children enjoy learning to swim; to encourage increased use of the pool and thus to make more money for the Council. Arguments against heating the pool include the heavy initial cost; the running cost; the tendency for heated pools to suffer from algal growth (i.e. green slime); the danger that swimmers will catch a chill when they climb out on a cold windy day. A few keen swimmers simply prefer unheated pools.

Either   As the secretary to the officer of the Council who has been instructed to prepare a report, draft a short document for your employer to use as a basis for his preliminary report.

Or   As honorary secretary of a newly formed swimming association you have heard of the possibility that the outdoor pool will soon be heated. Write a formal letter to the Council presenting your association's strong views (either for or against) and urging appropriate action. You should try to persuade the Council to allow a senior sports official to meet you so that you can put your views to him personally.

(30 marks)

2. Your employer is a house-builder. He shows you the following article
from *New Society* and says, 'Please give me a short summary of what
people think of their present kitchens and what changes they want builders
to make in future, with the reasons. I want to know what I could do to
help such people when I build houses.' Read the article carefully and
prepare a suitable summary in under 170 words.

Kitchen Misery

If housewives feel trapped, is it perhaps specifically the kitchen that traps
them? It is a place where women spend large parts of their day, and many
kitchens are not much bigger than large cupboards.

We interviewed three groups of people: 'men of ideas' (architects,
designers, journalists), estate agents and housewives. When we asked them
how kitchens should be, the 'men of ideas' wanted a large kitchen, the
estate agents a small kitchen, and the housewives a large kitchen with
enough room for family activities.

These were very contrasting views. The emphasis of the housewives on
size was impressive. A clerk's wife from Wales, said, 'First of all, it would
have to be a big kitchen — 15 square feet.' This was rather larger than most
of them had in mind. A labourer's wife from the west of England said,
'Twelve feet by twelve, I should think — a nice square kitchen.'

This did not seem to vary with the age or social class of the person we
asked. A young lawyer's wife said, 'I'd have it next to the dining room, but
the kitchen would be big enough for family informal meals. It would be a
big room — farmhouse style but streamlined and modern. It would be big
enough for the kids to play in. About twelve feet by sixteen.'

Only a third of the people we interviewed were satisfied with their
kitchen. The most dissatisfied group was that of mothers with two or
more children. Mothers with children at home are subjected to constant
frustration. A young doctor's wife told us, 'I'd want the sun to shine on
the back of the house, where the kitchen is, because a wife spends most of
her time in the kitchen preparing meals and washing up. If it's raining I'm
washing clothes and nappies for the baby, so I never use any of the other
rooms during the daytime except the kitchen.'

Our researchers went to inspect the most modern house designs they
could find. In every case the kitchen that was provided was a small one.
The salesmen on the site say, 'Well, of course, madam, the houswife of
today has more interests. She doesn't want to spend her life in the kitchen
any more.'

A kitchen that is too small is a burden and an irritation, most of all for
mothers. Builders and salesmen make the mistake of regarding the kitchen
as the catering centre of the home and nothing more. But it is a room in
which most of the housewife's time is spent and where she is often reduced
to misery. If builders understood this they would perhaps build large,
better-sited and more convenient kitchens. But then, there is a price to pay

for everything and, harsh though it may be, a housewife may prefer to suffer in a tiny kitchen rather than have no house at all. The present economic situation makes it hard for a medium-priced home to contain a decent size kitchen, and builders cannot risk bankruptcy through building houses that are too expensive to sell. (About 500 words.)

(Adapted from *New Society*, 28 January 1971)

(30 marks)

3. (a)   Read carefully the following extract from a *Cornmarket Careers Guide* for 1973, and then answer all the questions below it.

Information Science

Information science is particularly concerned with the task of obtaining scientific and technical information for specific needs, and therefore with the problems of evaluation as well as dissemination. Information scientists are employed in industry, government departments, universities and research associations.

Associateship of the Institute of Information Scientists requires, as a minimum, possession of two GCE passes at 'A' level including one scientific subject. In addition, it is necessary to have had five years' experience in information work, or two years' experience in information work plus possession of the Institute's Certificate.

Graduates in science and technology need only one year's experience in information work. There are also higher grades of membership for graduates.

(i)   The following two persons wish to make a career in information science. Write a *brief* paragraph advising each of them.

Miss A   She has just left school with five 'O' levels and an 'A' level in history, and has taken a job in a bookshop.

Mr B   He has excellent 'A' levels in mathematics, biology and physics, and has worked in a technical library for about ten years. He hopes to obtain a degree from The Open University in 1976.

(ii)   You read in a newspaper, 'Information scientists simply keep information and make it available to other people when it is asked for.' The extract suggests that information scientists do more than that. What?

(iii)   The last line of the extract speaks of 'higher grades of membership' than Associateship. Give an example of a higher grade.

(iv)   In a few lines, giving your reasons, say why you think this extract was or was not intended to be read by children leaving school.

(20 marks)

(b)   Read carefully the following extract from a review of children's books, published in *The Times Literary Supplement* on 29 March 1974, and then answer the questions below it.

Throughout this century a considerable amount of thought and effort has been given to the importance of art and good design in everyday life. Nowadays we have the opportunity to enjoy our visual surroundings. A child today is particularly fortunate; for special attention is devoted to both his practical experience of art and to his environment. Forty years ago, Britain was for him largely a drab brown, with his clothes a serviceable buff or grey; dull yellow prints hung on the walls of his home and school; oatmeal, cream or brown for the paintwork. If he went to a provincial museum he might well find faded photographs, mediocre Victorian paintings.

An irresistible tide of brilliance, extending from toys and book illustrations to fabrics and interior decorations, has swept away the muddy colours, and galleries and museums all over the country have lively exhibitions of original works of art as well as special displays and activities for schools. The young are the principal beneficiaries.

(i)   Why do you suppose the author chose to speak of 'muddy colours' instead of, say, 'rich earth colours' or even 'warm chocolate colours'?

(ii)   It is said by some people that children in the old days were dressed in boring colours because their parents had no imagination. What other reason is mentioned in the extract? In one or two lines, say how far you think it is a valid reason.

(iii) The extract is from a book review, not a history of children's clothes or schools. Why do you think the author begins his article in this way?

(iv)   The author gives the impression that people did not care for brilliant colours and lively art in the old days. Can you suggest any other reason, apart from fashion, why an 'irresistible tide of brilliance' has swept away the old colours?

(20 marks)

JUNE 1978
INSTRUCTIONS TO CANDIDATES

You are allowed 2½ hours and can obtain a maximum of 100 marks. *Answer ALL THREE questions.* Notice that the marks obtainable are shown below each question or section.

Put a line through any rough work.

NOTE: In this question, the town Z can be any suitable town that you know, or an imaginary town.

1. You are the secretary to Alan Webb, one of the partners of Robinson, Webb & Associates, a firm of financial consultants whose clients include a number of international companies. Your office is in the capital city of your country, but you often have to travel to business meetings in distant towns.

   Mr Webb is considering setting up a branch office in Z, a town about 200 miles away, to reduce the amount of travelling which he and his partners have to undertake. As many of his clients come from distant parts of the country, and from overseas, it is important that Z should have excellent transport and hotel facilities. It should also be suitable for business entertaining, and be sufficiently attractive to encourage secretarial staff to transfer there from your present office.

   You will shortly be attending a weekend business conference at Z. Mr Webb is unable to do so. He has therefore asked you to stay on for a day or two and to investigate Z carefully. He would like you to write a brief report for him, outlining any important facts about Z that he should know and assessing its suitability for a branch office. The report will be discussed by the partners after it has been circulated.

   Write your report. (30 marks)

2. Your employer is President of a local Residents' Association, and will shortly be giving a talk on safety in the home. For his (or her) benefit, prepare a summary, in not more than 130 words, of the following extract from an article by Dr Claire Whittington, published in *New Scientist* on 10 November 1977.

Safety begins at home

It has become something of a cliché to say that the home is the most hazardous place to be. This assertion is frequently based on little more than a vague impression that the chance of having an accident at home is somewhat greater than, for example, having an accident at work. But does the assertion have any substance? Even more important, what are the main types of domestic accidents that happen to people, and what action is taken to reduce the frequency and severity of these accidents?

Accidents in the home, even if they result in a fatality, are often undramatic and, with the exception of fires, generally involve a single individual rather than groups of people. Such factors combine to weaken the impact of such accidents. Nevertheless, home accidents are a major problem. In terms of numbers, they are comparable with the numbers killed and injured in traffic accidents. More people die in accidents in the home than in factories.

There have been certain surveys in the past, but the researchers have often only been concerned with only a limited aspect of the whole problem, such as the incidence of burns and scalds in young children. The failure to adopt a broad and systematic approach to the problem of home accidents has several unfortunate consequences. Among these was the duplication of research affort. Perhaps more important, the narrow approach meant that large numbers of accidents had to occur before the true scale of any particular problem was appreciated. Witness the avalanche of deaths and injuries due to inadequately designed or badly safeguarded paraffin heaters before a mandatory standard was imposed by parliament.

Although home accidents are frequently thought to happen primarily to the elderly and the young, nearly 44 per cent of the accidents recorded involved those in the active age groups 15 to 64. Unfortunately, government surveys do not classify accidents in terms of cause, but only in terms of the actual injury. In some cases, the injury will be self-explanatory, for example, burns or electric shock. But because falls or loss of balance (a common occurrence) can result in a wide variety of injuries, we do not know exactly how many accidents are caused by falls. Most surprising of all, in view of the results of other research on the subject, is the fact that only 0.2 per cent of all accident cases in the survey were due to poisoning.

Most home accidents occur either in the kitchen or the living/dining areas. Next on the list comes the garden (defined as part of the 'home' in the survey); and only then do stairs appear on the list (with 12 per cent of all accidents occurring on them). (450 words.)

(30 marks)

3. Read carefully the following article by John Lloyd, which was published in the *Financial Times* on 3 October 1977, and then answer all the questions below it. Remember that the answers to any *factual* questions are to be found in the article itself. Some words and phrases are printed in *italics* to help you locate them when you answer the questions.

Secretaries demand an electric typewriter

The major and obvious trend in the typewriter market is the shift from manual machines to electric machines, a trend which is extending itself to take in portables as well as office typewriters.

There, are, however, a number of special factors within this general shift which *qualify* the generalisation. In the first place, Britain lags behind the other advanced industrial countries in the speed of changeover and the distance travelled along the road to electrification. While the precise figures on machines in use are impossible to obtain, *informed guesswork* puts the ratio of electric to manual at around one-and-a-half to one.

This compares with a European in-use ratio of more than 2:1 and an American ratio of around 10:1 in favour of electric. Typewriter executives have no other explanation for it than *conservatism* on the part of British bosses, allied to the reluctance of Government departments, and especially local government offices, to invest in electric machines.

But these executives are hoping for the *efficacy* of another factor —

secretarial power — to hasten what they see as the inevitable course of events. The continuing shortage of skilled secretaries gives them a growing leverage, not just on rates of pay, but on conditions in the office. The office manager who refuses to replace the battered manuals with electrics may find himself faced, not just with complaints, but with *non-compliance.* This factor becomes stronger as the electric machines grow more sophisticated, increasing their attractiveness over manuals.

Third, though *the domestic market* is, reluctantly, going electric, there is a growing market in the developing countries which are at an earlier phase of office development, and which are demanding manuals in increasing numbers. More than 80 per cent of the manual machines which are made at a typewriter factory in Glasgow, for example, are for export.

Finally — a counterbalancing factor — innovation on manual typewriters has, according to the manufacturers, reached the limits of ingenuity.

The two basic types of electric machines, manufactured by all the big companies, are the 'typebar' and 'golfball' models. The typebar models are really electrified manual machines. However, the golfball models work on the principle of a single globe about one inch in diameter with all the standard characters *in relief* upon it. Pressure on the keys causes two movements: first an adjustment sideways and up or down, to select the character required, and then the movement to strike the paper.

The next challenge for the companies is perhaps the golfball portable with proportional spacing. In addition, there is a constant search for the noiseless typewriter and for keys which can be activated by the merest touch of a finger.

The speed of *the innovative process* is such that in many offices ageing typewriters with metal keys coexist with streamlined golfballs. This article was typed on one of the former sort, demonstrating either the conservatism of newspaper management or the fact the journalists have much to learn from secretaries on *office militancy.*

(a)   Prepare a brief formal office memo, correctly set out, to your employer, who is planning to buy a new typewriter (any kind you care to suppose). You would much prefer him to buy a different kind. Explain your preference, with your reasons, and ask him to reconsider his decision. Be sure to maintain a courteous and professional tone.

(10 marks)

(b)   Answer the following seven questions, which can obtain a total of 30 marks.

(i)   Suppose there are 12 million electric typewriters in Britain. How many manuals does Mr Lloyd guess there are?

(ii)   In your own words, explain the meaning of any THREE of the following as used in the extract:

> *qualify* (paragraph 2)   *conservatism* (paragraph 3)
> *efficacy* (paragraph 4)   *non-compliance* (paragraph 4)
> *in relief* (paragraph 7)

(iii)   In your own words, explain what you understand by any TWO of the following, giving where possible a brief example to make the meaning even clearer:

> *informed guesswork* (paragraph 2)
> *the domestic market* (paragraph 5)
> *the innovative process* (paragraph 9)
> *office militancy* (paragraph 9)

(iv)   Your employer thinks that Mr Lloyd may be a typewriter salesman, who has written this article to publicise electric typewriters. Say whether you agree or not, citing any evidence you find in the extract to support your view.

(v)   The librarian of a large industrial firm decides to cut out this article for his (or her) cuttings' file. Suggest your own choice of file heading which would be the most appropriate one under which to file the cutting.

(vi)   Would you expect to find a higher proportion of manual typewriters in central government or in municipal offices? Give your reason, based on the extract.

(vii)   Although it is expected that electric machines will become more popular, Britain is still producing a large number of manual typewriters. Do you think production will soon fall considerably? Give your reasons, based on the extract.

THE ROYAL SOCIETY OF ARTS
EXAMINATIONS BOARD
DIPLOMA FOR PERSONAL ASSISTANTS, 1978

COMMUNICATION
WEDNEDSAY, 14th JUNE (MORNING)
[THREE HOURS ALLOWED]

You have ten minutes to read through this question paper before the start of the examination

The number of marks allocated to each question is given in brackets

ALL *questions to be answered*

You may answer the questions in any order

1. EITHER
    Write an article of about 500 words for ONE of the following:
    (i)   the business section of a quality newspaper, either for or against the

view that sophisticated modern office equipment, such as word processors and dictating equipment, will never eliminate the need for the personal secretary.

(ii)   a women's magazine, criticizing the fictional representation of industry and commerce on television.
(You may restrict your comments to one particular programme.)

O R

(iii) in about 400 words prepare a press release for a British firm, announcing its first public showing of a new range of bicycles at the Hanover Cycle Fair on June 21st. (You may utilize the following information: production began in January with workforce of 50, some unemployed for long time, then re-trained at local government training centre; cycle manufacture is an operation on an assembly line in which frames and wheels, made in England, and other parts, mainly from abroad, e.g. tyres from the Far East, brakes from Switzerland, are put together; firm aims essentially at mid-market with conventional models from £70, but will sample reaction at Fair to revolutionary new cycle for housewives; from present range of production of 700 cycles per week target, by doubling workforce and increasing productivity, is 1000 by end of year; early production intended for export market, West Germany seen as promising.)

(25 marks)

2. You are personal assistant to Mr A.M. Millar, Managing Director of a small manufacturing firm employing 400 people making a small range of consumer electrical goods, notably heated trolleys, cabinets and trays for use in the home to keep food palatable until friends or the family are ready to eat it. The firm comprises a production side and a team of about 40 salesmen. He is exploring the idea of introducing a computer and has asked you to read the following two articles and prepare a summary to help him make his decision. In your summary he wishes you to take a critical look at past failures as well as future prospects and to offer practical advice to the prospective first-time user.

Read the articles below and prepare the summary for Mr Millar. (You may use note form.)

Nowadays any potential customer coming within scent of a computer salesman will be sung a new song. For the latest selling catch phrase is: 'We are not in the computer business but in the problem-solving business.'

The marketing wisdom behind the phrase is that there were two main failures in the 60's and early 70's — batch processing and software. Batch processing means that all work on the computer is processed at the main computer centre in batches. A better definition for this phenomenon is a bottleneck.

The other major problem was — and is — software. 'Hardware' means the physical computer machinery — a processor that can perform mathematical calculations at high speeds; memory, such as magnetic tape, magnetic discs, and punched cards to store information; and teletypes, printers, and visual display units to input information and receive results. Hardware developments have been unbelievable. One of the main developments has been the processor element. Electronic advances have made processors smaller, cheaper, and more powerful, leading to one of the most significant computer developments, the 'microprocessor' (commonly known as the micro). 'Software' is the program of instructions that enable those hunks of metal and electronic wiring to perform useful functions, like processing the payroll or booking an airline ticket. Hardware developments have been unbelievable. Progress in software techniques, however, has been virtually nil.

Online systems have now replaced many batch processing applications, giving direct online contact between a user and a computer, say via a visual display screen and keyboard linked by telephone line to the computer. Online systems cut through the batch bottleneck, placing the computer power close to where it is most needed — in a manager's office, on the shopfloor, in the accounts office.

Large complex centralised systems have begun to concede territory to smaller distributed processing systems, which mean, for example, that each division of a company could have its own local computer systems designed for local needs, with corporate information co-ordinated from a central system.

So computers now stand on the threshold of achieving much of their early promise. Gerry Fisher, president of the British Computer Society, recently said that it is time the British Government turned its attention from developing policies about the manufacturing of computers to the use of computers in manufacturing.

The potential for computers in manufacturing industry lies in the main areas of information management and direct control and supervision by intelligent machines or robot-like devices.

Computers are potentially the ideal information management tool because they have the ability to record and store vast amounts of information in an economical form. This information can provide reports in a variety of formats. Timely accurate reports available to management on current order and stock levels maintain the correct balance between customer demand and the company's cash flow needs.

In the field of information management, the user is unlikely to see immediately the impact of microprocessors. But micros will have a dramatic effect on the growing use of intelligent machines which will make it feasible to have the whole manufacturing process automated, with only one or two supervisors. Information from the computer system would then be fed automatically to robots for activation.

(Adapted from *the Guardian*, 18 July 1977)

For the small business man who is thinking of committing himself to the computer, here is a nutshell version of the computer community's advice:

Don't dive in the deep end: paddle in the shallows first. Don't rely wholly on the expert: understand the implications if not the technicalities. Know what you want — and why you want it.

There is a fair amount of cool counsel available to the newcomer — and he will need it as the advance of the micro widens the array of computer applications. The Department of Industry, which believes that the day has arrived for the computer in small business, is keen to see more micros develop.

On the manufacturing side, the Department has changed course in its efforts to encourage smaller firms to computerise. For four years now it has had an advisory team visiting factories but has been disappointed with the response. So it has decided that, rather than dealing direct with industry, it should encourage independent computer consultants who are ready to advise small and medium-sized firms.

Another provider of help to the innocent is the National Computing Centre Ltd, Oxford Road, Manchester M1 7ED. This is a non-profit distributing organisation supported by industry, commerce and Government: and its advisory services concentrate on the smaller organisation.

It provides comparative lists of available hardware and software — 'cold, without the advertising blurbs'. It will verify software packages, checking that they have been used satisfactorily before and that they are fully supported by the supplier's services. It also provides training courses for a computer user's staff.

The centre's director, David Firnberg, emphasises that the small business needs to be very clear what it wants done. Small firms cannot afford their own computer specialists, nor can they afford risks that larger organisations can ride. Therefore there must be maximum involvement and understanding from the business man and his staff (and this advice is echoed all round the trade).

Firnberg has doubts, at this stage anyway, about the suitability for the small maufacturer of a total system covering production and stock control, invoicing, payrolls, and company records. The strength of the total system relies on its reliability, but its weakness is a restriction on discretion. 'And the strength of the small business lies in their personal approach and in inventiveness.'

He suggests, therefore, that many small businesses would do well to enter the computer world not through buying their own system at once but by employing a computer bureau to tackle such chores as the payroll.

Alan Benjamin is director-general of the Computing Services Association, 121 Kingsway, London WC2B 6PG. (This is the trade association of the computer services industry. Details of inquiries received from businessmen are mailed each week to the members, who include computer service bureaus, software houses, and consultancies.) He, too, emphasises the importance of clear communication between supplier and customer and says that £2,000 to £3,000 spent on a consultant at the start could mean bigger savings later on.

Brian East is secretary of the first-time-user group of the British Computer Society, 29 Portland Place, London W1N 4HU. (This is the representative body of the computer community. It has over 20,000 members.) He goes further: without clarity between supplier and customer, software costs could eventually be double the sum mentioned in the sales talk.

East is yet another advocate of the gradual approach. The total system for small manufacturing industry is there in theory but the software, he says, could be costly because of the detailed analysis needed for production control. His estimate for a tailor-made system for a manufacturer employing around a thousand people and producing, say, highly specialised components, is between £150,000 and £200,000. But that would provide virtually total automation.

Micros — running in tandem with cheaper, more compact storage methods — could eliminate the cost barrier in a few years. But Professor Paul Samet, of University College, London, who is vice-president of the British Computer Society, thinks the micro is taking off faster than it should. Samet supports the Department of Industry's assessment that the day of the small-business computer has arrived, but, as a final cautionary note, he warns of a rebirth of the old delusion that the computer will itself solve all the problems, coupled with the temptation: 'Joe down the road's got one, so . . .'

(Adapted from *The Guardian,* 12 August 1977)

(25 marks)

3. You are PA to Mr A. K. King, Personnel Officer of a large insurance company soon to establish its national headquarters in the central area of another city.

Although generous relocation inducements have been offered, Mr King is very concerned because the staff, especially the junior members, have been put off the move by 'the ugly industrial image' of the new city.

He asks you to submit a circular letter for distribution to all staff updating the image. He tells you to show that with a rebuilding programme the city is blossoming into a lively and attractive place, although there are still some difficulties. He wishes you to mention especially the new shopping precinct, the leisure centre, the relatively cheaper homes for the first-time buyers, the motorway network opening up the whole region.

He adds finally, 'Pull out all the stops to keep the staff with us but don't make your letter read like a holiday brochure.'

With these instructions in mind, draft the letter.

(15 marks)

4. The table below shows the occupational choice of graduates. Consider these findings critically.

UNIVERSITY FIRST DEGREE GRADUATES
UK UNIVERSITIES 1976
(Non-medical Graduates)

	Total	Women as % of Total		Total	Women as % of Total
rst Degrees	1976- 57,246	35.4	Entering Production Management	1976- 1,864	5.8
tering Industrial Employment	1976- 7,891	14.0	Entering Management Services	1976- 1,422	24.3
tering Banking and Insurance	1976- 843	31.9	Entering Buying, Marketing, Selling	1976- 1,222	35.8
tering Other Commerce	1976- 1,701	41.9	Entering Personnel Management	1976- 272	61.7
tering Public Services	1976- 4,113	51.1	Entering Financial Work	1976- 3,185	22.7
tering General Traineeships	1976- 611	19.5	Entering Legal Work	1976- 877	32.0
tering General Management & Admin.	1976- 1,379	38.4			

(Adapted from *Universities Statistical Record*)

(15 marks)

5. Prepare minutes for the following meeting, amplifying the information given:

Langton's Sports and Recreational Society
Notice of Meeting

The meeting of the committee will take place in the Dining Room, Langton's Limited, on Wednesday, 8th March, 1978, at 2 p.m.

AGENDA
1. Apologies for absence.
2. Minutes of previous meeting.
3. Matters arising from the minutes.
4. Correspondence.
5. Reports.
6. Holiday Abroad.
7. National Theatre.
8. Christmas Party.
9. Competition.

Synopsis
Six of the seven members are present. In Matters Arising the Chairman announces the date of opening of the new squash courts. A letter is read

from the Social Club of Crescent's Ltd, with an invitation to a joint meeting in September which is declined. It is decided to send a letter to Mrs Mills, a founder-member of the society, who is retiring from company service. The Hon. Treasurer circulates his report showing a healthy financial position. The Holiday Abroad organiser says that Malaga has been selected but travel arrangments are not settled. She considers the cheap air fare a better financial deal than the express coach fare. One member asks about rail concession fares. The chairman wishes the details finalised by the next meeting. The Recreations Secretary mentions the good response to the National Theatre outing in late September, the advance block booking achieving a generous discount. It is decided to hold a Christmas social evening. Some members think it should take the form of a dinner-dance, some a social and one is in favour of a formal dinner. A sub-committee is formed. The Sports Secretary thinks that a team should be entered for the National Sportswomen Competition, explaining that it is a k.o. competition for teams of women representing firms all over the country. After much discussion the committee is unsure and the Sports Secretary says that she will write off for full details. The next meeting will be one month hence. The meeting ends at 4.50 p.m.

(20 marks)